Men Teaching Children 3–11

ALSO AVAILABLE FROM BLOOMSBURY

Changing Urban Education, edited by Simon Pratt-Adams, Meg Maguire and Elizabeth Burn
Education and Gender, edited by Debotri Dhar
Gender, Identity and Educational Leadership, Kay Fuller
Reflective Teaching in Schools, Andrew Pollard
Readings for Reflective Teaching in Schools, edited by Andrew Pollard

Men Teaching Children 3–11

Dismantling Gender Barriers

**ELIZABETH BURN
AND SIMON PRATT-ADAMS**

Bloomsbury Academic
An imprint of Bloomsbury Publishing Plc

BLOOMSBURY
LONDON · OXFORD · NEW YORK · NEW DELHI · SYDNEY

Bloomsbury Academic

An imprint of Bloomsbury Publishing Plc

50 Bedford Square
London
WC1B 3DP
UK

1385 Broadway
New York
NY 10018
USA

www.bloomsbury.com

BLOOMSBURY and the Diana logo are trademarks of Bloomsbury Publishing Plc

First published 2015

British Library Cataloguing-in-Publication Data
A catalogue record for this book is available from the British Library.

ISBN: HB: 978-1-4725-3484-2
PB: 978-1-4725-2735-6
ePDF: 978-1-4725-2660-1
ePub: 978-1-4725-2502-4

Library of Congress Cataloging-in-Publication Data
A catalog record for this book is available from the Library of Congress.

Typeset by Integra Software Services Pvt. Ltd.
Printed and bound in Great Britain

CONTENTS

ACKNOWLEDGEMENTS

We are greatly indebted to Professor Sue Lees, Elizabeth's original Director of Studies, who, before her untimely death, was such an inspiration to us, constantly challenging gender barriers through her own outstanding research in the field. We acknowledge with immense gratitude the wise and rigorous supervision Elizabeth received from Professor Meg Maguire at Kings College, London and her own lifetime commitment to developing equality in education. Professor Jane Martin, University of Birmingham, was Elizabeth's final Director of Studies, and the research has benefitted from her expert knowledge concerning the history of gender practice in education. Our book has profited from the knowledgeable and perceptive feedback these three scholars so generously provided, whilst Elizabeth was carrying out her research. Elizabeth also wishes to publicly thank Professor Diana Reay, University of Cambridge and Professor Pat Mahony, University of Roehampton, who examined Elizabeth's original PhD, ensuring her research was ethical and able to make a worthwhile contribution to scholarly research in the field. We would finally like to publicly acknowledge and thank Professor Ian Menter, University of Oxford, who has been so encouraging and supportive towards us over the many years we have been investigating gender injustices in education.

Introduction

This book is concerned with the work experiences of men who teach children 3–11 years of age. It critically examines a range of gender 'barriers' that these men may face and offers a number of strategies to help dismantle them. In the twenty-first century, when the roles of men and women in Western society have greatly changed, why does the teaching of young children still remain mainly women's work? We suggest that over time gender differentiation has become institutionalized within the occupation, creating symbolic 'gender barriers' that work to maintain a feminized workforce, ideally managed by the few men who are available for swift promotion (Jones, 2006; Weaver-Hightower, 2011; McGrath and Sinclair, 2013). These gender barriers are now embedded within the work culture and they are seen by many as 'normal', not worthy of comment, let alone scholarly research. Yet, as Foucault (1978) argues, it is these ordinary, seemingly insignificant, everyday practices and beliefs that we need to carefully examine if we wish to understand the operation of social practice and the power it wields: in this case, the power to recreate an imagined public patriarchal family.

In England, where our research was carried out, the latest national statistics (DFE, 2014) show that only 14.6 per cent of primary teachers in England are men (primary teachers teach pupils between 3 and 11 years of age). This is despite over a decade of recruitment drives; similar initiatives in other countries have also failed (Martino, 2008; Skelton, 2009). A range of biased assumptions about men and women are continuing to feed gender stereotypes that position the few men who do select to teach young children as 'Other' (Hepburn, 2013; Mistry and Sood, 2013; Mallozzi and Campbell Galman, 2014). The book analyses the work stories of a number of male teachers, in order to understand better how men experience the occupation. Data has been collected over time from men at different career stages and as a result this is a longitudinal study. Face-to-face interviews have been carried out by Elizabeth, and supplementary data collated from participant observation as well as commentary from professional peers in order to enrich the data set. (Appendix 1).

Four dominant male teacher scripts have been drawn up and are scrutinized in the light of other research and their historical roots identified. These scripts represent the legitimate roles available for men within the occupation and they are concerned with sport, discipline, role models and promotion. Chapters Three to Six examine these scripts in depth, drawing on the work experiences of the interviewees.

Our key informants teach in English inner-city state schools and peer commentary has been collected from a number of countries. Our intent is to move from analysis of gender practice towards practical strategies for change. The recommendations will be of interest to all involved in the teaching of children aged 3–11 years: training providers, teachers, parents, policy makers, governors and students of Education and Gender Studies.

The authors

We are two experienced primary school practitioners who subsequently moved into teacher education and we are united by a commitment to recruit talented people into this challenging and rewarding occupation, irrespective of their gender (or ethnicity, sexuality or class background). We believe that the main focus for recruitment, appointment and promotion must be on teaching ability (pedagogical practice) not gender. Prior to discussing the theoretical position adopted and the overall organization of the book, we briefly introduce ourselves and summarize our teaching experiences across the 3–11 age range.

A female and a male teacher collaborating in this area is unusual, a strength being that we can helpfully draw on our own lived work experiences when attempting to unpick the many complex and often contradictory ways gender practice can work to both disadvantage and advantage male teachers of young children (Thornton and Bricheno, 2000; Wadsworth, 2002; King, 2004). A short reflection on our own gendered career paths usefully sets the scene.

Elizabeth

Elizabeth qualified, with a distinction, as a primary teacher (3–11 years) in the North of England in 1970. She attended an all-female Training

College and the handful of male teachers she met during her three years training, were all Head teachers who had previously taught the older children in the Juniors (7–11 years). Although her college tutors were all male, the Principal, who ruled with a rod of iron, was female and after Elizabeth's first year of training, a third of her year group were asked to leave. Once qualified the first three schools she taught in were Infants (5–7 years) and all of the teachers were female so they carried out the sport, discipline, management and caring roles. Gender barriers were not in operation; it was only when teaching in Junior (7–11 years) and Primary schools that Elizabeth worked with male teachers. These few men were either: Head teachers, Deputy Head teachers or Year Six teachers (10–11 years) and they held specialisms in Physical Education (PE) or Mathematics. When she became a teacher advisor for mathematics and science at Key Stage 1 (5–7 years) no men in her Local Authority applied for the post, as they were all teaching Key Stage 2 (7–11 years). In her last school, Elizabeth held a Deputy Headship in an all-female staffed Infant school in London. Elizabeth has combined fourteen years of classroom teaching across the 3–11 age range, with career breaks as she has three children; each time she returned to temporary supply posts, despite previous promotions, holding specialisms in Mathematics, Art, Science and Nursery (3–4 years).

In interviews she was regularly asked about her family responsibilities and also told (off the record) 'of course you know Elizabeth they want a man'. The few male teachers who were working in her Local Authority, had all gained rapid promotion to senior management, and this gender practice is still replicated nationally (Powney et al., 2003; Jones, 2006).

It was when Elizabeth moved into Teacher Education in the 1990s that she met Simon and they began to collaborate on research concerned with gender practice in schools (Pratt-Adams and Burn, 2004). Elizabeth had already held a Teacher Fellowship at Newcastle University concerned with gender (Burn, 1989) and she realized that both female and male teachers must become involved in helping dismantle unfair gender practice. Elizabeth is now retired, yet the voices of the male teachers she interviewed for her doctorate (our key informants) have remained with her. So Elizabeth decided to write this timely book with Simon, as countries continue to search for strategies to increase male teacher recruitment. We hope that this book will contribute to the development of a more balanced workforce, by helping to expose the actual consequences of the gender barriers many of our male interviewees identified.

Simon

Simon trained as a primary school teacher in the mid-1980s. Although trained to teach across the full primary age range, he has mainly taught in

Key Stage 2 (7–11 years). Throughout his teaching career he experienced many gender-specific comments about being a man working with young children. The year that he moved from Year Six to teach in the Reception class (4- to 5-year-olds) several parents at the school thought he had been demoted and asked him what he had done wrong to be sent to teach the Reception class children. They were even more puzzled when he explained it was *his* career choice.

Whilst working in the East End of London, on several occasions parents complimented him on his ability as a male teacher and in particular said they were pleased that they had a man teaching their son. He can recall instances when parents suggested, because they felt he was a good teacher that he should go and teach in secondary school (11–16 years) and were surprised that he was not planning, or indeed trained, to do this. The parental perception was that as a man he should be working with older children – another common gender barrier faced by male teachers. Simon remembers the staff rooms being predominantly female environments and at times feeling uncomfortable and alienated by the conversation. Rather than spend his time in the staff room he would often go and sit and chat with the school keeper in his office.

As will be reported in Chapter Three, alongside other male teachers Simon was encouraged to run school sports clubs and take PE lessons on behalf of female colleagues. This was not a problem for him, unlike some other men, as sport was something he enjoyed. One consequence of this was that he would often wear a track suit around the school and there were many instances of visitors to the school meeting him in the playground or the school corridors and mistaking him for the school keeper. People did not associate the combination of being male in a primary school and dressed in casual attire as that of being a teacher.

Even during his own teacher training he can recall being sent disruptive children to discipline by female colleagues and while he attempted to use a range of strategies that encouraged children to reflect on their behaviour he well remembers other men using more traditional and stereotypical forms of chastisement and their voices booming out around the school and this seemed to be what was expected. One can only assume that because he was a man he would also be a good disciplinarian.

Simon was given his first post of responsibility after just one year of teaching. He became Deputy Head of his second school within five years of qualifying and was acting Head teacher soon afterwards when the Head of his school was seconded to work on a national initiative. He was first considered for headship after eight years of teaching and was enrolled by his local authority on a Headship assessment programme. On each occasion he was offered a Headship he turned the opportunity down as he was unsure this was the right direction for him at that time. On many occasions he was told by colleagues that his promotions were due to the fact that he was a man and he can recall some challenging and testing times from older female colleagues.

At this time he also completed his MA in Urban Education at King's College London, writing his dissertation about male friendship in the inner city which had a strong personal dimension and gave voice to other men's experiences of their male friendship. He received funding to study for a doctorate at King's where he further developed his interest in the field of masculinities and in particular the significance of the same sex peer group on the development of young males. This research was conducted in the late 1990s during a period of time when there was growing concern about the behaviour and academic achievement of boys, causing questions to be raised about the way masculinities are constructed and learned (Connell, 1995; Salisbury and Jackson, 1996).

While still working in primary school he also began to teach part-time on school leadership programmes at a local University and his career took a new direction when he left primary school teaching after just over a decade in the profession to work as a lecturer in a university Department of Education. His first class was teaching mathematics subject knowledge to thirty women trainee primary school teachers. It was here that he met Elizabeth and they subsequently team taught masters programmes and have co-researched, presented and published a number of articles in the area of men and masculinities. Since working in Higher Education he has held a number of senior posts including Director of Research, Head of Teacher Education and Deputy Dean for International Developments and External Income. He is currently Head of the Department of Education in the Faculty of Health, Social Care and Education at Anglia Ruskin University. He is involved in primary education as a trustee on the board of an Academy Trust. Furthermore, he keeps informed of developments in Primary schools coming from a family of 'female' primary school teachers.

The theoretical position

The book adopts a poststructuralist feminist position, focusing on the meanings given by the participants within a social situation (Skelton, 2011). It accepts that gender is socially constructed, context specific and interacts with other social relations (such as 'race' and class) over time. This means individual subjective accounts will be complex, contradictory and always open to future re-interpretation by participants, researchers and readers (Walford, 2001). Bauman and May (2001) discuss how instead of an essential 'self' the subject is constantly under production within a specific social context. So, in adopting this perspective, individuals are viewed as social actors who perform their public roles whilst negotiating their subject positioning (Hammersley and Atkinson, 1990). Hammersley (2003:125) cautions us all to be more aware of: 'what interview data can provide, and what they *cannot* provide.' The interview data drawn upon in this book represents the individual subjective experiences of a number of men who selected to teach young children and was not intended to (or able to) lead to generalizations. Rather it allows for a closer scrutiny of the complex and contradictory effects of certain gender practices. We accept 'what teachers "know" about teaching derives from the links between personal life history and professional career' (Thomas, 1995:11).

However, by following this path it does not mean we reject institutional as well as individual practices; both are implicated. Hughes (2002:14) suggests that avoiding the traditional 'binaried thinking' between agency and structure can be facilitated by recognizing the 'subject' as continually in production. Munro found that the women teachers in her study were not fully defined by the 'gendered norms inscribed in teaching' rather they were 'active agents in negotiating them' (Munro, 1998:4). So when analysing the data from our interview sample we are concerned with unpicking the complex and often contradictory ways male teachers experience, interpret and negotiate the established gender regimes in primary schools (Skelton, 2001; Jones, 2006; Mallozzi and Campbell Galman, 2014). Goodson (2000:15), who has long promoted life history methods when researching teachers', clearly views 'the school teacher as an active agent in the making of her or his own history' and we strongly support his argument (see Chapter Nine for a fuller discussion of feminisms, teachers and post structuralism).

The feminist standpoint adopted by this book is based on a recognition that overall men in Western society still benefit from an inherited patriarchal dividend (Connell, 1995). This dividend will vary, dependent on whether the individual man performs (or is able to perform) the required hegemonic masculinity (Connell, 2002). Ramazanoglu and Holland (2002:9) argue that 'investigation of gendered lives by feminists includes the study of men'. We subscribe to hooks (1984) belief that women and men working together can better tackle gender practice, which both men and women are implicated in. Gender practice may work to disadvantage as well as advantage men (and women) in particular situations. Male teachers during initial teacher training, for instance, can be vulnerable to 'attack' by female students resentful of male advantage (Chapter Two); qualified men can be advantaged in their careers due to their rarity (Chapter Six).

We employ male teacher 'scripts' as a heuristic device, allowing for a closer examination of the diverse, contradictory and inconsistent gender practices identified in our research data. Although there is a danger of over-simplifying volatile gender practices, the usage of gender scripts allows for a focus on the subject positions that may be made available to men. The male teacher 'scripts' can aid the identification of individual resistance and compliance, since men will both reject and claim these 'scripts' as they negotiate their work identities. There may be 'typical' male teacher scripts, but there certainly were not 'typical' men (as the easy stereotype claims); no two men in our research adopted the same position in response to the male teacher scripts menu. We have also identified the circulation of a pedagogic teacher 'script' as the ongoing struggle for gender 'truths' is played out within the occupation.

Overall, the data evidences how constructing the teaching of young children as 'maternal work only' is both validated and contested within the minutia of the everyday (Coffey and Delamont, 2000). In this book we are concerned to highlight the emotional costs of non-conformity to the accepted gender norms and several of the key informants openly discuss the ongoing pain of 'difference'; as Pulsford (2014:227) points out: 'the study of teacher's emotions and in particular their "emotional labour"...represents an important direction of research, especially with men.'

Our analysis of the data collected is greatly aided by the usage of Foucault's insightful work on discourses and their effects (Foucault, 1978) with certain caveats (see Chapter One). His careful analysis of the operation of social power helps us to better expose and refute the essentialist ideas these insidious gender practices attempt to promote and reinforce. Such practices have no place in twenty-first century schools, where the focus needs to be on teaching and learning not on outdated and discredited ideas concerning male and female teacher potentials.

In summary, feminist theorizing recognizes how gender is 'performed' (see Butler, 1990) and re-constituted in the everyday; as such, inappropriate gender scripts, once problematized, can be reworked. Post-structuralism posits that our identities are always in production (including our work identities) as we claim and disown the subject positions made available to us through discourse. These theories allow us to better understand how micro-power operates through everyday practices to maintain historic gender divisions within this occupation. They recognize how we can actively resist the subject positions offered, as some of our key informants' work stories clearly demonstrate, but not without costs.

We argue that if these ongoing gender practices remain hidden then they will continue to work to construct the teaching of very young children as female-only work (King, 2004; Cushman, 2010). It is important that we critically research the lived work reality of men teaching children 3–11 years of age. The selection of eighteen key informants teaching in inner-city London schools meant that in-depth face-to-face interviews were possible. These interview conversations (Corbetta, 2003), with Elizabeth, were able to probe, allowing for discussions of sensitive gender issues that do not normally surface in impersonal questionnaire responses. We acknowledge that there is no such thing as 'doing perfect research' (Griffiths, 1998:97) and all research methods will have limitations, no matter how rigorous and self-reflective the researchers. For example, the focus on 'gender' alone is artificial; as the data analysis evidences, the intersectionality of 'race', class, sexuality and other relations are all implicated in the gender practices discussed by the informants (Skeggs,1997; Brah and Phoenix, 2004).

As teacher-researchers we are advantaged: teachers of young children talking to each other, irrespective of gender, have a shared vocabulary that greatly aids communication (Nias, 1989). We too have experienced gendered comments in staffrooms, received comments from parents and have been placed in certain classes because of our gender rather than because of our teaching expertise. So, when teaching in Primary schools, we have also had to negotiate some of the gendered 'barriers' that this book is concerned to make visible and change. We are very grateful to the male (and female) teachers and students, who have disclosed their own work experiences to us, making this book possible, and we profusely thank them.

The organization of the book

The book is organized in four interconnected sections. The first section provides the historical origins and theoretical issues in order to contextualize what is to follow. The second section examines four historical male teacher scripts that also emerge from our research findings – namely the role of sport, discipline, male role models and promotion. In the third section, the focus turns to recent moral panics surrounding men working with young children, international experiences and women teachers. The final section offers strategies for dismantling gender barriers and the book concludes with a reflection of effective pedagogical practices which stand in contrast to the gender practices previously examined.

At the end of each chapter, we provide discussion questions, which allow the reader to reflect on what they have read in the chapter, as well as to draw upon their own knowledge and experience, in order to critically consider the issues raised.

Chapter One

In Chapter One, we offer a short examination of the historical origins of this occupation in the England and we find that, at the start of the nineteenth century, the first Infant teachers were actually men! It was only men at that particular time who were seen as having both the moral and physical strength to teach young children in the public sphere. A clear example of how wider societal beliefs about women and men will influence what is deemed as gender appropriate employment. Also how the occupation itself is viewed matters; at that time it was seen as of importance to the nation and as such had high status in England and Europe. The chapter traces how powerful maternal discourses then emerged, claiming that only women had the qualities necessary to teach young children. Indeed by the end of the nineteenth century there had been a significant gender shift: women were now teaching in the Infants, whilst men were needed for senior management and the teaching of the older boys in the Juniors. The teachers of the children of the poor were increasingly being constructed as 'public parents', with the patriarchal father firmly in charge. These historical maternal and paternal discourses are still in circulation and staffing patterns in many state Primary schools today continue to replicate this outdated Victorian model (Alexander, 1988).

Chapter One also provides a brief discussion of 'discourses' and the many complex ways they can operate to 'normalize' certain practices in the daily ongoing struggle for social power. We examine how dominant gender discourses have been laid down over time within this occupational culture and conclude by identifying four key 'male teacher scripts', concerned with: sport, discipline, role models and promotion. These scripts are clearly visible in the accounts given by our male informants; we address their effects in Chapters Three to Six.

Chapter Two

Chapter Two is concerned with the training experiences of a group of men who selected to enter this occupation and as we write, it is becoming a historical route as in England the training of primary teachers is under-going radical change and new teacher training paths are evolving. As such this chapter provides a unique glimpse of the cumulative way ongoing gender practices can impact over time and work to undermine a person's confidence. The data was collected by Elizabeth from our participant observation in a male student support group over an academic year. The support group had developed from a wish to tackle the high male student dropout rate during initial training.

These male students found that they were subject to gender stereotyping and 'attacked' for being men; they had unwittingly crossed the accepted gender barriers by entering into 'women's work'. Chapter Two includes a consideration of 'stereotypes' themselves and how they work to 'Other' the minority group, in this case, the few male students still on the course.

Chapter Three

The legitimate male teacher script we examine in Chapter Three is the one that works to construct all male teachers as 'natural' and willing sports men, especially needed to teach the older boys football. We critically examine initiatives that set out to engage failing working class boys in literacy through the usage of football; some of our key informants discuss their own involvement in these sport programmes. A number of the male teachers interviewed strongly reject this script, whilst others support it. Several of our informants hold a PE specialism which is still seen as a legitimate 'male' subject and linked to boys and an acceptable 'masculinity'. In common with the other male teacher scripts, the masculinity of the men is 'on the line' if they fail to uphold this sportsman script. Chapter Three includes a review of research into 'masculinities', which argues that men are being measured against an 'idealized' heterosexual norm (including participation in male sports) and any failure to conform and perform the required 'masculinity' results in sanctions being applied.

Chapter Four

In this chapter we examine 'discipline' – another historical script that is still being applied to male teachers today. Our research data evidences that men can experience being 'sent' boys to discipline even during initial training. We explore the actual beliefs behind this gender practice and again constructions of a particular type of legitimate masculinity are implicated. Another finding from our data analysis concerns the way pupils may offer male teachers more 'respect' than their female teachers. The majority of our key informants disown the male discipline script but they still find that parents may expect male teachers of young children to possess a 'natural' authority. It means that men are often given the oldest children to teach (10- to 11-year-olds) regardless of their age range specialism, as it is believed that they will be 'better' at discipline. The few black teachers in our sample are assumed to be able (and willing) to discipline the older black boys and issues of 'race' and class difference are visible in the data collected. Again there is no overall consensus about this gender belief. A number of our informants are happy to claim the discipline script, arguing that their male physicality and depth of voice are 'assets' in the classroom or nursery. Once again, as with the sports script in the previous chapter, the focus of the discussion is on the older boys and it is assumed that boys' behaviour will be a 'problem' which requires correction by men.

Chapter Five

Chapter Five examines a fractured and complex script concerned with constructing male teachers as role models. The chapter begins by examining how in the 1930s men secured their promotion advantage by drawing on the idea that men were needed as 'role models' to stop boys being damaged by 'unnatural' spinster teachers. The male role-model script (needed for boys) continues and new discursive formations have now emerged. Societal changes in family structure have meant that derogatory discourses about single-parent families (which are always assumed to be female-led) are today positioning male teachers as 'needed' father substitutes. A number of our informants actively claim this script and again issues of class and 'race' cut across these gender practices. Several of our key informants strongly reject this replacement 'father' role, which is working to perpetuate the 'public patriarchal parents' construction unearthed in our historical review. A few of the interviewees aim to become role models for 'teaching' itself and this emerging pedagogic discourse also appears in the women teachers' interviews that we present in Chapter Nine.

Chapter Six

Chapter Six examines the male promotion script that is still in operation today although two-thirds of our key informants either deny or ignore their inherited promotion advantage, despite the statistics. Male teacher 'rarity' supports the continuation of this script and there remains an expectation that men will quickly rise up the career ladder (Hepburn, 2013).

Chapter Six also includes a short discussion of 'patriarchal relations' which this promotion script seeks to maintain. Several of our informants understandably find it insulting that when they gain promotion the suspicion is it is due to them being a 'man' rather than because of their ability. Some men have stepped off this fast promotion ladder in order to develop their classroom teaching expertise (embracing the pedagogic script). When women justifiably voice resentment of male promotion paths, men feel 'attacked', blame 'feminism' and retreat into victimhood. These 'attacked man' discourses also surfaced in the student support group (see Chapter Two). Thus the promotion script serves to drive a wedge between male and female teachers, reinforcing gender barriers; and men find that unless they do gain early promotion they may be viewed as 'failures'. We find evidence that men are being told, both prior to application and during training, that they will achieve quick promotion (whether they want it or not) as the 'needed man' discourses continue to circulate within the occupation.

Chapter Seven

This chapter is concerned with gender discourses that were not visible in our historical trawl – discourses that evidence a moral panic surrounding men, young children and child abuse. The majority of our key informants raise this as a significant issue and believe that the fear of being stigmatized as a potential paedophile prevents many men from entering this occupation. We recognize the raising of this sensitive subject may actually serve to reinforce the moral panic surrounding men and young children; however, the discourses that link paedophilia to all men who select to work with young children must be challenged. There is also evidence of suspicion being attached to men's sexualities and homophobic innuendos are reported. Many of our key informants live in fear of being alone with a child in case allegations are made. We rightly have clear safeguarding policies in place for young children in school, but where are the safeguards for the men who teach them?

The painful conversations we report in this chapter need addressing as a matter of urgency. We hope Chapter Seven will help open up this 'taboo' subject for wider debate and ways forward found, so that men feel able to pursue this career without a constant fear of false accusations.

Chapter Eight

Chapter Eight provides a concise review of recent research findings in other countries, concerning the occupational experiences of men who teach young children, aged 3–11 years of age. These international research findings are compared and contrasted with the present own research findings; and again gender discourses are identified and their effects scrutinized. The chapter also examines a number of recruitment campaigns and initiatives in other countries, aimed at redressing the gender imbalance in this occupation. These recruitment strategies include suggestions that male teachers should be given higher salaries and other advantages in order to attract more men into the workforce.

Chapter Nine

We thought long and hard before including this chapter which is concerned with women teachers' experiences, since the focus of the book is on men who teach young children. We also wish to avoid maintaining gender practices within this occupation by ignoring the 'voice' of women teachers. Our data also shows women teachers are involved in upholding or rejecting gender barriers. It is women teachers, for instance, who may select to send male teachers boys to discipline and it is women staff who are making both the supportive (we need a man) and critical (a typical man) comments discussed by many of our informants. So, Chapter Nine provides an analysis of interviews carried out with two female primary teachers, identifying the female teacher scripts that they have been subject to due to their career choice. Elizabeth also critically reviews feminist theorizing and research, drawing on her own work experience where relevant. Chapter Nine demonstrates how the gender stories of both male and female teachers need to be analysed if progress is to be made in dismantling gender barriers within the occupation.

Chapter Ten

Chapter Ten offers a range of strategies that we believe can help challenge and dismantle the gender barriers that we examine in this book. We are certainly not providing a simplistic 'check list' to evict these damaging practices and beliefs; as Chapter One clearly evidences, these gender discourses have been laid down over time and they will take time to remove. Our data demonstrates how gender practices operate in different ways in different contexts and in the light of this we recommend a multi-faceted approach to challenging them.

It is in the daily school practices that change can be most readily achieved; for instance, sending the 'male' teacher children to discipline, can be disrupted by female and male teachers refusing to engage in this practice in the first place. It can be tackled by effective school policies on discipline being in place; this exemplifies how senior staff and governors can practically contribute to the development of equitable practices in schools and nurseries. The chapter is of relevance to inspectors, teacher trainers, policy makers and parents, as well as practitioners: the most appropriate strategies can be selected (or adapted) once the gender barriers are identified by the school community.

Conclusion

We conclude by reflecting on the wider implications for teaching and learning of the numerous gender practices and beliefs, which have been examined in this book. The gender stereotyping of male (and female) primary teachers impacts on the young pupils that they teach. The stereotype of 'a bloke in a track-suit bantering with the boys about football', as discussed by one of our informants, is a very different construction to one of a primary teacher who is concerned with young children's intellectual development. So, when discussing the possible educational consequences of gender barriers within the primary school we provide a brief overview of research into effective pedagogical practice, focusing on early reading and mathematical thinking (helpful for readers who are not primary specialists). We leave the final words of this book to Carl and Jeff, two of our key informants who strongly resent being subject to occupational stereotypes; they believe that they should be judged on their teaching ability, not on their gender.

CHAPTER ONE

The Historical Background

Chapter One examines the historical gender legacy 'inherited' by male primary school teachers in English schools today. It traces significant gender shifts in staffing patterns. At the start of the nineteenth century, the first Infant school teachers were radical young men who aimed to change society. In the twenty-first century, gender discourses are working to construct the teaching of young children as a female only occupation, which is largely managed by men (Alexander, 1988; Acker, 1994; Reay, 2001; Weaver-Hightower, 2011). This chapter argues that as long as these historical gender beliefs and practices remain only of historic interest or are seen as of little importance today, they will continue to reinforce existing gender barriers within the workforce.

It is not possible in one chapter to adequately cover the turbulent historical period which finally 'birthed' in 1870 a system of state schooling, for the young children of the poor (Beddoe, 1983). Instead we will take as our starting point the opening in 1817 of the first Infant school by Robert Owen

(Peltzman, 1998; Giardiello, 2014). However, for clarity, before we start to unpick the complex gender and class discourses that were circulating when these early Infant schools were set up by men, we provide a brief discussion of 'discourses'.

Discourse: Constructing regimes of truth

The 'regime of truth' (Foucault 1978) that teaching young children always has been and always will be women's work is a social construction that still has powerful effects on the recruitment and retention of men into this occupation. Mitchell and Weber (1999:168) argue:

> The layered sedimentation of past images is churned up every now and then by social events permitting old teacher images to rise to the surface to be reborn and shared with a new generation.

Powerful and contradictory public 'images' of present-day male primary school teachers are part of research findings in a range of countries (Pepperell and Smedley, 1998; Fraser and Yeomans, 1999; Carrington and Skelton, 2003; Gosse, 2011; McGrath and Sinclair, 2013). There are negative images of male teachers as potential 'perverts', co-existing with positive male 'role model' ones (Lewis and Weston, 2002; Skelton, 2011). Foucault (1978) would assert that the widespread circulation of these well-known 'discourses' is not insignificant; rather, it is indicative of the complex and unpredictable ways social power operates in the every-day to govern our beliefs and behaviours, drawing on past discourses to increase their effects. Foucault views 'discourses' as:

> Tactical elements or blocks operating in the field of force relations; there can exist different and even contradictory discourses within the same strategy. (Foucault, 1978:101–102)

Raphael Reed (1999:94) has employed Foucault's ideas about discourses and power, when examining the moral panic about failing boys needing male teachers:

> Discourse is more than a matter of ideas. It arises out of and affects practices; it mediates and adumbrates actions; it speaks of history and context.

This chapter demonstrates how historical specificity matters when tracing gender discourses about primary teachers; at the time of the early Infant school movement for instance, women were not seen as morally or physically able to perform such an important public role (McCann and Young, 1982).

Foucault (1978) insists that we need to recognize the contradictory ways multiple 'discourses' circulate within a culture. They are laid down and will be taken up as part of a tactical strategy to win social power. We must recognize that discourses are fragmented; new ones will become attached to existing formations, in ways that are both incongruous and diffuse. In the development of state teaching, powerful class discourses were laid down alongside gender ones to construct 'ideal' type teachers for the children of the poor (Sutherland, 1971).

Foucault (1978:101) argues that discourses are volatile: they transmit and produce 'power' at the same time as providing 'a starting point for an opposing strategy'. So, no discourse is ever fully successful and there will always be opposition to the dominant strategy of the time. These discursive formations are concerned with the wielding of social power; they operate to help legitimate and 'normalize' certain practices and 'knowledges' as 'common-sense truths'. A very influential discourse works to construct Early Years teaching as women's work only, since women are 'naturally' caring. This long accepted common-sense 'truth' has worked over time to exclude male teachers, as well as to devalue women who work in that sector (Aspinwall and Drummond, 1989; Martino, 2008; Skelton, 2011).

In agreement with Hughes (2002:21) we found that Foucault's ideas about social power were helpful when we attempted to unpick the many contrary gender discourses that circulate about 'primary teachers', many of which we have been subject to ourselves when we were primary teachers. Griffiths (1998:60) also considers that Foucault's theorizing of the micropolitics of 'power/knowledge' is of value when examining gender practice:

> Two aspects of Foucault's theory have been particularly useful. One is the emphasis on locality and particularity. The other is the analysis of knowledge in terms of regimes of truth.

These 'regimes of truth', carried through discourses, become internalized and we monitor and control our own behaviours against them; they have an unconscious 'disciplinary power' (Burr, 1995:65). For instance, the long-held 'truth' that men are 'naturally' good at discipline is to be found in the historical teacher accounts of Spencer (1938) and England (1973). These two male teachers both measured themselves against this male discipline 'truth'. England claimed a talent to enact 'male' discipline whilst, in contrast, Spencer believed he had 'failed' to perform the discipline script required by this particular regime of truth (Burn, 2005).

We acknowledge that feminist researchers have criticized Foucault's sexism due to his 'analysis of men or Man in isolation from the analysis of women' (Mills, 2003:123). It is important to recognize that gender practice in schools involves men and women (Burn, 2002), which is why we include the voices of women teachers in Chapter Nine, and we decided to collaborate on this book.

We have employed Foucault's ideas concerning 'discourse' to help us unravel the way male teachers of young children can be positioned and how they also seek to position themselves in the light of gender beliefs and practices. However, we share Mills (2003) concerns and agree with Ramazanoglu and Holland (2002:56) who argue that accepting multiple accounts of 'truth' claims from a relativist position offers 'a direct challenge to modern feminism'. Feminism can itself be seen as just another competing 'truth' claim. Ramazanoglu and Holland (2002:57) point out it 'matters which accounts of reality are believed'. Hughes likewise considers it is important from a feminist research perspective not to abandon all 'ethical positions' (Hughes, 2002:122). The career discrimination that women primary teachers continue to experience cannot be written away as yet another competing 'truth' (see Chapter Six). With these important provisos in place we employ Foucault's analysis of the operation of social power to help us to examine the historical gender and class discourses laid down within this occupation, alongside substantial feminist retheorizing in this area. Healy (2000) usefully summarizes four aspects of Foucault's usage of 'discourse':

1. *Discourses involve 'rules' that legitimate certain statements (and practices) at specific times while excluding others.*

    Tropp (1957) reflected the prevailing discourses of the 1950s when writing the history of the teaching occupation. These discourses worked to construct primary teaching as an 'ideal' occupation for married middle-class women (after the marriage bar had been lifted). This new set of discourses had been brought into play at the end of the Second World War, when there was a large rise in births and a shortage of Infant teachers.

2. *Discourses and power are 'interconnected'* (Healy, 2000:40).

    'Regimes of truth' will set out to define what is seen as 'good' practice within teaching at a particular time. The London School Board policy in the late nineteenth century, for instance, promoted the ideas of Froebel in Infant departments (Martin and Goodman, 2004). This policy contributed to establishing the taken-for-granted 'truth' that women are the 'natural' teachers of young children, due to their inherent 'mothering' qualities. Middle-class women employed these highly influential 'nurturing' discourses when attempting to secure the entrance of women into the public sphere (Widdowson, 1980).

3. *Discourses are complex and their effects cannot be predicted.*

    In any context there will be a multiplicity of competing discourses. For example, two powerful sets of discourses are implicated in the public 'status' given to primary teachers. This state occupation has become historically constructed as a 'good' one for women to enter, seen as an extension of their 'domestic maternal duties' (Miller, 1996). In contrast, discourses concerned with upholding wider patriarchal power have also been working to construct the same occupation, as a one that only 'failed' men would enter. The salary was seen as not 'good enough' for men, seen as the 'natural' breadwinners.

4. *We need to consider the actual 'effects' of discourses rather than search for 'deep truths'* (Healy, 2000:11).

When England (1973) became a head teacher in an urban school the 1950s he did not allow parents' evenings, in order to 'protect' his female staff. England was adhering to dominant social class discourses at the time, which constructed the urban poor as undesirable and potentially violent.

We now examine some of the influential gender and class discourses which were circulating when the first Infant schools were opened by men, at the beginning of the nineteenth century.

The laying down of familial discourses within the occupation

The 'birthing' of Infant schools: Growing a different society

Robert Owen, 1817

Robert Owen, a self-made man, set up the first Infant School for the children of his factory workers at his cotton mill in New Lanark in 1817 (Peltzman, 1998). A social reformer, Owen had travelled in Europe and was impressed by the writings of Pestalozzi (Hahn, 1998) and other men who believed that early childhood was the time to influence young minds. Owen was concerned with creating a co-operative commonwealth and fairer society. Today Owen is acknowledged as one of the founding fathers of the Co-operative Movement.

Gaffin and Thoms (1993:8) consider that:

Owen, challenged the underlying tenets of the capitalist system, advocating an economic and social order which stressed co-operation and harmony ...

In contrast to the strict 'monitorial' church schools, set up by Lancaster and Bell in 1790s to ensure the future workforce would be disciplined (Sutherland, 1971:10), Owen employed both men and women teachers, provided they were 'kindly'. Owen disagreed with physical punishment and the curriculum aimed to develop good habits and kindness to others. The subjects offered included music and dance; he introduced playgrounds and even provided parenting classes (Giardiello, 2014). May (1999) records that by the time the school building in New Lanark was completed in 1817, Owen had employed twelve unqualified teachers to teach 194 children and his school was viewed as a model of enlightened pedagogy. In common with the radical teacher Thomas Spence, who had developed a phonic alphabet thirty-five years earlier in Newcastle upon Tyne (England), Owen believed in political as well as written literacy for the children of the poor (Thompson, 1963).

Samuel Wilderspin and the Infant School Movement, 1825

The Infant School Society was established in 1825 for the education of working-class children. Clarke (1985:75) reports how gender roles were being redefined in the middle-class home: 'the separation of spheres into male-public and female-private'. At this time Victorian middle-class men were being constructed as the public guardians and educators of young vulnerable children. Samuel Wilderspin, the leader of the Infant School Movement, drew on essentialist beliefs about men and women's 'natural' characteristics to justify why men were best suited for teaching in these Infant schools. The male head of his family, would 'exercise a greater degree of authority over children', confirming patriarchal relations (McCann and Young, 1982:175). Clarke (1985:81) argues that these schools aimed to 'reproduce the structure of the family in the public domain of the school'. Powerful paternal discourses were now in circulation, supported by religious beliefs, working to position men as the 'natural' moral leaders and teachers of young working-class children (Hall, 1995:78). Wilderspin believed that women did not possess the spiritual and intellectual powers, or the physical strength to run Infant schools. This Infant School Movement can be seen as a moral mission set up to ensure that social class hierarchies were maintained (Sutherland, 1971). The Infant schools intended to teach 'obedience, cheerful subordination, cleanliness and order' (Clarke, 1985:79). It could be argued that the early Infant School Movement served to symbolize male authority in public, maintaining male intellectual and spiritual superiority.

These early schools for the children of the poor demonstrate how complex and completing discourses operate to construct 'ideal' teachers. Owen's vision was infused with political discourses working to achieve a different society and the gender of the teachers was not an issue, as long as they were able to be 'kindly'. Wilderspin did follow a liberal curriculum, yet he employed gender discourses to argue that it was only men who had the moral strength to save these children (aged 2–6 years) from 'neglect and contamination' (Curtis, 1967:120). Powerful social class discourses concerning the need to 'civilize' the children of the dissolute poor were becoming more influential

(Purvis, 1989) and contributed to the establishment of 'public parents' who were needed to rescue these children.

The development of the 'mother' teacher and the 'male' expert

In the early nineteenth century, there were powerful maternal discourses emerging about the 'unique' role of the 'mother' in educating 'infants' (Cunningham, 2000). The male infant teacher may have been able to claim superior spiritual and intellectual qualities, but it was only the female teacher who could publicly enact the mother-made-conscious (Steedman, 1992). Alexander (1983:9) identifies how the mother was seen as 'the pivot of the family, and consequently the guardian of all Christian (and domestic) virtues'. This 'maternal' role was now being constructed as essential for the development of a Christian society and was in future 'to be learnt artificially' (Harris, 1993:80). The Christian Mothers Magazine by the early 1840s was using the word 'parent' to mean mother 'rather than being ambiguous or meaning "father"' (Clarke, 1985:84). Hall (1995:75) considers that by the 1840s 'the definition of women as primarily relating to home and family' was in place. New labour markets were developing for men and women as industrialization increased. The poorly paid jobs made available for women, including teaching, reflected their domestic role (Hall, 1995:99).

The removal of men from Infant teaching

Wilderspin's movement was short lived and by the late 1830s, male participation in infant teaching had 'all but died away' (Clarke, 1985:74). Men moved into the position of removed experts and the teaching of infants became constructed as suitable 'women's work'. This public reworking of the female maternal role has resulted in a widespread and long-lasting acceptance that Early Years teaching is a suitable occupation for women-only, due to women's 'natural' and nurturing qualities. This key gender shift was supported by influential campaigns led by middle-class women, who promoted the educational writings of Froebel. Froebel believed that the teaching of young children was maternal work (Cunningham, 2000; Martin and Goodman, 2004). Froebel believed that women 'possessed an innate maternal tendency' that should be employed in teaching young children (Hilton and Hirsch, 2000:12). Froebel had also developed a complex theory of directed play, in contrast to the rote instruction in many of the early voluntary schools. His philosophy was taken up by committed middle-class German women and as 'early as 1854 a private kindergarten was started in London by a leading Froebelian' (Hilton and Hirsch, 2000:13). Powerful maternal discourses were further developed as male and female roles continued to be renegotiated during this time of vast social, political and economic change (Steedman, 1992). The writings of Darwin and others also reinforced essentialist discourses 'about sex and gender' that drew a great deal of support from many women as well as men (Harris, 1993:26). The Froebelian movement in England was composed mainly of middle-class women who developed popular discourses of 'spiritual motherhood' in order to carve out a place for themselves in the public sphere (Brehony, 2000:186). Froebel believed that: '(the) teaching of young children was, ideally, the mother made conscious' and this allowed middle-class women to claim teaching as their 'maternal' right and duty (Moriarty, 1998:1). Harris (1993) argues that 'good' mothering, as defined by the new middle-classes, was increasingly constructed as contributing towards the welfare of the nation and empire. Louisa Hubbard campaigned widely in the 1870s to recruit lower middle-class women into teaching to serve the nation by becoming 'a mother to her pupils' (Widdowson, 1980:31). The 'progressive' educational methods advocated by Froebel were increasingly gaining ground in England and The Council of the National Froebel Society was established in 1874. Although during the 1870s there were roughly equal numbers of male and female state teachers (Steedman, 1992; Miller, 1996), teaching was now beginning to be increasingly constructed as an 'ideal' occupation for middle-class women to enter into and men started to exit (Copelman, 1996).

The school population continued to grow, from 751,325 in 1860 to 871,309 in 1866. Tropp (1957:96) reports that 'education' was the leading issue of the day. The voluntary schools were providing schooling for 261,158 pupils, but a further quarter of a million children now needed schooling (Copelman, 1996:65). The 1870 Elementary Education Act brought in a state education for all pupils in England and Wales up to the age of ten (Beddoe, 1983:55), setting up School Boards. The 1870 Act 'gave women the right to serve as representatives on the thousands of school boards being set up' (Martin and Goodman, 2004:85). The discourse of public 'mothering' continued to be employed as a strategy by female middle-class campaigners to support the entrance of more women into the public sphere. Martin (2000:179) reports how women members of the influential London School Board were drawing on: 'the rhetoric of familial femininity'. Froebel's ideas concerning the teaching of infants were increasingly incorporated into School Board policy (Steedman, 1992; Bloomfield, 2000). Martin (2000) also offers a short excerpt from Florence Fenwick Miller's unpublished autobiography, *An Uncommon Girlhood*, which clearly demonstrates the usage of 'maternal' discourses, in order to support a campaign for the employment of married women:

> I believed that mothers would very likely be the most efficient teachers, partly because the sympathy of young women is often dormant until they have children of their own, when they understand and sympathise better with all the little ones. (Quoted in Martin, 2000:179)

Florence Fenwick Miller was one of the twenty-nine women who served on the London School Board. It was not only in London that Froebel's ideas were adopted: Bloomfield (2000:168) refers to a report written in 1882 by William Abel, a school board inspector in Nottingham, that employs Froebel's imagery of the 'garden' in order to argue against the continuation of mechanical rote teaching in the Infant departments. In many areas, lectures were held on child development based on Froebel's usage of 'gifts' and training and certificates were offered for women infant teachers. Bloomfield reports that by 1910 the national membership of the Froebel Society had risen to 2,600. Steedman (1992:185) asserts that Frobel's ideas have contributed to the teaching of young children as a 'conscious and articulated version of mothering'. Men would in future be excluded from Early Years teaching due to their inability to enact the role of a public 'mother' (Walkerdine, 1992; King, 1998; Wadsworth, 2002).

The association of maternal discourses with Early Years teaching was also accompanied by the development of a set of powerful paternal discourses that this time contained sex-typed assumptions concerning 'male' qualities. If women teachers were now to be the bearers of 'feminine' qualities such as 'caring' then male teachers would need to be responsible for 'masculine' qualities. Paternal discourses affirmed the 'good' but firm heterosexual father who was required to lead the school 'family' (Epstein and Johnson, 1998). In 1880, state schooling was made compulsory and the curriculum offered was itself highly gendered. Boys were now to be prepared for occupations such as skilled manual jobs, factory work and military service: and the girls were to be offered domestic training skills (Skelton, 2001:14). Male and female elementary teachers were given separate and distinct roles to play in the regulation of the children of the poor, as well as receiving different salaries and status.

The state curriculum imposed on elementary schools in the nineteenth century was gendered as well as classed (Paechter, 1998). The imposed curriculum reflected assumptions that male and female teachers were suited for teaching different age ranges and different subjects. The curriculum promoted mixed sex infant classes and then aimed to separate the older boys and girls. Discourses that argued older boys would require men to teach them were already in circulation and Bergen (1988:52) discusses how women 'were only gradually allowed to teach male children' and this was when male teachers were not available.

The move from the mixed sex infants into the juniors 'meant physical separation and a new school identity as girl or boy rather than infant' (Davin, 1996:119). Many of the old board school buildings still have separate entry and playground signs chiselled into the concrete, for the older boys and girls. Davin (1996:121) describes how a Richard Church, born in 1894, found the change to male teachers in the juniors very upsetting and she suggests that by this time: 'masters were seen as exerting tougher discipline'. The use of corporal punishment in these early elementary schools was the norm and the working-class pupils were routinely caned. Clegg (1972:19), who was born in 1888, has highlighted the central role corporal punishment played in these schools when he described his headmaster as: 'a hard worker. For one thing, he did several canings a day'.

The curriculum that was established in these state schools continued gendered practices that had been found in many of the charity and voluntary schools previously set up for working-class children (Miller, 1996:148). Miller (1996) offers evidence from the records of a school founded in 1824 in South London, where the girls' curriculum was focused on needlework rather than arithmetic, which was often only taught to the boys by men. Sewing activities for girls could earn money to help support the running of the school and the sewing teacher would always be female. Beddoe (1983:52) refers to the 1827 Report for the Girls National School in Lambeth that shows how girls engaged in sewing for four afternoons a week. Beddoe (1983) also reveals that by the early 1860s, school readers for girls were full of anecdotes about good and bad housemaids, reflecting the growing employment of female (working-class) servants amongst the middle-classes. A Boer War (1899–1902) recruitment drive found many working-class men were unfit-for-service due to diet and hygiene (Beddoe, 1983:58). In consequence, domestic subjects were further developed for girls in school to ensure they acquired better housecraft skills: 'poverty and malnutrition were attributed to a lack of domestic management' (Paechter, 1998:82). This focus on girls and domestic subjects again drew on maternal discourses that positioned women teachers as extending their 'natural' home-making skills within the public sphere (Paechter, 1998). Male teachers could not be part of this 'maternal' work; they were expected to teach 'boys' subjects that were separate from domestic chores. The older boys were to be offered craft subjects in order to 'labour cheerfully at the tasks that were his lot' developing positive industrial habits (Paechter, 1998:83).

The division of physical education for girls and boys further supported the creation of two separate spheres for male and female pupils and their male and female teachers. It imposed a 'divergence in both syllabus and classroom experience' (Davin, 1996:121) for pupils and teachers. Military drill encouraged boys to respond to discipline and the girls were offered Swedish drill based on gymnastics. The need to regulate and control what was seen as the uncivilized sexuality of the poor was a feature of this provision, despite the over-crowded living conditions at home where girls and boys would have mixed freely (Davin, 1996:119). This highly gendered and classed school curriculum was concerned with inculcating the values of a bourgeois 'respectability' including separation of the sexes as well as of subject content. Connell (2002:117) discusses how, during Victorian times, the 'separate spheres of men and women were powerfully emphasized' in schools. This was the time when long-lasting gender scripts were laid down in society and men and women were clearly given different roles, including occupational ones.

Male sports were intended to guarantee a well-disciplined male workforce and to produce men who would be healthy enough to be able to serve the empire in times of war (Paechter, 1998). Male teachers developed football for working-class boys as an important part of school life. In the 1880s football clubs had been set up in London and were very popular. Football itself 'drew many boys to school and to school activities' (Walvin, 2000:62). The popularity of football attracted boys into school at a time when many pupils truanted in order to earn money (Beddoe, 1983; Walvin, 2000). Male sports quickly expanded and 'by 1895 nearly every important town had developed a school organization for the promotion of football and cricket' (Curtis, 1967:299). Discourses about men being needed for boys' sports were laid down at this time and are still circulating today (Raphael Reed, 1998; Pratt-Adams and Burn, 2004). In Chapter Three, we explore further how sport continues to feature in the male teacher 'scripts'.

In order to ensure strict discipline, as well as for the teaching of crafts and boys' games, male teachers were clearly valued in these early elementary schools. Research shows that gender discourses concerning 'male' sportsmanship, role models and ascribed management and discipline qualities continue to position the 'scarce' male teacher as a valued asset in primary schools, reinforcing gender barriers (Connolly, 1998; Skelton, 2000; Jones, 2006).

The numbers of poorly paid female 'supplementary' teachers employed grew rapidly after 1870. These women had no qualifications as they were uncertificated and they were placed mainly in Infant classes (Widdowson, 1980:58). By 1899 there were: 'six certificated teachers to five uncertificated teachers' (Ozga and Lawn, 1981:72). Partington (1976:4) reports how 'the typical infant mistress was the untrained supplementary teacher'. Tropp (1957:171) considers that at this time the 'alarming increase in uncertified and untrained female teachers' led to a cheap pool of unqualified labour. Ozga and Lawn (1981:72) argue 'women were used increasingly as cheap labour in the education system'.

This increasingly gendered staffing policy meant that:

> the elementary schools were divided into three departments, infants, girls and boys, the first two staffed by women and the last by men. (Copelman, 1996:50)

Copelman is referring to London schools; in rural areas this staffing pattern was not always feasible due to pupil numbers. Where possible, men taught in the Juniors; they received higher salaries and were already advantaged in promotion. This is evidenced in the first headship promotion list drawn up by the London School Board in 1886, when they:

> ... recommended fifty men and only twenty-seven women at a time when there were 2,076 men and 4,065 women in the teaching force. (Copelman, 1996:50)

It is worth noting that women teachers did not receive equal pay until 1961 and, as Jones (2006:62) points out, in 'the UK primary school there are disproportionate numbers of male headteachers at primary level'. Male teacher career advantage continues within this workforce, aided by rarity and gender stereotypes of men as superior at: keeping discipline, teaching sport and providing male role models for the boys (Burn, 2005; Martino, 2008).

The decline in the recruitment of male teachers to elementary schools continued as further employment opportunities became available for men. So, by the start of the twentieth century the teaching of young children had become predominately female work. In 1895 there were 24,948 girl pupil teachers compared to only 6,384 boy pupil teachers (Tropp, 1957:170). This was a major gender shift and since then this occupation has continued to attract mainly women teachers (Widdowson, 1980; Bricheno and Thornton, 2002; Skelton, 2011).

Maternal and paternal discourses seeking to replicate the patriarchal family were drawn on to further justify the higher pay and increased promotion that male teachers were given from the beginning of the occupation (Miller, 1996). The 'nurturant and caring' female teachers (Reay, 2001:153) together with the large numbers of young female unqualified teachers were positioned as merely re-enacting their domestic roles in public and in need of management by 'rational' men. These powerful gender discourses (Blackmore, 1999) positioned male teachers as suited to instruct older pupils, maintain strict discipline, teach male sports and carry out school leadership roles, thus reaffirming wider patriarchal relations (see Chapter Six).

The maintenance of Early Years teaching as women's work in the twentieth century

Early Years teaching became further consolidated as a female occupation during the twentieth century. Davin (1996) has drawn from inspection reports to document the increasing separation of the boys and girls and of the infant and junior departments in schools. Davin quotes from a report by female inspectors in 1906: 'little children are subjected to military rather than maternal influences' (cited in Davin, 1996:117). The report further promoted the teaching ideas of Froebel and criticized the traditional formal 'instruction model' of teaching in the Infants. In contrast male elementary teachers were constructed as the 'instructors' especially needed for junior boys who were believed to benefit from drilling and the stricter discipline men could 'naturally' provide (Littlewood, 1995:47).

The Education Act of 1902 had set up Local Education Authorities (LEAs) and replaced School Boards, establishing municipal secondary schools in England and Wales and reinforcing the elementary/secondary divide (Beddoe, 1983:59). The shortage of entrants into elementary teaching intensified further after 1902, due in part to the new Education Act, which now gave responsibility for training to the newly established LEAs (Curtis, 1967:319). The old pupil-teacher system was now to be abandoned and replaced by new entry routes. Tropp (1957:189) argues that between 1902 and 1914 there was a 'complete transformation of the method of recruitment to the profession'. Trainee teachers were now required to go to college at sixteen, after being offered a scholarship to secondary school, thus delaying their earning potential. The lengthening of teacher training resulted in a severe drop in entrants and Tropp (1957:186) tells us: 'the decline was particularly serious for boys'.

The First World War in 1914 meant 'the virtual cessation of the recruitment of men into the profession' (Tropp, 1957:208). Curtis (1967:339) records that classes were depleted of male teachers during these war years and women teachers were teaching large classes of boys as well as girls. When the war ended, a government scheme of 'special training' brought 1,000 ex-servicemen into teaching (Tropp, 1957:223).

The influential Nursery pioneer Margaret McMillan served on the Council of the National Froebel Society (Moriarty, 1998:1). The 1918 Education Act allowed Local Educational Authorities (LEAs) to set up Nursery schools and in 1919 McMillan opened a training school in order to train young girls as the natural 'nurturers of small children' (Steedman, 1990:83). In the 1920's, a time of increasing male unemployment, the majority of these female 'nurturers' of children would be unmarried. Increasingly the LEAs imposed marriage bars, which meant women teachers were required to leave on marriage; the belief that a women's place was in the home once again gained high currency (Beddoe, 1983). Martin and Goodman (2004:128), drawing on Manchester Education Committee records of the time, discuss how some women opposed this marriage bar, whilst other women supported it. Men were increasingly being constructed as 'failures' if their wives had to work outside the home, because they could not financially support them. Powerful 'male breadwinner' discourses came to the fore, justifying further the higher salaries male teachers still received. Women, who did not marry and continued to teach, were being positioned as unnatural 'spinsters' (see discussion of male union campaigns at this time in Chapter Five).

Gender barriers within this occupation were being cemented and a Report on Infant and Nursery Schools in 1933 used the female pronoun throughout when referring to staffing. The report recommended that young girls could support the headmistress, whilst learning how to better run a home in future (Burn, 2005). The link between the future female domestic role in the home and working in Nursery and Infant schools was explicit. Barriers to prevent men teaching this age-range were once again publicly reaffirmed. The policy to employ young girls on poor pay continued the 'normal' usage of cheap female unqualified teachers that was widespread at the start of the twentieth century (Tropp, 1957).

The Second World War (1939–1945) once more saw women teachers teaching the older boys and as men enlisted the marriage bar was informally lifted. The cessation of the Second World War once again saw the introduction of 'emergency' teacher training, including men from the armed forces. The post-war rise in the population now meant far more teachers needed to be trained. The number of male teachers recruited increased by 55.5 per cent and women by 22 per cent (Tropp, 1957:256). Tropp (1957:262) comments positively on this increase in male entry: 'the profession has shed its mass of cheap untrained female labour'. There was a continuing configuration between 'female' cheap labour, unqualified staff and Infant teaching. Tropp's view conjures up memories of the poorly paid, unqualified 'supplementary' women teachers of the late nineteenth century.

Oram (1989:25) suggests that the 'sexual division of labour in the schools became more rigid' after the Second World War. Her research shows that male teachers became further advantaged in promotion and 'appointing panels often preferred a headmaster if they could find one' (Coffey and Delamont, 2000:114). The recruitment policy once again reflected the historically held 'truth' that it was women who taught the infants and men were required for teaching the older boys. There is also evidence that women teachers were being devalued and seen as 'problematic' especially for the older boys. Agnew (1989) shows how this largely female workforce has long been positioned as deficit:

> No country should pride itself on its educational system if the teaching profession has become predominantly a world of women.
>
> (Langeveld, The Year Book of Education, 1963,
> quoted by Agnew, 1989:67)

Whilst, Acker (1994:77) reports that:

> In the 1950s and 1960s, a number of commentators expressed concern over the disastrous consequences they supposed would follow from the predominance of women in teaching.

As late as 1957, a male teacher union was still arguing that women only came into teaching as a precursor to getting married, further cementing existing maternal discourses (Coffey and Delamont, 2000). This attack on women teachers by a male-only union had previously surfaced in the early 1930s (Limond, 2002). The discourses worked to ensure that men continued to gain promotion advantage since women teachers only saw the occupation as 'fitting-in' with their childcare responsibilities. If women did return to teaching after child-bearing, it would be their maternal qualities that would be valued rather than any consideration of their actual teaching talents (Steedman, 1992). Tropp (1957:263) describes the occupation in 1957:

Teaching, with its short hours, long holidays and opportunities for part-time work is the most convenient occupation for middle-class married women, and teacher training is perhaps the most profitable investment for a girl whose aspirations include marriage and motherhood.

This 'most convenient occupation' for women served to further construct the female teacher as essentially preparing for motherhood. Male teachers were more suitable for headship, since this particular 'regime of truth' constructed married woman teachers as primarily concerned with obtaining part-time work to fit in with their domestic responsibilities. The familial discourses were firmly back in circulation, working to construct 'ideal' primary teachers: the male junior teacher 'father' receiving authority and respect due to his rationality and superior discipline skills, in sharp contrast to the comforting infant teacher 'mother'. The Plowden Report (CACE 1967), a highly influential report into Primary schools, valorised ninety-seven male Infant teachers for their bravery:

> In infant schools in 1965 there were only 97 brave men out of a total of 33,000 teachers. The tradition that women are better suited than men to work with younger children also affects the allocation of classes within schools. The National Survey shows that 90 per cent of teachers of first year juniors were women as compared with 55 per cent of teachers of fourth year juniors. (CACE, Volume 1, 1967:313–314)

The Plowden Report considered that more male teachers were 'needed' in all Primary schools and also suggested men could become further involved in the teaching of young children:

> There are both educational and practical grounds for urging that as far as possible there should be men teachers in all primary schools. Some young children, particularly boys, may respond better to teaching from a man than from a woman. (CACE, Volume 1, 1967:324)

The Plowden Report specifically identified how it would be young boys who would be the main beneficiaries of increasing the number of male teachers. The historical discourse of 'boys need male teachers' has resurfaced internationally in recent years (see Chapter Eight) and been employed in teacher recruitment campaigns (Sargent, 2000; Mills et al., 2004; Martino, 2008; Skelton, 2009). 'Male teachers as role-models' is also part of this male gender script.

In the 1960s Hoyle (1969:49) had argued:

> The concept of the infant school teacher as a mother figure is an appropriate one since one of her main tasks is to wean the child away from its psychological dependence upon the home.

'Weaning' reaffirms the image of a maternal nurturing female teacher concerned with the emotional needs of the young child. Hoyle's educational textbook was widely used on Teacher Training courses; it was one of Elizabeth's texts during her training. In contrast, the male junior teacher is described as: a father, grandfather, elder brother, uncle or 'a rather wayward cousin' (Hoyle, 1969:66).

(Steedman, 1992:186) examines how, in the 1960s and 1970s D.W. Winnicott (a respected child paediatrician) advised 'teachers of young children to model themselves on good – or good enough – mothers'. This belief, supported by very influential theories of maternal deprivation, again argued mother figures were vital for young children and they were widely publicized through radio broadcasts as well as books. In this particular gender construction there is no room for men to be actual teachers of young children; they are to be the senior managers and experts. Steedman (1992:188) posits that gendered discourses of the 'good' mother have 'urged teachers to take upon themselves the structures of maternal thought'. Maternal discourses are still in circulation within the occupation; for example, when researching the training experiences of 'Philip', Oyler et al. (2001:374) found Philip was being positioned as a 'father' figure, in order to 'enter the domestic and maternal world' of teaching. It is worth noting that just as many female teachers resent being constructed as substitute mothers, male teachers can also resent being cast as substitute fathers (Cameron et al., 1999; Burn, 2002). Historical gender 'scripts' work to strait-jacket both men and women who enter into this occupation and they need to be made more visible and challenged today.

Blackmore (1999:23) argues that regimes of truth have been historically established within teaching, that work to link 'rationality to masculinity in leadership, and thereby emotionality with teaching and femininity'. Jones (1990:75) suggests that the transformation of the urban teacher into 'a good and nurturing mother' by the end of the nineteenth century was clearly concerned with providing 'a moral exemplar' for inadequate parents in the 'urban abyss'. However, Jones (1990) does not discuss what this construct of teaching as 'mothering' means for men; we have already argued that the only subject position left available for male teachers is 'fathering'. These historical 'patriarchal parent' roles have been covertly affirmed by staffing practices and beliefs that still exist (King, 1998). Alexander (1988:167) argues that the 'ideal' Victorian family is still symbolically represented in primary schools today:

> The (usually male) head, 'kind but firm', is the school's father figure, head of the household ('my school'); the (usually female) class teacher is mistress of her particular domain ('my class', in effect 'my kitchen') in which the child receives warmth, comfort and even protection from the fiercer excesses of the head/father. This I realise is a very Victorian and possibly sexist image, but then the power available to the primary head

resembles nothing so much as that of those middle-class Victorian fathers who conceived of and established those elementary schools ...

Staffing and promotion patterns within Primary schools continue to largely correspond to Alexander's insightful description of the 'Victorian' paterfamilias.

Although we recognize that there is still an ongoing public perception that the teaching of young children is akin to mothering and as such defined as 'caring' rather than teaching, it is important to acknowledge that all primary teachers do not agree with these sex-typed beliefs. In the following chapters we offer research data from male and female teachers which evidences that some teachers will challenge these gender assumptions, whilst others will uphold them. Acker (1994:120) found in her research that women primary teachers were actively making 'patriarchal bargains' in order to 'negotiate' their own work identities within the many structural constraints that they were faced with, rather than just becoming passive victims of the system. In the same way as middle-class Victorian women claimed that women were the 'natural' teachers of Infants as part of their campaign to establish women in the public sphere; the claiming of 'natural' female qualities may have developed as a long-term female strategy in order to keep ownership of Early Years teaching. It may also serve to demonstrate how gender discourses can be upheld by both women and men in our present-day society. Yet, many male and female teachers do refute these gender practices (Reay, 1990; Wadsworth, 2002) and this book explores both resistances to and acceptances of the long-established gender norms in primary schools (see also Epstein, 1993). These gender norms have become embedded within this occupational culture even though they no longer reflect the roles women and men occupy in today's society and in fact can be viewed as working to reinforce outdated sexist views concerning the potentials of men and women.

Conclusion

Chapter One has examined how constructs of male and female primary teachers have been shaped by powerful gender (and class) discourses, which have long promoted essentialist ideas about men and women. It shows how familial discourses have been laid down over time, working to position male and female primary teachers as public 'patriarchal parents'.

Maternal discourses have constructed Early Years teaching as female-only, and men have been excluded due to their 'lack' of care, which is constructed as a female-only quality (King, 2004). The 'strictly relational character of power relationships' (Foucault, 1978:95) suggests that if women teachers are positioned as 'mothers' then the only subject positions available for male teachers are as 'fathers' who are in charge. The chapter has shown how 'symbolic public parents' have been historically constituted in order to control the children of the poor and their influence can be seen in the gender barriers that have become 'normalized' within the occupation (Skelton, 2001; Cushman, 2005a; Jones, 2006; Mistry and Sood, 2013).

Paternal discourses have also worked overtime to give male primary teachers status, pay and promotion advantage, providing they fulfil the sex-typed subject positions allotted to them. The four main historical 'scripts' ascribed to male teachers are concerned with: sport, discipline, role models and promotion. Male teacher scripts that can be assumed as 'ordinary' practice; gender was largely invisible for the ninety-nine primary teachers that Nias researched. However, she did find that:

> Nearly a third used the family as a metaphor or an analogy for their favourite schools…'we're almost a mummy and daddy, with a family': another said he treated the children in his class as he did his own children, 'behaving like a dad to them'. (Nias, 1989:185)

We now examine these historical taken-for-granted gender beliefs and practices within the occupation, drawing on the data we have collected from men who have selected to become primary teachers.

Discussion questions

1. Duncan (1996:169) argues that dominant discourses can be challenged once they are 'exposed, rendering them open to change'. Reflect critically on your own early schooling; can you identify some of the gender/class discourses discussed in this chapter? If so, what effect did they have and how did you respond to them?

2. We have discussed how 'unqualified' women were employed as cheap workers in infant classes at the end of the nineteenth century. Consider the number of (mainly female) classroom assistants employed in many English primary schools today: are there any parallels?

CHAPTER TWO

Men Training to Teach Young Children

Chapter Two draws on data obtained from our participation in a voluntary Male Student Teacher Support Group. The data collected from this Male Support Group indicates that the ongoing project of gender identity construction is itself highly problematic, cut across by class, sexuality and 'race' difference (Showunmi, 1995; Skeggs, 1997; Reay, 2001; Pulsford, 2014). In contrast to a single in-depth interview, the research data was collected over an academic year; so we had time to become 'involved' with these men and we had also established a professional relationship with several of the participants prior to the group's establishment. These male students were reflecting on gender (and other) practices within one particular teacher training establishment. The research method offered an opportunity to listen to and reflect critically on, how a small number of male student teachers 'negotiated' the complex, emotional, contradictory, conscious and unconscious processes implicated in the ongoing production of our internal and external 'selves' within a specific context and at a particular time (Walkerdine and Lucey, 1989; Burr, 1995; Wieler, 1999).

Research suggests that the training experiences of male primary teachers can be problematic and the data we collected supports these research findings (Smedley, 1999; Thornton, 1999; Lewis, 2001). A significant feature of the group meetings was the disclosure and often emotional discussions of 'being stereotyped' experienced by the majority of the male students. After providing the background details of these students, we briefly discuss 'stereotyping' itself and then present the five key issues that arose from the data analysis. Chapter Two concludes that long-established gender regimes, current gender discourses about 'male' primary teachers and a backlash against 'feminism' itself are all implicated in these men's interpretations of their particular gender experiences, whilst training to become teachers of young children aged 3–11 years of age.

Background

The Male Student Support Group was initially composed of seven men who were at the start of their second year of study on a Bachelor of Education (B.Ed) degree in primary teaching. Their School of Education was part of an inner-city university in England that had an explicit policy of recruiting mature students from non-traditional backgrounds. Many of these student teachers had entered through Access schemes targeted at working-class and ethnic minority groups, and middle-class students entering from traditional A-level routes were a distinct minority.

The Male Student Support group enlarged, after the third meeting, when four men from Year Three of the degree joined the group. A total of eleven male students attended the group over the academic year. The seven 'mature' entry students were aged twenty-five or older and had all entered university through non-traditional access routes. Appendix 1 provides details of the male students, indicating how many meetings they attended and their year of study. The sessions were about an hour in length and held in university rooms, with tea and coffee available.

When we set up the voluntary Male Student Support Group we were not involved in teaching these male students during the second year of their studies, although Elizabeth had taught the students mathematics the previous year. We were aware of and concerned about the higher dropout rate male students on the B.Ed faced nationally during initial teacher training (Thornton, 1999). A research paper, which Elizabeth had presented about gender and teacher training, had been reported in the press and Adam, one of the male Year Two students, stopped her in the corridor: 'Why are all the men failing, Elizabeth?' We decided to see if setting up a male support group would help more of these at risk students complete their training.

There were now seven male students in Year Two, since five of their male colleagues had already left. Colleagues were supportive and we booked a room and asked Adam to invite a few of the men along for a cup of tea and a chat to see if they were interested in meeting on a regular basis. The male support group met for a total of seven times over the year in-between school placements. Elizabeth attended all of the sessions, whilst Simon attended four sessions due to timetable clashes.

In the first meeting, to our surprise, all seven of the Year Two male students turned up and we made it clear this was 'their' group, and if there were things they wanted to talk about without tutors present, we would leave and in a couple of sessions we did withdraw for a time. The male students all believed research was needed since nearly half of the men in their year group had already left. The men willingly agreed to the keeping of field notes and several offered themselves as 'role models' prepared to speak to other men who wanted to enter primary teaching.

We did not direct the discussions, but we did offer comments and contribute verbally when the men asked us for our views or wanted some advice. The moral panic around men teaching young children arose when the male students asked us for advice about supervising children during PE lessons. Dave disclosed, 'it's terrible that people could think I'm some sort of pervert'. Simon's school experiences and advice were significantly different from Elizabeth's who had never considered that she might be accused of child abuse. After this upsetting session (with the group's permission) we took their concerns to the school experience tutors, who drew up student guidance in this matter. However, most of the sessions were not as focused, they were very informal, relaxed and friendly. Their main purpose seemed to be to provide an opportunity for the male students to 'safely' talk through their experiences at university or during school placements.

It was during the first meeting that the 'attacked' man script became visible. We had advertised the group on the student notice board; but the men asked us if we could send details and date of subsequent meetings via their e-mails. Several men had received mockery and negative comments from women students who had read the initial notice. Dave was asked: 'What do YOU need a group for? It's alright for YOU! They'll let YOU through.' An indication perhaps of how some female students resented the way they saw these 'male' students were being favoured.

The current 'role-model' discourses were constructing these male students as 'assets' to the occupation: at the same time these discourses were making the men targets of female student resentment and jokes, that often drew on wider stereotypes about 'useless men'. Stereotyping and its effects were constantly discussed; these men felt they were always viewed as 'Other'.

Stereotyping and the concept of the 'Other'

When Mike told the support group: 'I'm sick of being stereotyped,' we all understood that Mike meant that because he was a white middle-class man he was expected to 'behave' in certain ways. Stereotyping involves the drawing up of social boundaries: attributing fixed essentialist 'qualities', usually negative, to certain groups (Hall, 1997; Barker, 2000). These ongoing classifying practices are concerned with the operation of social power in specific contexts (Foucault, 1978). Stereotypes can be viewed as 'weapons', which are employed to uphold or contest wider structural relations (Barker, 2000). Pickering (2001:12) believes that stereotypes

> operate within a given ideological field, not for all time but in relation to definite social needs and conditions that may change.

Pickering (2001) argues that the complexities and effects of stereotyping can be better understood when considered in connection with the related concept of the 'Other'. In her classic text *The Second Sex*, de Beauvoir (1988) explored the way sex stereotypes have historically operated to reduce women to the 'Other'. The man is the subject and the woman is the object.

> She is defined and differentiated with reference to man and not he with reference to her; she is the incidental, the inessential as opposed to the essential. (Simone de Beauvoir, 1988:16)

Feminists and other social justice campaigners have taken up the notion of the 'Other' in order to represent how groups and individuals can be excluded and stigmatized. Paechter (1998) provides a very helpful discussion of the multifaceted ways 'Othering' can occur. These excluding practices are culturally and historically specific; they may result in symbolic social exclusions and have real material effects. Epstein (1993:18) has researched the complex ways both individuals and organizational cultures engage in the business of Othering: 'It is by drawing boundaries and placing others outside those boundaries that we establish our identities.' Everyone is somebody's Other and identities are constructed in relation to an idealized or deficit Other who can be both desired and loathed (Orner, 1992; Skeggs, 1997). These asymmetrical power relations operate to establish dominant social and national groups, which will exclude, assimilate or appropriate the Other:

> The marking of Other is not just a method of providing a distinction between two groups, but a way of institutionalising hierarchical difference and power.
>
> (Cameron et al., 1999:21)

Pickering (2001:77), exploring the racialized Other, describes the pain and psychic damage these processes can inflict on the 'object' who is being Othered:

> The indelible effect of this recognition of yourself as Other creates a twoness of vision that allows you to see yourself only through the eyes of others.

So, racism (and other excluding practices) can result both in internalizations of the negative stereotypes applied by the more 'powerful' group, as well as resistances (King, 1998). Pickering (2001:69) believes that the concept of Othering helps provide a fuller recognition of how stereotyping is 'implicated' in maintaining wider structures of power: 'the two concepts can be taken as complementary'. Stereotypes can work to both advantage and disadvantage; for example, the same maternal stereotype that affirms women as naturally 'caring and sensitive' and therefore 'ideal' teachers of the youngest children will also work to exclude them from senior management since they are too emotional and non-rational.

Othering operates in groups as well as through institutional practices, it is supported by stereotyping and the developments of powerful social myths, such as women are 'better' at Early Years teaching due to their natural caring abilities (Sargent, 2000). These established 'truths', built on sexist stereotypes, can operate as effective social control mechanisms, to legitimate or exclude:

> Who is the Other at any given place and time depends of course on who is being defined as the Subject. There are innumerable Others, as there are innumerable sets of power relations between groups, and many people experience Otherness in multiple and sometimes conflicting ways. (Paechter, 1998:7)

The men in the support group occupy a more 'privileged place' in wider society due to their gender (de Beauvoir, 1988:169), but in this student body they are very much a minority group. They are often the only man in a teaching session, or on a school placement and this may make them at risk of becoming the temporary Other (Cameron et al., 1999). When the college tutor or class teacher is female there is a reversal of the 'normal' patriarchal power relations. Initial training could be one of the few times in their teaching career, when these men may feel institutionally 'powerless' in a female group. Women students and staff will also be aware of these 'unusual' social power conditions, since we are all involved in the 'structures of gender relations' (Connell, 1995:82) as we struggle to claim and disown our social identities (Skeggs, 1997:28).

When these men started their degree studies and found that there were very few men, how did they project 'a definition of the situation'

(Goffman, 1959:23)? Goffman argues that these initial performances will be significant for later group acceptance. Coleman (1990:192) notes that a 'familiar criticism of Goffman is that he can be seen as presenting people as consciously pursuing strategies of impression management'. Yet, Goffman (1959:18) does discuss the complex and sometimes misunderstood elements of a public performance: a person 'may be neither consciously nor unconsciously disposed to create such an impression'. Goffman (1959:45) argues that individuals may attempt to present an idealized performance in order to be accepted, which 'will tend to incorporate the officially accredited values of the society'. This 'social script of expectations' (Goodson and Sikes, 2001:61) includes notions of 'acceptable' masculinities and male and female students will be aware of the social expectations that 'real' men are meant to 'perform'. Gutterman (1994:223), discussing the 'doing' of masculinity, points out:

> As members of any particular culture, community, or group, individuals are given a vast array of scripts that together constitute them as social subjects.

The 'masculinity' of the male students appeared to be under the spotlight and they felt that they were being 'judged' by the women students and staff, when they were in lectures or on placement. Their gender 'minority' position during training produced a strong sense of 'male' exclusion, and resulted in self-exclusions. The men's position as the stereotypical Other due to their gender was filtered through layers of 'race', sexuality and class difference. The five major 'issues' that were identified through scrutiny of the field notes collected by Elizabeth are likewise mediated through our own subjectivities as two experienced primary teachers who have moved into academia.

Issues raised by the male students

Issue one: The isolated and 'attacked' male student

In the first group session 'stories' of isolation and comments made in teaching sessions by women students and tutors were told and this became a regular feature of all of the meetings.

A public re-telling of these often-painful feelings and events seemed to offer a safety valve for the male students. In this group they could disclose a sense of isolation and difference and receive support and validation for their feelings from the Other male students. The men may have found it easier to disown some of the comments, when they heard what the Other male students were experiencing. It was less about them as individual men and more about the complex gender dynamics that can arise for men in predominately female groups. Cameron et al. (1999:70), researching Early Years staff, found:

> Staffrooms as a site of gendered discussions was highlighted by four men and two women. These discussions were described as 'women's talk' or 'intimate conversations', from which men are generally excluded ... Being excluded from conversation is a powerful means of dividing staff; and being excluded on the grounds of gender is a powerful means of dividing men and women ...

The researchers report how Early Years workers told them that male staff could often find themselves 'slightly ridiculed' and 'stereotyped' (Cameron et al., 1999:67). Mulholland and Hansen (2003:221) also report that some male student teachers in Australia experienced being mocked by women students during training; one student disclosed: 'I've come across one big stereotype in the course that because you're a guy, you're dumb.'

In the Male Student Support group it was possible for these men to openly talk to other men about not 'fitting in'. Gavin disclosed: 'When I know I'm going to be the only man in the group (p) I feel different.' These men had already spent a year studying with women students, so their present sense of social unease indicated a continuing tension. Colin's account suggests that he finds many of the mature women students quite intimidating:

> Often, I'm the only man in the discussion group and the women all boss me. I'm told I have to do the feedback (p) then the female tutor attacks me for dominating.

In this School of Education, the gendered staffing patterns of the primary school are clearly replicated: the majority of men are in senior management (see Coffey and Acker, 1991:255, for discussion of staffing in Schools of Education). Women tutors teach many of the actual teaching sessions and these eleven male students often find themselves the only male in the room.

Colin's comment about being 'bossed' hints at female bullying whilst he is attempting to make friends and 'fit' into the student group. Colin also feels vulnerable to female tutor allegations of dominating the group due to his gender. A story told by Bill supports Colin's claim of being directed by women students to carry out stereotypical male roles. In Year One each of the four curriculum groups had to select a student representative for the Board of Studies. A women student had told Bill: 'You do it. We haven't got the time. We don't ALL have a wife to pick up our kids.' When Bill went to the meeting, he met Dave, Colin and Frank since each individual group had voted for a man. The female year tutor was horrified. Bill complained: 'they told us to be the reps. then they blame us for taking over – you can't win!' There was an assumption and an accusation that these students as 'men' would have no childcare or domestic responsibilities. At the end of this session Frank, who had gone to wash the cups, came back with tray in hand and announced:

> I do look after our 3 children, just as much as my wife. She has to work part-time but they're ALWAYS saying 'I don't know what it's like to look after a family' but I do!!

Out of the seven men in Year Two, three of them had young children and fully shared family responsibilities (Frank, Dave and Bill). However, as 'men' they had also received verbal 'attacks' from female students who implied: 'it's all right for you lot'. These stereotyped gender jibes are, as Fraser and Yeomans (1999) in their research into ITT argue, cumulative.

The male students were aggrieved by the way some of the female students attacked them as 'typical' men. However, they also found that some female students were highly supportive and 'felt sorry for us' (Colin). In gender practice there will be male and females who uphold the 'norms' whilst others will seek to challenge them. In course discussions about sexism the individual man may feel he has very few resources available to 'defend' himself with when given the full responsibility for wider male oppressions. hooks (1989:133) suggests that feminists need to 'make a space to dialogue with men' rather than reversing the oppressive 'subject-to-object' relationship. Gender barriers can cause alienation on both sides.

Overall, the data collected indicates that these men felt that they were being held responsible by women for men's bad behaviours in society. None of the students identified how men can also benefit from 'institutionalized power relations' (Walby, 1990:32), the patriarchal 'dividend' men can inherit (Connell, 1995: 82). Their gender 'stories' were focused on the way the women students 'blamed' men and they greatly resented these 'unfair' jibes.

King (1998) interviewed a male teacher in the United States of America, who described a training session in an all-female group, where he had experienced abusive comments about 'men' in general. The man's reaction parallels many of the stories told by the group:

> I slipped out of class, confused, disturbed, but unable to identify the source of my disquiet...I had been on the receiving end of blatant sexism... I found myself thinking, 'Well. OK, I guess I'm supposed to take this – after all, I'm sure that they've been the target of this kind of treatment often enough,' as if rationalizing it would take the pain and inherent wrongness of it away. (King, 1998:37)

This man did complain to the female tutor but the response of the group was to say they were 'just kidding' and afterwards he felt he was increasingly 'subjected to various hostilities' (King, 1998:39).

The sense of a collective female 'attack' on individual male students was highlighted after the four 'Year Three' students joined the support group. There were some very long and emotive discussions about how 'every man is made to feel guilty' (Mike). When Fraser and Yeomans (1999:7) interviewed male PGCE students, they reported:

> At some time in their training each had to cope with stereotyping and prejudice in some form, even though sometimes it had been mild in impact (presented as humour) and discriminatory in intent.

Elizabeth was very aware that she was a woman tutor listening to men admitting in public to being actually 'wounded' by sex-stereotyped comments made by women. The male students often seemed to forget that she was present; these men were actively involved in attempting to re-establish and protect their own conflicting masculine identities in the face of ongoing comments about the 'failures' of men. Once, when the men were discussing the regular comments about 'useless' men that they were receiving, both in schools as well as in college, Dave quietly explained: 'it's not bias Elizabeth, it's persecution'.

The constant striving to reclaim, understand and then establish a type of 'masculinity' that was acceptable to them, as well as relating to the women they were studying alongside, was an ongoing feature of the men's conversations. They demonstrated how problematic and complex it can be for men to 'do' masculinity (Mills, 2001; Morgan, 2002). The public 'performance' of an 'accepted' masculinity is fraught with contradictions and ambiguities. Smedley's (1999) research recommends that during ITT male students need to talk about and theorize their experiences as 'men' and the data collected from the men's group likewise indicates that training can be a stressful and upsetting time for 'male' student teachers.

The two lectures on Gender that the B.Ed students had received so far had impacted in negative ways for all of the men in the support group. The gender lectures were usually an hour in length followed by a short seminar; they were infrequent due to the many other demands of the ITT curriculum (Cole, 1999). Mike felt: 'the gender lecture was TOTALLY unfair! It made me feel worthless!'. Kevin told the group:

> In sessions we're expected to represent men and take the flack. It's male bashing on this course.

Kevin, a Year Three student, attended the support group twice before walking off the course and not completing his degree. On both visits Kevin had expressed very clear anger about: 'a war against men' and the Year Two men were surprised by the strength of his bitterness. Skelton (1989:54) suggests 'we know very little about how gender issues are (or are not) tackled on ITE courses'. Aspinwall and Drummond (1989) argue that:

> The stereotyping of male and female qualities that pervades our society has serious implications for initial teacher training. (Aspinwall and Drummond, 1989:16)

The gender lectures had not served to open up a male/female discussion about the need to challenge inequitable gender regimes in primary schools. Instead, as Thompson (1989:74) found in her study of ITT, it seemed: 'antagonism to gender issues' continued to exist.

There were clear differences in how the men interpreted the ways the curriculum tutors positioned them in class. Kevin felt the tutors did not respect him because he was gay; Dave told the group that he had personally found all of the tutors very supportive and Frank and Ian strongly agreed with him. However, John and Henry believed that the only way to 'survive' was to remain silent; otherwise you were 'labelled'. Mike disclosed: 'I'm already labelled because I answer back – the tutor doesn't like me'. Again the sense of wanting to fit in, to be liked, by the female students and tutors was a feature of many of the men's conversations. These male student teachers seemed to be largely unable to establish a fully 'credited' social self within the wider female group (Goffman, 1959:245). The 'psycho-social' costs of this were apparent in the very emotional discussions that occurred in several group meetings (Walkerdine et al., 2001:15).

The reason we thought the group both enlarged and lasted over the year (see Thornton, 1999 for discussion of her male student support group's poor attendance) was because of the strong friendships that these men forged and cemented. At times the group seemed to perform the role of self-therapy, where an individual sense of 'male' isolation and difference could be spoken about, accepted and indeed mediated through discussion with Others. It became 'their' group and the men often e-mailed each other and 'protected' other group members, forming a safety net when individual men expressed a wish to leave. These male students remained highly fearful about non-completion and would monitor their male colleagues' attendances at university. Despite their many differences due to ethnicity, age, sexuality and class, it was gender that united these male students in a visible and powerful way.

Gutterman (1994) suggests that gender identities are always being fought over and all of these eleven men had disclosed being 'made to feel uncomfortable' in college or schools, as reported by Ian, due to being a 'man'. The men had a shared sense of 'not belonging' which helped develop strong group empathy amongst them. The voluntary Male Student Support group provided a safe space where these men could let down their masculinity 'shields' and express pain, anger, bewilderment and uncertainty without making themselves vulnerable to ridicule (or challenge) for not upholding socially acceptable hegemonic 'masculinities'.

Issue two: Social class difference

Ramazanoglu and Holland (2002:147) discuss the dangers of focusing on gender alone when examining social practices and argue that gender relations 'are difficult to separate in practice from other power relations'. Although we have divided the main issues that these male students raised into categories for analysis purposes, the strands are interrelated. Connell (1995:80) identifies how:

> The interplay of gender with other structures such as class and 'race' creates further relationships between masculinities.

Social class itself, as a concept, has become increasingly problematic and Savage (2000:156) argues that in Britain today there has been 'a profound remaking of the relationship between class and claims to individuality'. However, this does not mean social class has disappeared in today's 'risk' society. Beck (1992:99) in his highly influential analysis of changes in the labour market, argues:

> Class does not disappear just because traditional ways of life fade away. Social classes are rather emancipated from regional and particularistic restrictions and limitations as a result. A new history in the chapter of class is beginning.

This 'chapter of class' continues to produce educational inequality and Reay (2003:311) has researched the 'powerful processes of class-based exclusions' in Higher Education. A focus on 'processes' is particularly relevant for Mike's story, which we retell below. It shows how Mike's middle-class social 'status' became transformed into a 'stigma' within this particular setting. Mike believes he was Othered by the tutors, due to his gender, class and ethnicity.

Out of the eleven male students in the support group, Mike and Ian are the only two men who fit into the middle-class bracket from a socio-economic perspective. Mike was the only man in the group to speak openly and proudly about his social class background. These two young men achieve high academic grades, but whilst Ian is quiet and non-confrontational, Mike is angered at the way he perceives he is treated within the university. Mike is very supportive towards the other men in the group and he showed a particular empathy towards Colin when he disclosed to the group how the mature women students had bullied him in class. Articulate and self-confident, Mike seems more able to resist being 'directed' by the female students; however, his relationship with the female tutors is far more problematic.

After a couple of support meetings, the 'men' started to drop into Elizabeth's office to discuss issues that had occurred; it was as if they were looking for help to make sense of some of the comments and behaviours they were experiencing as men. These male students' claims of discrimination stand in contrast to Thornton's (1999:44) findings:

> Club participants did not identify any ways in which they felt discriminated against or disadvantaged by their primary ITE course.

Simon did not receive any of these 'informal' visits from the men in the group. One could hypothesize that the men were positioning Elizabeth as a 'mother figure' or that they found it easier to talk through emotionally stressful events with a mature woman rather than talk to a relatively young man. Also Elizabeth had taught several of these men, so they had already formed a relationship, whilst Simon did not teach on the B.Ed degree.

It was during one of these unplanned-for visits that Mike revealed a very angry and highly distressed sense of his minority social class position within the student body. Colin knocked on Elizabeth's office door and asked if she could 'spare a minute? I've brought Mike to see you, he's going to walk out'. The usually confident Mike was very upset. He sat with his arms folded, his head down, and he seemed to be shaking. Mike then looked up and burst out:

> I'm PROUD of being middle-class and when I'm qualified I'm going to SUE this University.

Mike sat back and knocked his head on the bookshelf; Colin and Elizabeth both laughed and the 'tension' was broken when Mike joined in. Mike felt then able to discuss the 'incident' that had made him so upset, angry and ready to leave. In one lecture to a whole year group, the white female middle-class tutor had asked a question and when nobody else answered, Mike did:

> I was accused of (p) 'oh, it has to be the white middle-class man who speaks' (*mocking voice*). JUST because I ANSWERED the question!

By speaking his account, his version, Mike was able to distance himself from the actual event, and he regained a calmer self. One explanation is that Mike, due to his white middle-class inheritance, would have the social confidence to answer the tutor's question. Leonard (1994:169) has found that mature working-class students may be 'intimidated by the sophisticated language' used by tutors. Mike spoke in the same language register as the middle-class tutors and he did not lack confidence when speaking in public. When no other student answered in the session, Mike could have felt he was trying to support the female tutor (or the year group). Another interpretation is that the female tutor was trying to prevent a man from dominating the discussion, which research shows can occur in mixed sexed groups (Mahony, 1985; Spender, 1990). hooks (1994) discusses how power dynamics in HE can operate to silence some students, recognising the complexity of these exclusionary practices. For these men gender barriers co-existed with those of class, 'race' and sexuality.

Certainly Mike was very alienated by what he felt was open bias from the tutor, resulting in a very public shaming; Mike then calmed down and he and Colin went off for lunch. This story shows how: 'the politics of everyday life is being constantly debated and worked out' (Lees, 1993:21). Comments about individual identity can both affirm and, as in Mike's case, wound: they are personal and context specific (Burn, 2000; Hey, 2003). Skeggs (1997:93) discusses how 'class hatred is not just one way' and in this particular context it was Mike's social class 'difference' as well as his gender and ethnicity that were highlighted by a female tutor. Mike is studying at a School of Education where it is mature working-class female students who are the 'norm'. The emotive pain of class difference is evident in Mike's account and Ball (2003) argues:

> The distinctions and identifications of class are embedded in non-cognitive dispositions as well as in the minutiae of the everyday perceptions and fears. In one form, class struggles are realized within the everyday interweaving of diverse tapestries of behaviour. (Ball, 2003:177)

Mike never mentioned this particular incident in the support group meetings (the other men had all witnessed it) but he became increasingly cynical, self-excluding and often voiced a survival strategy of not talking in lectures. He was not going to risk a repeat of the tutor's public accusation that had so hurt him. In fact, he became silent in the taught sessions. The rest of the support group did not encourage Mike to continue speaking; it seemed that the men tactically supported his decision. The cost of course continuation for Mike was a retreat into silence as a 'survival' strategy; gender barriers had effectively muzzled him.

Ian, the other middle-class student, adopted a non-confrontational strategy of befriending tutors and being quiet, which served him much better during his training. Ian was also quiet in most of the group sessions and never contradicted other 'stories'. After qualifying (with a First Class Honours degree) Ian gave Elizabeth a helpful collection of newspaper and web site articles about male teachers, which he thought would be useful for her research and thanked her for being so supportive. Ian had just accepted a first teaching post with an extra allowance for science, although this was not his subject specialism, because they 'wanted a man in the school'. Recruitment of more men continues to be a government priority. The needed man and role-model scripts work to advantage male teachers once they are qualified (Mills et al., 2004). Duncan (1996), in her New Zealand research, agrees with Thornton and Bricheno (2000) that 'rarity' can bring rewards for male teachers in both appointments and promotion; however, it may also bring female teacher resentment that can surface during initial teacher training, when men are not yet in positions of authority.

Issue three: Homophobic innuendoes and heterosexual flirtations

I've been told by a female tutor to lower my voice in class. I know I'm not masculine enough. Colin.

The men in the group were shocked when they heard Colin's story and told him that his voice was perfectly all right. Colin a gay man, could have been measuring himself against dominant heterosexual masculinity, and he is judging himself as not 'male' enough (Hearn, 2002). In our society men will be expected to continually prove their allegiance to the 'hegemonic' norm (Pratt-Adams and Burn, 2004). Among the many hierarchies of masculinity, it is gay men who occupy the lower rungs (Mills, 2001). Colin's self-definition that as a member of a subordinate masculinity he was 'not masculine enough' evidences this constant pressure to evaluate his performance against the socially accepted masculinity script (Epstein and Johnson, 1998).

The female tutor's advice may not have been connected to Colin's sexuality alone. The day following this group meeting, at the end of a PGCE math's session, a black heterosexual student disclosed that he had also been told to 'lower' his voice in school, by a female teacher. The similar advice these two male students had received could have been part of the discipline man script (see Chapter Four). This script encourages men to employ their physicality (including a loud voice), in order to assert a paternal authority. Another interpretation is that the advice was merely intended to help these students develop appropriate 'teacher' voices, rather than as a specific criticism of the men's 'masculinities'. It would be interesting to research whether or not female students also receive advice to change their voice tones.

Staff room stories were shared that indicated mild sexual flirtations or taunting could sometimes occur, which corresponds with the research findings of Fraser and Yeomans (1999). Dave described how the women teachers in his school placement had arranged a 'date' for a young male teacher; they had then turned up at the wine bar to mock him.

The male students who were placed in schools with an all-female staff reported more of these sex-typed conversations. The male students were just as 'visible' in primary schools as in the university classrooms. Whether the men were given praise, such as, 'it's great having a man in the Infants' or censure: 'it's alright for you, you'll be a head in five years', their presence in schools was noticed and commented on. Remarks, linked to role-model and promotion scripts, often embarrassed the men. Adam, Mike and Ian, the three younger white heterosexual men, were positioned by some female staff as favourite sons, or as handsome princes, a target for mild sexual flirtations. Research in Scotland also reports male students resenting being 'mothered' by female teachers during their school practices (Hepburn, 2013).

The men's gender minority status serves to position them as 'male' students rather than as student teachers; it was noticeable that if there was already a male teacher on the staff he would often 'protect' the male student during practice, offering him advice and support.

The gay men in the group seemed particularly vulnerable to stereotyped comments that hinted at the need for 'real' men in classrooms and in schools they felt under the closest scrutiny. Seemingly insignificant comments caused these men to reflect on what they saw as their personal inadequacies. These gay men were not challenging their treatment in schools; rather they were concerned that staff, parents and pupils would accept them.

King (2004) has examined the culture of silence and suspicion surrounding male teachers and their sexualities. This can cause men to carefully monitor their own behaviours for possible censure. King (1998) discloses how, when a class teacher, he internalized homophobia:

> I internalised the monitoring of my homosexuality that I imagined others were doing. I remember deciding what to say to other teachers, whom to sit with at lunch, how artistic I could be…I was often embarrassed because I was certain they could tell I was gay. (King, 1998:116)

A couple of weeks after Colin had described being told to 'lower' his voice in school, he came to Elizabeth's office with a newly shaven head: 'why have I done this Elizabeth (p) is it about me being a man?' For Colin it would seem that the need to renegotiate and reaffirm his 'masculinities' is an ongoing issue. Perhaps Colin was attempting to 'maintain a manly front' in the light of his recent school experience (Kimmel, 1994:132). These complex identity performances are not easily explained nor are they fully understood by the 'performer' or the audience (Goffman, 1959). One of the heterosexual male teachers interviewed by King told him 'they'll think I'm weird or maybe they'll think I'm gay' (King, 1998:111). The linking of homosexuality with perversion remains a powerful and destructive public discourse (see Chapter Seven).

Issue four: Discipline men

After school experience visits, the male students talked with dismay about how they were 'expected to be good at discipline' (Dave). The older men, especially the black men, were all assumed to be very good at discipline – which they were not, at this stage of their training. Their presumed masculine authority was on the line, if they did not perform the 'required' male discipline script. Henry told the group 'I never became a teacher in order to shout at children.' These male students did not wish to perform the authoritarian role but found some women teachers were expecting them to carry out the discipline role in school. John was sent the disruptive black boys and disagreed strongly with this practice: 'just because I'm black myself!' Adam felt that the pupils, female staff and parents, all gave him extra status because of his physical size, regardless of his wishes (see Chapter Four).

Epstein (1997) suggests that dominant masculinities are being re-affirmed in schools and some men do embrace this discipline role. A white female student, Elizabeth was supervising, reported a comment made by a young black male Junior teacher. His classroom was full of football posters and the 'naughty' black boys were regularly sent to him (by white female teachers) to be disciplined. This male teacher had told the female student 'every school has a bastard, and I'm happy to be it'. In contrast to John, this particular black male teacher was happy to claim and perform the discipline man script.

The gender stereotype that men are naturally 'good' at discipline, certainly disadvantages them during training when they may be 'sent' naughty boys from other classes to discipline; however, the positive aspect of this stereotype means that men can also be advantaged in appointment and promotion due to the gender stereotype of men's 'superior' ability to discipline pupils (Cushman, 2005a).

Issue five: Men, mathematics and ICT

Nine out of the eleven men in the support group had selected to study mathematics or ICT (Computer Science) as specialisms. There was no longer a PE specialism, which in the past had also been favoured by male students. Frank had selected maths because: 'there's less essay writing'. All of the working-class men in the support group had expressed doubts about their writing abilities. Students can see mathematics as a subject area where there is less essay writing and as Hutchings (2002) discusses, maths can still be constructed as a 'male' subject.

ICT, like mathematics, is a subject that can also be stereotyped as 'male' (see Jenson and Brushwood, 2003). It is worth noting that most of these male students had large student debts and were in severe financial difficulties; yet they were all very e-mail and computer skilled. There is a shortage of mathematics and ICT specialists in primary schools. Once qualified these two high status specialisms may give male teachers even more promotion advantage (Chapter Six). All of the men in the group reported female teachers in schools were already valuing them for their computer expertise.

Conclusion

This chapter has focused on one group of male trainees; although it cannot be generalized from, it can help us understand better how gender stereotyping can both disadvantage and advantage men who enter this occupation. It indicates that women students and teachers can resent the advantaged career prospects these men will subsequently inherit, provided they are prepared to follow the legitimate male scripts (discipline, sport, role models and promotion).

The pain of 'gender' isolation that these men discussed in their group discussions agrees with other research concerned with male student teachers (Pepperell and Smedley, 1998; Fraser and Yeomans, 1999; Lewis 2000; Mulholland and Hansen, 2003). The majority of the men in the group felt unjustly 'attacked' by some of the women students (and some of the female tutors). All of the men found that they were subject to the 'discipline man' script when in schools and they all strongly rejected this role. The gay men in the group seemed more sensitive to public censure and all of the male students felt very vulnerable to being seen as potential child abusers (see Chapter Seven for further discussion of this issue).

The 'role-model script' also surfaced and the men were aware of their rarity; on teaching practice, all of them had been made 'welcome' as needed 'men' (with their computer talents). However, some of the men reported feeling uncomfortable at the way older women teachers 'mothered' them in the staffroom or made sexual allusions. Several of the men positioned themselves as needed and necessary 'role models', not only for male pupils in school but as student 'mentors' willing to encourage other men to enter the occupation (see Chapter Five).

The men's reactions to lectures on gender were emotive and negative. None of the men showed any awareness of wider patriarchal relations. They felt they were being 'persecuted' but at no time did they reflect on wider male advantage in society. These male students had started their teacher training well aware of and in agreement with government recruitment policies that affirmed the 'need' for male teachers (especially for older boys). They may have expected to be greatly 'valued' during their training, and in the school context many were made welcome. However, the response from some female students and tutors to their own understanding of themselves as potentially important additions to the occupation was far more divided. These men did not have knowledge of gender theorizing in order to engage in debates: instead they retreated into victimhood. Public discourses of the 'attacked' and endangered man are highly influential, as Lingard and Douglas (1999:9) discuss:

> Newspapers and magazines throughout the western world have been full of articles about the reconstitution and defence of masculinities under dual pressures from feminism and changing labour markets.

The students knew that they were at higher 'risk' of non-completion due to being 'men'. They defended their position by creating a strong network of male support and by positioning themselves as innocent 'attacked' victims, drawing on the ongoing backlash against feminism (Mills, 2001; Connell, 2002). The painful distress many of these male students subjectively experienced, during their training, needs to be both acknowledged and tackled.

Discussion questions

1. Have you ever been the only man or woman in a work or study group? If so, did you receive comments about your 'gender' and what was your response?

2. The training of primary teachers in England is undergoing change, with more school-based routes now available. What opportunities could this present for reconciling gender tension between the students?

CHAPTER THREE

The Role of Sport in Upholding Gender Practice

Chapter One showed how particular subject positions for male primary teachers have been constructed over time, through the circulation of powerful paternal and maternal discourses. These discursive configurations have produced a set of legitimate male gender 'scripts', which work to maintain male advantage in status and promotion, providing the male teachers adhere to them.

One of the gender 'scripts' laid down in the late nineteenth century, worked to construct male teachers as 'sportsmen' needed and necessary for the teaching of football and PE to working-class boys (Walvin, 2000). In this chapter, we examine research data, from present-day male teachers, that evidence this sportsman script is still in circulation today. It also reveals a resurgence of 'football' as a tool to engage 'failing' boys (Pratt-Adams and Burn, 2004). Government campaigns, aimed at recruiting more men into primary teaching, have employed these sport discourses, with slogans such as: 'Every good boy deserves football' used to inspire more men to sign up for PGCE courses (Pratt-Adams and Burn, 2004:244). It can be argued that by drawing on this gendered script, men who do not want to be bearers of outdated forms of hegemonic masculinity could find this advert patronizing; rather than encourage recruitment, it may actually work to alienate men further from entering the occupation (Skelton, 2009). We conclude this chapter with a critical examination of 'football' initiatives in primary schools and the gender practices they can inadvertently reinforce (Raphael Reed, 1999:63).

We do not wish to criticize the sport, and we have both enjoyed teaching football to girls and boys, when we were still classroom teachers; rather it is the linking of football to hegemonic masculinity that we challenge. Jeff, one of our key informants, believes: 'the football culture in schools can be very aggressive and elitist'. Connolly, researching racism in three inner-city primary schools, found that: 'football was a very male affair. Girls were systematically excluded...' (Connolly, 1998:85). Connolly also reports that the focus on boys and football marginalized women staff, which supports Messner's (1992:19) view that: 'the hegemonic conception of masculinity in sport' reinforces men as separate and superior to women.

Prior to discussing our male teachers' differing responses to the 'sportsman' script, and the gender practice it produces, we provide a short discussion of research into 'hegemonic' masculinity itself and its continuing ability to defend male institutional power.

Male primary teachers and masculinities

Wadsworth (2002:42) argues that present-day constructions of male primary teachers are still derived from 'rigid concepts of what masculinity is', which work to reinforce the belief of innate sex difference (Connell, 1995). We have demonstrated how familial discourses have historically attempted to 'fix' masculinity in opposition to femininity, drawing on established 'oppositional binarisms':

> A framework of oppositional binarisms has historically provided the governing logic of identity formation in the West. This framework has grounded identity in a series of either/or categories within which individuals are expected to exist. (Gutterman, 1994:220–221)

In primary teaching, these gender binaries require both male and female teachers to value a 'hegemonic' masculinity which must be upheld for the protection of wider 'patriarchal relations' (Weedon, 1998:108). Connell (1987:187) defines contemporary 'hegemonic' masculinity as 'the global dominance of heterosexual men' which is affirmed through the institution of marriage and 'often involves the creation of models of masculinity which are quite specifically fantasy figures' (Connell, 1987:184). So, 'hegemonic' masculinity actually represents men's social and institutional power, rather than individual men, but all men will be measured against it. It is historically and culturally specific and it is a winning strategy for maintaining 'men's dominance over women' (Connell, 1987:185). In the operation of 'hegemonic' masculinity, men claim power over women and subordinated masculinities, such as gay men, will be attacked ideologically.

Research into men and 'masculinities' indicates that there are a number of competing subject positions for men: 'males very rarely demonstrate a coherent or consistent form of masculinity' (Mills, 2001:21) any more than women will all adhere to one version of 'femininity'. Men will have 'multiple identities and interests' (Hobson and Morgan, 2002:18). Morgan (2002:280) further argues that despite the plurality of masculinities, powerful sanctions can be applied to punish men who transgress against the 'hegemonic' masculinity that is currently legitimated within a particular society:

> The idea of hegemonic masculinity suggests that, despite the apparent range of ways of 'doing masculinity,' there remain deeply embedded and subtly coercive notions of what it really means to be a man.

Researching how male primary teachers select to describe their gendered work experiences involves a reflection on the influence of 'hegemonic' masculinity on their work subjectivities (Cockburn, 1991). Our analytic framework of 'legitimate male teaching scripts' has been designed to allow for a closer scrutiny of male teachers' claimed and denied 'masculinities'. The scripts (see also Chapters Four to Six) were drawn up after coding the data collected from the key informants to allow for better scrutiny of the gender practices we seek to challenge. We need to move beyond description as at present we still know 'very little about the *masculinities* of male teachers' (Skelton, 2000:15). The 'scripts' allow for a more systematic examination of how these male teachers are negotiating their gender identities within specific contexts; recognizing that the claiming and disowning of subject positions is ongoing, complex and contradictory. Kaufman (1994:147) supports the social constructionist perspective that:

> Gender is not a static thing that we become, but is a form of on-going interaction with the structures of the surrounding world.

Connell (1995:71) argues that gender relations remain highly significant; they are 'a way in which social practice is ordered.' These social practices involve 'interactions' with other major power relations, such as social class and 'race'. We focus on gender in this book, whilst recognizing that to understand gender relations better 'we must constantly go beyond gender' (Connell, 1995:76). As the data evidences not all male teachers will benefit equally from male power. Connell (1995:198) suggests researchers need to recognize the:

> Complex structure of gender relations in which dominant, subordinated and marginalized masculinities are in constant interaction.

In this way the 'doing' of gender is a 'fluid and hybrid construction' cut across by 'race', class and other identities (Pratt-Adams et al., 2010:29). Some of the male teachers we researched have not had the same access to patriarchal dividends due to their other social identities as gay, black or working-class (Connell, 2002).

Derek, one of our key informants, described how when he was inspected by a white middle-class male Ofsted inspector, he was told he was 'rarer than hen's teeth'. Derek could not decide if the Ofsted inspector was referring to his gender, as he is an infant teacher; his sexuality, as he is gay; his ethnicity, as he is Black; or his social class, as he is working-class. In this instance, Derek's strategy for being positioned as the 'Other' is to turn this experience into a humorous story. However, later in the interview he angrily discloses that after six years of teaching: 'I feel like a pawn in the game, I'm just a token really.' Skeggs (1997:121) points out how:

> The sexed and gendered subject is constructed across a multiplicity of discourses, positions and meanings, which are often in conflict with one another and are inherently contradictory but which are circumscribed through access. We do not all have equal access to positions in discourse.

The male teachers interviewed who did not conform to the hegemonic norm, that is, they were not white, heterosexual and middle-class, discuss exclusionary practices concerned with their other social identities, alongside gender. Hearn (2002) acknowledges Connell's (1987, 1995, 2000) major contributions to theorizing a plurality of 'masculinities' with unequal power relations existing between men. Hearn agrees with Connell, that despite the status differences between men, male social, economic and institutional power still continues to be upheld by 'hegemonic' practices. These practices are enshrined in the legitimate male teacher scripts, of which 'boys sport' is one.

This short consideration of research into men and 'masculinities' indicates that male teachers will be positioning themselves (and be positioned) within the established hierarchies of male power. We are aware that 'hegemonic masculinity' with its required heterosexuality and whiteness will be institutionalized and well-defended by 'the cultural machinery' that operates in the public arena (Connell, 1995:241). Men who follow the approved gender path will expect to gain both approval and rewards. This has clear implications for the male teachers who do not wish to (or, like Derek, cannot) 'perform' the legitimate male scripts:

> the claim that we all perform our gender might mean, for example, that when a man behaves in ways that are socially acceptable for men, then he feels more convinced than ever that he is a 'real' man. (Moi, 1999:55)

Male teacher scripts, like the Sportsman Script, function as upholders of the socially approved 'hegemonic' masculinity, which continues to be heterosexual (Jackson, 1998; Mallozzi and Campbell Galman, 2014). These dominant male teacher scripts will be 'constructed in relation to various subordinated masculinities as well as in relation to women' (Connell, 1987:183).

Men who enter primary teaching may still be subject to these masculinity scripts since they have 'inherited' historical 'gender patterns' (Connell, 1995:86). Edley and Wetherell (1995:211) propose that:

> men are constrained by the range of different theories of masculinities made available by a culture... the individual man might have further constraints placed upon him by the fact of his physical shape and occupational status.

Male teachers' physicality has historically been seen as an asset within the primary teaching occupation, required for disciplining the children of the poor and sport. The discipline script constructs the 'physicality' of male teachers as necessary to 'control' the older boys (see Chapter Four). The sportsman script constructs men as needed for teaching older boys sport, in particular football. Male physicality also works to exclude men from the Early Years; they are constructed as powerful and as such, unable to perform 'caring' roles (King, 1998). Butler (1990) has radically critiqued the social construction of the gendered body and its linking to essential sex difference; rather performances of 'masculinity' are discursively produced within particular cultural and historical periods.

Unfortunately, these essentialist beliefs that construct male primary teachers as essentially different and superior to women primary teachers, continue to surface in research findings. Cushman (2010:1215) reports interviewing Ronnie, an English primary teacher, who describes how he can discuss watching football with young boys, in a way women staff cannot: 'you have to be a man to know all about these things... it's a man subculture. Women aren't into these things'. Again, not all men share this gendered belief, Cushman (2010:1215) also interviewed Kris, who disagreed that men are necessary for sport: 'I could say undignified things like "men are better at sports" but it's simply not true'. Our data showed the same contradictory responses and we now examine our male teacher resistances to, as well as acceptances of, this historical 'sportsman script'. Responses which demonstrates how, as Moi (1999:350) asserts: 'Just as all women are not feminist, not all males are patriarchal.'

Research findings

Interviews with eighteen key informants

Eight out of the eighteen male teachers who took part in in-depth interviews had either studied PE as a subject specialism whilst training, or had gained promotion for sport. Eight of the male teachers openly disagreed with the sportsman script; five supported it; and five did not raise it as an issue. This diversity (in response to the scripts) is found in all of the research data we collected and demonstrates how the negotiation of our public identities by the claiming or disowning of subject positions is complex, inconsistent and also context specific. Research concerning male primary teachers in Scotland reports similar contradictory findings (Hepburn, 2013). Context also matters, in Infant or Nursery schools, where football is not on the timetable, male teachers will not be expected to 'naturally' perform the sportsman script. Pat, one of the five men who did not discuss the sportsman script, is Head of a Nursery school (3–5 years) where all of the other staff are female; the playing of team sports is not on the curriculum. Three out of the five men who did not mention sports were Newly Qualified Teachers (NQTs); and four out of five were Early Years trained.

In contrast, Jeff, who was soon to take up a deputy headship in a Primary school, found on his pre-interview visit: 'the other male teachers in the school were the PE or the rugby teacher, or the sports teachers'. Jeff is aiming to challenge this 'typical' staffing pattern when he takes up his new position on the senior management team. These 'reforming men', who want to dismantle gender stereotypes in sport, were teaching both in Infant and Junior classrooms. Football was the sport they identified as potentially excluding and problematic; they also challenged the linking of football to working-class boys' educational achievement.

We first discuss the eight male teachers who are attempting to resist the sportsman script and 'rewrite' sports as inclusive of girls and female staff; then we introduce the five men who saw teaching football as a 'normal' part of a male primary teacher's work identity and raised no issues about gender practice.

Reforming men

Carl does not accept being: 'a bloke in a tracksuit' and in his interview he discusses how football is being increasingly used to 'motivate' working-class boys in school:

> It's not going to work (p) you have to make learning attractive rather than 'you'll get a game of soccer [football] at the end of it'. It's wrong, if we're good teachers and blokes it's by-the-by, we're just good teachers...
> (Carl, a Year Five supply teacher)

Carl is denying that being a 'bloke' is synonymous with being a 'good' teacher, and argues that learning itself should be the focus rather than sport (Skelton, 1996). Carl's subject specialism was history/geography, yet he has held a promoted post for sport in the Juniors and he increasingly contests this 'sexist' role.

Derek believes:

> The day a boy comes into my classroom carrying a book instead of a football is the day I know I have succeeded. (Derek, a Year Two teacher)

Jeff also considers that government drives to develop football in schools, as a way of engaging working-class boys in literacy, is very problematic:

> Is it not reinforcing a stereotype, you know? And what about those boys who aren't very keen on football? (p) I actually don't like the football culture in school (p) my crusade is to improve the playground (p) to take away football, to bring back other games, because I think it's very competitive, I find it very aggressive... it can be quite damaging (p) I actually think it could reinforce stereotypes. (Jeff, a Year Five senior teacher)

Jeff has found in his eight years of teaching that he has often been expected to take boys sport and in particular football, due to his gender, although his subject specialism is Religious Education. He actively contests this gendered practice: 'I've always told people don't give me football!' Jeff demonstrates clear agency and resistance throughout his interview and alongside his 'crusade' to dismantle the sportsman script, Jeff is also rejecting the discipline man script (see Chapter Four). Despite resistance from female colleagues, he moved into Infant teaching for two years, because he wanted to become a 'very good teacher' and learn his craft. This reforming discourse of 'I want to be seen as a good teacher, not as a male teacher' that works to disown the current gender regimes in schools, surfaces in many of the interviews, and is supportive of Skelton's (2009) argument that recruitment drives should be focusing on the challenge and satisfaction to be gained by becoming a good primary teacher, rather than highlighting essentialist notions of male-only qualities (see also Cushman, 2005a).

In common with Carl and Jeff, Oliver (Head of an Infant school) enjoys sport but he 'hates football.' Oliver challenges the belief that all men like football; Wadsworth (2002:42) also rejects: 'the authoritarian, unemotional male who is obsessed with football.' Oliver's Infant school has started two clubs, and at the moment it is only boys who are outside playing sport. The girls have selected to attend the textiles club, which is taught by a woman teacher. Oliver is very concerned about this and he has now decided to teach textiles himself in order to try and develop mixed sex groups in both clubs. This is an excellent example of how teachers themselves can actively challenge damaging gender stereotyping.

Neil's Infant school has started recorder, art, football and board games clubs. Neil (Deputy-head of an Infant school) was told he had to run the football club 'but it was over-subscribed' and the one girl left when she found she was the only girl. Neil enjoys sport but worries about giving 'sexist messages' to the children. Neil hopes to soon 'relinquish' his football club responsibilities to two female teachers. These women teachers took a session last week and 'the boys were absolutely gob-smacked that women were playing football.' We need to recognize how children, parents and governors are involved in promoting and upholding gender practice (Burn, 1989; Thorne, 1993) and our strategies for dismantling the male scripts include recommendations for the whole school community (see Chapter Ten). Neil's account also evidences that when women and men teachers work together gender practice can be more effectively challenged. Wadsworth (2002:43) recounts, how when he was an infant teacher, he was likewise expected to 'publicly demonstrate' his masculinity by teaching the older boys football and cricket. Again, thanks to a female teacher, he escaped this 'uncomfortable role' by being invited to play netball with the girls and some parents. These gender alliances are useful in evidencing how female and male primary teachers can actively resist the limiting stereotyping that teacher gender scripts seek to impose (see Chapter Nine). It would be valuable to see if the majority of teachers thought sport being segregated along gender lines was a problem. In order to maintain power, discourses must always recruit new 'subjects' and if other teachers support our Reforming men's refusal to be bound by limiting and outdated beliefs about males and females and sport; then this narrow male sportsman script will unravel. We believe girls and boys both need access to a wide range of sporting activities and female and male teachers are needed to teach these sports. Sport is no more 'male-only' than reading is 'female-only' yet gender stereotypes can work to construct them as so (Burn, 1989).

In his first school, as a young male who liked sport, Roger (Head of a Primary school) enjoyed taking boys' football. In common with Neil, Roger became increasingly aware that he was: 'accidentally reinforcing these stereotypes.' Roger recognized that male sport in the school served to marginalize the 'talented' female deputy head, with the male sports teacher and the male head teacher actively excluding her from senior management discussions (Roger's experience parallels research by Connolly, 1998; and Skelton, 2000). Roger is clearly identifying how gender barriers can have real material consequences. Roger has also held a promoted post for sport; yet, his training specialism was history/geography.

Quentin has previously held a promoted post for sport, although his subject specialism was also history/geography. Quentin feels an increasing tension between teaching football, a sport he really likes playing, and continuing sexist stereotypes:

> I love sport (p) but I have to be careful that I don't sit there perpetuating the male stereotype. Which is HARD. At the end of the day I'm a product of my society, so I'm a bloke who does like to (p) go down the pub, who

does like to play sport, who does like to watch sport, who hates loading the dishwasher you know. (Quentin, a Deputy Head of a primary school)

Quentin shows the taking up of multiple subject positions is fraught with tensions: the subject positions available to us at any one time are contradictory and fought over. His interview data demonstrates the 'insecurities' identified in recent Scottish research (Hepburn, 2013). Gender identities are 'precarious and vulnerable' and Quentin is clearly aware of these ongoing dilemmas (Alvesson and Due Billing, 1997:98). In his interview, Quentin positions himself as 'totally' against the 'sexist stereotypes' as well as being bound up in them:

If you're a male teacher you're expected to have control (p) discipline and be good at sport and probably good at IT.

Quentin easily identifies several of the current legitimate male teacher scripts (including sportsman) which the Scottish research also found to be in widespread circulation (Hepburn, 2013). The legitimate male teacher scripts for men work to uphold a certain 'type' of masculinity; Mills (2001:6) discusses how 'sport plays a major role in the construction of masculinities'.

Stuart (Lecturer in HE) has a great deal of experience of teaching a physical activity in primary schools; however, in contrast to the other male teachers, it is not football. In fact, Stuart found that his choice of activity has received censure as it does not conform to the accepted 'male' sportsman script. Stuart is a keen folk dancer, and he really enjoyed setting up country-dancing clubs in schools for girls and boys, instead of the 'expected' and approved football ones. Many of the boys would not attend 'because they thought it was too sissy for them.' A father stopped one talented boy from attending: 'his dad thought dancing was too effeminate.' Stuart actively challenges this gendered belief and he discussed this with the boy's mother and eventually the father 'relented.' Once again a male teacher is actively refusing to be strait-jacketed by outdated gender practices and he persuades the child's mother to support him.

The gender profile of dancing is very different to football, which, as a socially approved 'male' sport, works to uphold present-day constructions of hegemonic masculinities. Stuart, by engaging in a collaborative physical activity that is often labelled 'female' only, is symbolically challenging dominant constructions of men as aggressive and competitive. Stuart (and the boys he recruits) risk becoming femininized and hence 'sissy', since the 'cultural scripts' demand that normative masculinity is publicly defended at all costs (Gutterman, 1994). So, the sportsman script will only sanction the historically approved 'male' sports that operate to affirm male power and superiority. Hepburn (2013) reports how Darren, a primary teacher, in common with Stuart, taught dance instead of the 'expected' football. He also found that the boys were shocked that a 'man' was dancing.

These Reforming men are crossing gender barriers and as such they invite pupils to also widen their understanding of male and female potentials. Cushman (2010:1215) interviewed Jonas, a Swedish male primary teacher, who like Jeff, one of our key informants, is on a 'crusade' to dismantle sport stereotypes: 'part of our mission was not to classify sports as female and male'. Cushman (2010) concludes her research by identifying how men can be successful agents of change in schools; this is clearly evidenced by our eight 'Reforming' male teachers, who are all actively attempting to resist and dismantle the male sportsman script.

Conforming men

Leo (a Year Six senior teacher) has always enjoyed teaching football and holds a promoted post for sport in his primary school, where he has now developed links with a local football club. Leo's training specialism was Religious Education. Leo does not raise any gender issues and finds 'the guys who come in and do sport are absolutely fabulous'. The sessions are open to girls and boys, but Leo finds 'obviously' there are fewer girls attending since the boys 'tend to be trusted to walk home on their own and that sort of stuff'. Leo does not identify the lack of access given to the girls in this statement and accepts the gender imbalance as 'normal'. Thomas (lecturer in HE) also reports the enjoyment he gained from teaching football in schools and, in common with Leo, does not raise any issues of gender inequality in relation to the teaching of football in primary schools.

Alan (NQT, Early Years) claims all of the legitimate male scripts throughout his interview, including the sportsman script. Alan is convinced that men are needed in schools for the boys and as a mature student he responded to the campaign to recruit more men as 'they're crying out for male teachers'. He subscribes to essentialist notions of gender, where men and women have different qualities. Alan was assured by 'everyone' that as a man he would do very well in teaching. His subject specialism was sport and shortly after completing his probationary year, Alan started working for an ICT consortium advising schools. This is a very fast promotion and ICT is another subject where male teachers remain advantaged in appointment and promotion (Hutchings, 2002). Hepburn (2013) reports a male teacher, who, in agreement with Alan, strongly believes that men are naturally better at football skills and as such needed for teaching older boys. This man, who is now a Director of Education, displays a similar confidence in gaining swift promotion; he actually applied for a headship whilst still in his probationary year (see Chapter Six, for an examination of the male promotion script).

Ken (a Year Five teacher) selected PE as a training specialism and enjoys teaching football to the boys. However, Ken does challenge some of the other male teacher scripts in his interview, as 'I don't believe in JUST putting a man in the classroom'. In common with most of our key informants,

Ken challenges some gender practices, but ignores or supports others. Like Leo, and Thomas, he does not identify any gender issues in the teaching of football in schools.

George (NQT, not currently teaching) a former footballer, selected to study PE as his training specialism, however at the time of interview he had not yet started teaching. In his interview, George discusses how he believes his previous career will help him relate to 'failing' boys, especially black boys, as he himself is black. George is upholding the discourses that work to construct sport as a way of controlling and engaging disaffected working-class boys in education (Mac An Ghaill, 1994; Sewell, 1997; Pratt-Adams and Burn, 2004).

The data collected from our key informants, evidence how some male teachers are conflicted, finding it problematic to reconcile their own enjoyment of football, with their recognition of how football activities in schools can serve to marginalize both girls and women teachers. The Reforming men dislike the 'macho' culture football can promote in schools. Other men accept and perform the male sport script with no problems, whilst some men (especially in the Early Years) do not discuss teaching 'sport'. The interview data also indicates men are gaining promoted posts for sport (and other 'male' subjects) whether they hold a subject specialism or not (Hutchings, 2002). In summary, the eighteen key informants are demonstrating resistance to, acceptance of and ignorance of the historic sportsman script which has become embedded within the occupational culture.

A serious issue surfaced in these interviews, concerned with how many of the men felt vulnerable to accusations of child molestation when pupils were changing into their sports clothes, due to inadequate changing facilities and this issue is addressed in Chapter Seven.

Professional Peer Responses

Eight of our key informants challenged this male sportsman script; they were concerned that it was 'perpetuating the male stereotype' and marginalizing girls and women teachers. In contrast only one of the twenty-two professional peers, who identified the sportsman script, openly rejected it, whilst one man described how other teachers 'try' to give him the role. In fact, many of these male teachers volunteered to take sport; they accepted the teaching of sport 'out of choice' (England, NQT) and a third of these men held PE specialisms. None of the professional peer responses gave any consideration to how this sportsman script, with its focus on boys' sport, may work to side-line girls and female teachers (Connolly, 1998).

The men reported that as men: 'there was a definite expectation that I would be better at teaching sport than female counterparts' (England, 9 years); and half of the forty men were happy to claim this 'truth', whatever their subject specialism.

The belief of 'male' superiority in sport was upheld by some women staff as well; men reported being glad to accept the role. This teacher (England, NQT) claimed:

> I am able to engage boys within discussion about sport due to having an interest personally, and the boys appear to engage in this due to the nature of sharing 'banter'. I do not believe this would be as frequent with a female teacher, even if they had a keen interest in sports.

Whilst, another male teacher, who is also in his first year of teaching volunteered for sport, since:

> … other staff know that if there is an event that they need help with then I would always be willing to help or guide them. (England, NQT)

Here is the 'needed' man, able to 'guide' the rest of the staff. He is already being told by both female staff and parents that the boys 'love to tell' him about their sports and hobbies, now that they have 'a young male teacher' (see role model discussion in Chapter Five).

The need to ensure all teachers are competent to teach a range of sports may also be a factor in the positioning of male teachers as 'naturally' superior in teaching this subject. As the following informant indicated:

> Recently I was asked by a young female colleague to referee a football match as she was unsure of the rules… (England, NQT)

Another relatively new teacher may be showing resentment of the sportsman script when stating how he is 'definitely expected to take on football purely because I'm male' (England, eighteen months). One of the limitations of peer commentary is that the researcher is unable to 'probe' further to find out if this teacher agrees or disagrees with the male sportsman script that he finds himself subject to. However, other informants clearly voice their agreement with the script and essentialist beliefs about boys requiring sports teaching by men are a feature of the data:

> Usually sports groups are different for girls and boys… And it is natural and common, that teachers for girls are women, and for boys they are men… (Finland, 8 years)

Finland also has a predominately female teaching force (Chapter Eight), so it will not be possible that all boys will be taught sport by men, however this gender 'truth' continues to circulate. In common with Simon's experience (see Introduction) some of the men discuss how they were 'given' sport to teach even when training – these men are quite happy to accept it:

> I have been given the role of P.E. planner for a whole year group for a term whilst on placement. (England, trainee teacher).

Once again, football was the 'male' sport discussed:

> My time as a male teacher has been enjoyable and fulfilling, as the kids keep me active and creative, (and they're easier to beat at soccer than adults). (New Zealand, 23 years)

This experienced teacher does not state whether the 'kids' are boys or girls, but he does disclose that he really enjoys teaching sport and has 'even taken netball', the assumption being that it will be girls playing and he has crossed gender barriers in order to teach them.

These male teachers are being positioned by women staff and they also are positioning themselves as needed 'sportsmen'; female teachers are being constructed (and some construct themselves) as second-best in teaching this subject. The twenty-two informants who mentioned this script reported how 'sport is something males are expected to take' (Finland, 10 years).

The professional peer responses were collected two years after the Olympic Games were held in England in 2012, where there were many superb female and male athletes. The majority of men who claimed this gender script are NQTs and trainees who are teaching in England; it is disappointing that so many of these new entrants claim the gender 'truth' that men are the best sports teachers for young children (especially boys). Another reading of the responses could be that as these men are new to the occupation, they may still be adjusting to working with mainly women and they are employing their knowledge of football to 'defend' their 'masculinity'. It could be a tactic to ensure status; several men did indicate that they found it difficult to adjust to 'being a male in a female dominated environment' (England, NQT). One man disclosed (England, trainee):

> I find staff rooms alienating and I certainly know of other men who feel the same. I feel there is an expectation to be the joker, put on a performance or dominate conversation. Quite often male teachers will spend lunch time in the four walls of their classroom...

As we discussed in Chapter Two, being the 'Other' can be very isolating and it could be argued that by demonstrating expertise in football these men are gaining both respect and approval.

We would like to remind the reader that games such as football, netball and cricket are only part of the PE curriculum for young children. We both enjoyed teaching PE across the 3–11 age range and we recognize how important this subject is for all children. It can contribute to young children's physical well-being; teach them to follow rules; set challenges for themselves; persevere; and collaborate with other children. To see a young child enjoy (and for some, also excel) at dance, for example, is to recognize the curriculum limitations of this particular male sportsman script, with its narrow focus on boys and football.

This historic gender script works to limit opportunities for girls and boys to gain equal access to developing their enjoyment of a wide range of physical activities. It also reinforces biased gender practices that construct all men as 'naturally' willing and able to play football with the older boys, reaffirming the required hegemonic masculinity.

We leave the last words to the one man who, like Wadsworth (2002), did not want to play the game and also managed to escape the male sportsman script:

> ... I'm not the sportiest of people! I was asked to help run the football club during my BA2 placement (*second year under-graduate training*), but politely asked if I could join another club instead. (England, trainee)

Conclusion

We conclude this chapter with a consideration of the way football has been recruited to uphold a hegemonic masculinity, which works to maintain gender divisions within the occupation. Curriculum initiatives involving local football teams, such as the one discussed by Leo, are rooted in popular discourses about 'boys' failure' due to the feminization of teaching (Martino, 2008; Skelton, 2009). The 'backlash' against feminism is found in other western countries with women being constructed as endangering 'masculinity' itself (see Lingard and Douglas, 1999; Mills, 2001; Connell, 2002). This is not a new discourse, in the 1930s male unions suggested women were a 'danger to young boys' (Miller, 1996; Limond, 2002). This pejorative discourse works to maintain male teacher promotion and appointment advantage, providing the men uphold the legitimate male teacher scripts, such as male sport. So, these male teacher scripts are continuing to maintain gender barriers within the workforce.

The 'feminized' classroom, with its assumed bias against boys, is once again being blamed for working-class boys' underachievement in schools (Acker, 1994; Leake, 2001; Martino, 2008). It was during the media 'panic' in the late 1990s (Pratt-Adams and Burn, 2004) that football initiatives were introduced in English inner-city schools as a panacea to 'help' the failing boys. The Learning FC Guide, for example, uses football to teach English and maths (Henry, 2000). Skelton (1996) argues that the role of football in primary schools is implicated in promoting a homogenized view of boys (and we would suggest, their male and female teachers). Raphael Reed (1998) discusses how notions of masculinity are embedded in this male teacher sportsman script. The fact that women can enjoy playing football too is ignored.

The simplistic 'failing boys' discourses employed to blame female teachers for all boys' underachievement are not based on actual data on exam success, and not all boys are failing. Thrupp (2000:4) argues that lack of academic achievement in inner-city schools is not due to female teachers but social class, it is: 'a reflection of the middle class bias in schooling in capitalist societies'. Osler and Vincent (2003:16) point out that many white and black working-class girls are also underachieving (despite all these women teachers) and she reminds us that the 'gender gap' between girls and boys educational success is far less than 'those associated with ethnic origin and social class'. Tomlinson (2000:241) argues that in recent years there has been a widening of 'social class segregation' in state schools. There is a need for an examination of the intersection of gender, class and ethnicity when identifying which pupils are 'failing' in schools (see also Plummer, 2000; Walkerdine et al., 2001). In short, statistics do not support this simplistic gender discourse that proposes ALL boys are failing, so more football and more male teachers are needed to address this 'problem'.

This brief overview of how football, taught by men only, can be employed as 'compensation' for disenfranchised working-class boys raises issues for pedagogy as well as for the men 'expected' to perform the script. Instead of providing tokenistic boy-focused football worksheets linked to basic skills; male and female teachers could usefully work with all pupils in exploring the origins of this popular game and promote girls and boys becoming involved in the sport. For instance, pupils could research how during the First World War, working-class female football teams in the North East of England were very popular, attracting large crowds (Brennan, 2007). The recognition that all pupils can enjoy this game (alongside other sports) can be very productive, helping to re-capture the 'beautiful' game as an enjoyable and inclusive team sport that does not promote a damaging hyper-masculinity in schools.

Discussion questions

1. This chapter has critiqued the way sport can be used as a way of asserting a hegemonic masculinity. Select three popular newspapers and examine the sports pages: are images and headlines that promote hyper masculinity still in circulation? How much coverage is there of female sport?

2. Review your own experience as a child of learning sport in school: do you agree with mixed-sex sport? Discuss.

CHAPTER FOUR

Male Teachers and Discipline

Chapter outline

The discipline script works in combination with the sportsman script, examined in the previous chapter, to legitimate and uphold notions of hegemonic masculinity. It has also been laid down over time to publicly reflect the idealized patriarchal family, with the father in charge (see Chapter One).

The hegemonic man

Quentin, a Primary deputy head, in common with the majority of our male interviewees, rejects: 'the myth: wait till your father gets home'. This male teacher is clearly identifying the historical practice of giving men the discipline role, both in the private and public spheres. Men are positioned as being able to instil good behaviour due to fear of their physicality and their inherent violence if they are not obeyed. In teaching, the discipline script harks back to the times when corporal punishment was allowed and seen as needed in order to control pupils, in particular the older boys. Again, as with the sportsman script, the older boys, as future bearers of hegemonic masculinity, are constructed as potentially problematic if their essential male unruliness is not 'tamed' by a 'stronger' man. So, symbolically the male teacher is being constructed as the representative of male power and authority within wider society.

Thorne (1993) has shown in her perceptive study that children are also subject to the legitimate gender rules alongside the teachers who teach them. So, irrespective of the male teachers' wishes and beliefs, pupils can themselves reinforce this script as part of their own gender compliance. Gender rules may be also upheld and reinforced by other members of the school community: such as parents, governors and female teachers. Mills (2001:146) argues we need to:

> examine the way in which schools implement discipline strategies and the extent to which teachers' behaviours legitimate/disrupt existing gendered relations of power.

This particular gender script labels men as essentially 'aggressive' and as such, works to affirm male teachers as 'non-caring' and as such not suited to teach very young children (Skelton, 2011). Research in Scotland likewise reports men who resent being given this discipline role and the assumption is that young pupils are scared to misbehave if they are being taught by men; again all male teachers are being constructed as potentially violent due to their 'inherent' masculinity (Hepburn, 2013). The data we present from our key informants evidences some of the gender practices that this pernicious script produces and the problems faced by male teachers who do not agree with being positioned as the feared 'disciplinarian' figure within a school community.

Research findings

Discipline was an important issue for the majority of teachers interviewed; only two of the eighteen men did not mention it in their interviews. It was also discussed in the male student support group when some of the men were sent boys to discipline during their school teaching practice (Chapter Two). Thirteen of the key informants did not believe that men were any better than women at establishing discipline; whilst three of the men, who were all NQTs, did support this gender script, believing that male teachers would be 'naturally' better at discipline, due to their innate male qualities. The two informants who did not discuss being expected to carry out the school 'discipline' role were Brian, an NQT, and Pat, a Nursery head. Again the 'ethos' of an individual school could be of significance in preventing the identification or operation of this script. In the schools where female staff do not send male teachers pupils to discipline, the power of the script may be muted. Elizabeth has personally not taught in schools where women teachers selected to send pupils to male teachers to be disciplined; whereas in the schools Simon has taught in this practice was commonplace. The less male and female teachers (and other members of the school community) agree to perform these damaging gender scripts, the less power they will be able to wield. However, if the few men teaching young children are to be found predominately in senior management (Jones, 2006) then this in itself will serve to reinforce the belief that it is male teachers who are the 'natural' discipline and authority figures: none of these male teacher scripts stand alone and both individual and structural practices are implicated. Unfortunately research continues to evidence that the historical discipline script, which positions male teachers as 'naturally' intimidating pupils, is still in circulation within this occupation (Cushman, 2010; Mistry and Sood, 2013).

A key practice produced by this gender script is one where women staff will 'give' the male teacher authority and responsibility for pupils' behaviour. Many of our key informants have experience of being sent children from other classes (in particular boys) to discipline. King (1998:43) in his interviews with male teachers also reported this practice; Steve, a male Early Years teacher interviewed by King, complained: 'I don't enjoy being the heavy.' Steve's usage of the word 'heavy' indicates how the actual physicality of the man may be identified and deferred to by the school community, irrespective of his wishes. There is evidence in our data of the role parents' may play in reinforcing this gender stereotype and Gregg another Early Years teacher interviewed by King, also reported receiving comments from parents:

> There is this notion that a male teacher will straighten out that child who is a discipline problem. A large number of parents have said to me that their son or daughter has been a problem and a male teacher is what the child needs. I guess what they are saying is that there aren't any female teachers who have good classroom or discipline techniques. (King, 1998: 52)

This American Early Years teacher is highlighting gender binaries: if men are good at discipline then women are not. Several of our key informants referred to women teachers who were 'real shouters' (Thomas) when criticizing the male discipline script. These men are concerned to show that some women teachers' can also perform the 'discipline man' in the sense that they can also use loud voices that may frighten pupils. Thomas is acknowledging how both men and women can 'perform' behaviours (such as aggression or caring) that can still be stereotyped by wider society as male or female behaviour only. The type of 'discipline' this male script demands is certainly not good practice; rather it is connected to the sergeant-major role that England (1973:90) carried out when he was 'a one-man police patrol' for his female head teacher.

Kaufman (1994:148) argues that men are required to 'suppress' nurturing and caring in order to prove their 'manhood' and the discipline script works to affirm this 'suppression'. The script constructs discipline as being achieved through a threat of possible male violence and a man's physical size is seen as an asset. Ken and Carl, both teaching nine-year-old children, link being given the discipline man role to their physical size, telling Elizabeth that they are over six foot in height.

Skelton (2001, 2007, 2009, 2011), who was herself a primary teacher and has published widely in the field of gender practice within the occupation, has also identified how physicality and sexuality can be conflated in the gender stereotypes applied to teachers of young children. Skelton (2009) describes how Georgina, a lesbian primary teacher, is given little sympathy when a male visitor to the school attacks her and breaks her nose. Georgina discusses her physicality and how 'in comparison' to the rest of the female teachers 'she appeared to be "built like a brick s***house so she can handle it" ...' (Skelton, 2009:47). This exemplifies how a physically larger woman may also be expected to perform the 'male' discipline script. Georgina's non-conformity to the required heterosexual norm means that she receives little support from her female colleagues. The compulsory construction of heterosexuality for all teachers is endorsed (Epstein, 1993).

Reforming men

Quentin, a primary deputy head, likewise refers to physical size when he disagrees with the script, he describes a teacher: 'a massive bloke was dreadful...it's not about your physical appearance'. Quentin then discusses his partner, who is also a primary school teacher:

> ... I would say that my partner is 4 foot 10 and she is as good with behaviour as any men (p)..... it's a lot to do with society (p) it's playing on the stereotypes.

Quentin identifies the continuing stereotype of the disciplinarian father figure; affirming historical patriarchal discourses (see Chapter One). Quentin also refers to the duality between male and female teacher stereotypes that seeks to construct the school as a symbolic public family with female 'mother' teachers:

> If you go 'I'm a women and a teacher' people see you as 'pretty mumsy', wants kids blah, blah (p) my mum used to say the great thing about being

a female teacher is the holidays and it is one job that you settle quite well into with kids.

Quentin feels this 'mumsy' type image of primary teaching still persists, despite the recent marketing campaigns to 'make it a yuppie job'. Quentin believes that the public perception of teaching has still not changed, quoting the 'old' adage:

If you're a young girl and you like kids (*p*) and you're a bit thick you become a nurse, and if you're a bit clever you become a teacher.

We wish to make it clear that both Quentin and ourselves totally disagree with this insulting stereotype; however, if we do not make visible such stereotypes, it is impossible to challenge them effectively.

Throughout the interview Quentin remains angered by these 'sexist' teacher stereotypes. He argues that they are very harmful to male and female teachers of young children:

There is no evidence to suggest that the stereotypes that parents or people entering teaching may hold are borne out. But they DO matter (*p*) because people make some very dangerous assumptions about male or female teachers' practices.

Quentin also offers several examples of the practices the discipline man script can produce, for example:

White Anglo-Saxon working class parents or ethnic minority parents say: 'I'm really glad he's got a male teacher this year 'cause that'll sort him out' and you DO get that, you do get that, I don't care what anyone says, you get it!

In common with Quentin, Thomas, who is now lecturing in HE, discusses receiving many comments from parents about discipline and boys. Fathers would come into school and tell Thomas that if their boys misbehaved he had their 'permission' to punish them and Skelton (2001:30) reports 'discipline and punishment are part of the role of being a male primary school teacher'. Thomas like many of the other informants, 'always knew that the head really wanted me at the top end of the school'. The gender message is men are 'needed' for Year Six teaching and discipline, irrespective of their teaching experience, specialism or personal wishes. Thomas felt he was labelled as the discipline 'man' in his last school and he found himself 'more and more involved with behavioural and disciplinary matters'. Once Thomas became the Deputy Head he was officially given the 'main responsibility for issues around behaviour' and:

at times it didn't sit comfortably with me (*p*)I actually felt I was in some ways used as a threat (*p*) when I recently left the school one of the things the children wrote about me was 'we have to come and see you if we're naughty'.

These male teachers are describing a web of beliefs and practices, involving women teachers, head teachers, parents, governors and pupils themselves, that ascribe to them 'natural' male discipline qualities based on their physical size. They contest this construction; they do not wish to be positioned as the 'scare' figures; preferring to become good teachers of young children, rather than school 'bully' men.

Jeff, a primary supply teacher, was very distressed that being a male teacher could result in him being constructed as 'frightening' by the young children. Stuart, now a lecturer in HE, likewise still remembers how in schools some parents thought he might be 'cruel' and also frighten their young children. Stuart, like Thomas and Quentin, has experience of parents telling him how pleased they are that their sons are getting a man at last, 'to sort them out'– a perpetuation of the stereotype of strict male teachers needed to 'frighten' boys in particular.

Boys are being labelled as potentially badly behaved and the girls are invisible. Stuart denies that he is that 'type of teacher' and describes some women teachers as 'real battle-axes'. Stuart describes how some parents would come to see him in school 'to size me up really'. Stuart refused to act the stereotypical discipline man, 'I have a loud voice, in the class I always speak quietly and stay calm.'

Roger, a Primary head, trained to be a teacher twenty-seven years ago, and his grandmother called him the 'master' as she 'assumed' he would be only teaching the boys, echoing back to the elementary single-sex schooling system. Roger and Oliver (who is an Infant head) both strongly disagree that male teachers will be 'better' at pupil discipline. Oliver found, even during his teaching practices, several parents accredited him with superior discipline, especially needed for the boys. They:

were pleased that there was a male teacher and they thought that was a good thing, even though the strongest teachers I've ever seen in terms of behaviour management (*p*) were women, you know.

Many of the key informants had been moved to Year Six in order to 'perform' discipline, by both female and male head teachers, again irrespective of their age-range specialisms or previous experiences. These men felt under pressure to act as substitute authoritarian fathers; rather than develop their pedagogy and become good classroom teachers. They are claiming a 'pedagogic script' that requires all teachers, irrespective of gender, to gain class 'discipline' by demonstrating expert teaching, instead of physically 'frightening' pupils. Yet, they find, they are being expected to 'perform' an outdated male discipline script by the rest of the school community.

It was only when Leo became a deputy head that he faced any discipline issues. Leo shows a clear rejection of the discipline 'script' which he believed the female head teacher performed. Leo expected the pupils to talk, but they 'had been brow beaten into silence' and at first the pupils 'couldn't quite handle' it. Leo challenges the strict discipline approach and prefers to gain pupil attention by appropriate teaching; so he is claiming the pedagogical script. Leo eventually resigned and moved into supply teaching in order to gain more classroom experience, study for his MA and develop his pedagogical practice.

Fred had recently accepted a first teaching post in Year Four when he was interviewed. The male deputy head then phoned Fred to tell him he was being moved to Year Six in order to establish discipline:

> They were quite open about it! The reason I got Year 6 was because 'they want a man in Year 6'.

Year Six (10–11 years) is again seen as the 'ideal' age range for the male Primary teacher to teach in and Fred as an NQT felt he 'couldn't start challenging' but he strongly disagrees with male teachers being placed with older children for discipline. Fred clearly challenges the male discipline script and he argues it is a very damaging 'practice'. It invokes for Fred painful memories of 'wait till your father gets home' which he was told as a child. Fred also experienced being sent boys from Year Six to discipline even when he was still on student placement, in common with some of the men in the student support group.

Eric, an Infant teacher, uses practically the same words as Henry in the male support group, when stating:

> I don't feel comfortable (p) I always said I never became a teacher to shout at children and I've stuck to it.

In his Infant school Neil, the deputy head, finds some pupils and some of the female staff have positioned him as 'the strictest teacher' apart from the female head. The female deputy would often send him boys to be disciplined. Neil does not understand why some of the boys will 'kick' the female teachers, including the head, but when he arrives they calm down and this makes him feel very uncomfortable: 'I don't know why.' Neil senses that some boys may show men more respect; again patriarchal relations are confirmed. Now the school has another teacher who is labelled the strictest: 'and it's a woman and it's marvellous'. No longer does Neil have to perform the discipline man script and be sent pupils 'to tell off in the morning'. His account exemplifies how volatile and unstable discourses are and shows, despite the longevity of the male discipline script, it can be interrupted. We support Mills (2001) in his argument that an examination of discipline practices in schools may help reveal (and dismantle) these unfair gender practices that reinforce essentialist beliefs about the assumed talents of (and roles ascribed to) male teachers.

Ken, a primary teacher, in common with Neil, acknowledges his 'given' discipline advantage in schools:

> I believe you get 'easier' discipline if you're a man (p) I think it's an advantage (p) especially the boys (p) I remember speaking to some Muslim boys and they don't respect female teachers (p) their power and position of authority. Also parents come in and see my size (p) I'm quite tall and 15 stone (p) and I can use it as well (p) if the children are fighting I can physically get in their 'space'.

Ken is employing a 'strong man' discourse, but Ken both mocks and qualifies it by stating clearly that many women teachers are excellent at discipline and in common with the other reforming men, Ken thinks the discipline male script is 'very wrong'.

Ken and Neil have both found that pupils can actively position them as being more capable of enforcing discipline, than their female teachers. They believe that boys may 'give' men more respect and societal attitudes still 'hold women in lower esteem than men' (Bradley, 1989: 214). Once again men are being constructed as essentially violent, in opposition to women teachers who will be essentially 'caring'. These gender practices are attempting to reinforce patriarchal regimes within schools. Jeff, who is now a supply teacher, discusses this negative construction of male teachers as harsh and 'non-caring' and reports that: 'even the parents perceived you as … VERY strict'. These male teachers are well aware why they are still being 'given' the discipline role in schools and they link it to wider societal beliefs about males and females; sexist beliefs that they disagree with strongly.

Derek, as a black man finds, like John in the student support group, that he is expected to help 'discipline' black boys in the school; drawing on 'racist stereotypes' of black men as being essentially violent (Connolly, 1998: 78). Derek, who has been teaching for six years, now refuses to perform the discipline man script and for Derek issues of racism and class as well as gender practices are involved. Derek feels that working-class black boys are 'significantly over-represented' as discipline problems (Wright, 1992; Connolly, 1998). Derek discusses how he has:

> … different techniques for dealing with those children (p) those difficult black boys and I will NOT hate those little black boys like some teachers I feel do (p) I hear comments all the time, everyday you know, I was a child here once (p) a difficult child, so my last teacher said (laughs). There's still some hope you know (p) you can't write people off just because they're difficult at school.

Derek's believes that instead of dealing with black boys by the stereotyped performance of black discipline man, wider structural issues, such as racism and class, must be addressed. Derek also discusses the need to examine racist practices in initial teacher training (Crozier and Menter, 1993; Siraj-Blatchford, 1995).

The 'female Year Five teacher who can't hack it' sends black and white 'naughty boys' to Carl, a white supply teacher. The male music teacher also asks Carl for help with discipline. He cannot remember ever being sent 'naughty girls' to discipline. Carl is a 'bit fed up' with this discipline script, but:

> Physically I'm very big so the kids feel a bit (*p*) not afraid but they look at me and see me and I'm quite a size (*p*) so I guess I'm a bit overpowering

Carl can enact this discipline role due to both his physical size and voice and even the other male teacher in his school defers to his physicality: 'I can speak quite loudly' also 'I know the kids.' Carl has had a 'few incidents' with fathers concerning discipline:

> I had an angry father who came in because I'd told a child off and 'it wasn't my place to be telling his son or daughter off' but it was OK for the female teachers (*p*) I've had that a few times since and its more likely to be with the fathers (*p*) and sometimes I'm told 'I'm their father NOT you' and they do see that as a threat (*p*) the fact that their child is being told off by another man.

After qualifying Jeff taught 8-year-olds in a Welsh village school and some parents positioned him as a 'very strict' male teacher. Jeff, like Fred, disagrees with this male discipline 'label' and challenges the gender stereotypes that can construct men as 'uncaring' and even 'cruel'.

Jeff, like Derek and Fred, has also been sent boys to discipline: 'you know really tell them off'. Jeff, in agreement with Carl, Fred and Quentin, links this to the historical stereotype of the authoritarian father figure:

> Is this what people are thinking (*p*) if you're the male in the school, you're the daddy in the school, even if you're not the head you're still the daddy and everybody else is the mummies?

Jeff strongly refutes this 'daddy' role despite the institutional power it gives him and, like Carl, he likewise criticizes the 'mummy' role given to women staff. He is clearly identifying the 'familial structure' (Oram, 1989:31) that works to construct primary teachers as symbolic patriarchal parents. Epstein and Johnson (1998:128) discuss how:

> the sexual landscape of the school is familiar, tracing the contours of patriarchal relations between men and women, girls and boys.

When Jeff discusses the Early Years he identifies maternal discourses:

> It's still perceived as a nurturing role (p) it's an extension of the mothering role (p) it's not seen as having professional status. You know the academic challenge of an Early Years teacher planning an Early Years curriculum! It's very skilled (p) all the management skills, but it is perceived as child minding …

Jeff strongly refutes both male and female teacher scripts that can construct Early Years teachers as dim mothers (Aspinall and Drummond, 1989; Steedman, 1992; Miller, 1996). The female teachers, whose stories we present in Chapter Nine, certainly agree with Jeff about the devaluation of Early Years teaching. Jeff has already stepped down from senior management and although he has now accepted another deputy headship, he is determined not to accept the male 'discipline' role in his new school (see Chapter Six).

In Sweden Cushman, who also has a substantial portfolio of research in this area, interviewed Max, who, in common with these reforming men, argues male teachers 'are not better at disciplining…I can't stand it' (Cushman, 2010:1216). In Sweden (see Chapter Eight), despite teachers of young children being explicitly required to consider gender equity, Max, still experiences being given a class that needs discipline, just because he is a man!

Conforming men

Three NQTs are happy to claim the discipline script and intend to use their physicality in order to gain good behaviour in the classroom. Alan, an Early Years teacher, believes that men are naturally 'better' at 'child discipline' and he is proud of his performance in schools and nurseries during his teaching practices:

> The children were getting used to having the females really shouting and (p) males having a deeper voice they just have to use their voice as a weapon.

Alan is clearly enacting the discipline script that constructs male teachers as more able to assert authority in a classroom, by using their 'male' voice (and body size) as a 'weapon'. In common with Carl, he knows how to employ his voice and size. Alan may be drawing on the discipline script as a way of publicly affirming his 'masculinity' which could be under threat since he has entered a workforce that can be viewed as 'woman's work' (Allan, 1993).

Mulholland and Hansen (2003:217) interviewed a male student in Australia who described how, during training:

You felt all the eyes on you. I thought, when I first walked through that door, they were saying there is a male in Early Childhood. 'What's he doing here?'

The male students in Chapter Two also discussed the painful effects of being the Other; and Alan's derogatory description of 'females really shouting' may be indicative of his continuing 'difference' within this sector. Alan's view stands in stark contrast to Jay, a male Early Years teacher, interviewed in North America by Mallozzi and Campbell Galman (2014) who actively refutes the discipline role he is 'given' by the female staff.

Harry agrees with Alan that men are really needed for enforcing discipline in schools. On Harry's second school practice his male class teacher in Year Four told him 'they were glad they were getting a man' as he believed 'it was better for discipline'. Harry had Year Six on his final practice, and another male teacher, who also reaffirmed the male discipline script. Harry is quite happy to claim and perform this stereotyped role.

George also taught older pupils during his school teaching practice, and like Harry he was given a lot of praise by staff for his 'discipline' as a man in a Junior classroom. George was told in several schools: 'we need more male teachers' by both female and male staff and they all supported the 'need' for boys to be disciplined by men. It is of concern that three new recruits into the occupation so easily claim the male discipline script and report a great deal of support in schools for adopting this stance. The essentialist beliefs held by these three men challenge the assumption that as society changes 'new' men will emerge, who are less likely to embrace outdated gender stereotypes. Again, there is no 'typical male teacher'; rather typical gender practices, which are being claimed by some men and rejected by others.

In this data, there is clear evidence that some female teachers are selecting to confer on male staff responsibility for discipline enforcement; one explanation could be there is female resentment concerning male promotion advantage within the occupation. Women staff may feel that if men are going to gain swift promotion and higher pay, then they should shoulder the added responsibility for managing discipline problems (Burn, 2005). An alternative interpretation of this particular gender practice could be that some women teachers agree with Alan, Harry and George that men are 'naturally' better at enforcing discipline, especially needed for the boys. Also, as Neil, Ken and Quentin identify, if certain boys 'give' more respect to males, then women teachers can be disadvantaged when disciplining boys; and men will find it easier.

The actual practices of placing men in Year Six, irrespective of their specialisms and sending them boys to discipline even when in training, need to be challenged. As Healy (2000) argues, it is the actual effects of gender discourses that we should be concerned with. The majority of our key informants were upset that they are being expected to perform 'fear' in order to discipline boys: they want to be recognized as teachers of young children not law enforcers. It is also worth noticing that the needs of girls seem not to be on the agenda of the discipline script; as with the male sport script, the needs of the girls remain marginalized.

Another feature of the discipline script is the expectation that older boys in particular will always be badly behaved and therefore need male teachers to control them through threat. In the next chapter, we will examine discourses about male role models, another gender script which stands alongside the discipline and sports scripts in promoting male teachers as needed for boys; again boys are constructed as 'needing' men and the expertise of female teachers of young children is disregarded. As long as the emphasis remains on hegemonic masculinity, rather than on pedagogy, the focus will be on boys and the men who teach young children will be judged according to their stereotypical 'masculine' performances rather than on their actual teaching ability (the pedagogic script).

It is worth noting that our eighteen key informants were teaching (or had taught) in multi-lingual inner-city schools, with pupils from economically disadvantaged homes. In common with the historical establishment of state schools that aimed to 'control' the children of the poor (Copelman, 1996; Davin, 1996), these pupils (and their families) may still be subject to negative social class discourses that label them as in need of correction and therefore strict discipline is required and 'bully men' are needed to enforce it. Is the male discipline script also circulating in affluent schools and private schools, where pupils are not seen as deficit; or will the focus in these schools be fixed on pupils' academic achievement (a pedagogic script) that can be performed by male and female teachers irrespective of their physical size or ethnicity?

An examination of gender practice (in this case discipline) necessarily involves a reflection on the culture of a particular school community. Where the school's culture is concerned with giving all pupils' quality education then differentiation between male and female teachers should not be on the agenda; but when it is still concerned with creating symbolic, public patriarchal parents then the actual gender of the teacher will indicate the 'areas' of expertise. In this script men are cast as the 'natural' disciplinarians and this again has educational consequences. How much time are some of these male teachers spending on having to see boys to 'tell off' (Neil) rather than engaging in quality teaching? The male discipline script is still in operation and as Quentin argues in his interview:

> … it is perceived, isn't it, that male teachers are stronger on behaviour, by some parents. It's a total myth, a total myth.

Professional Peer responses

In contrast to the majority of our key informants who strongly challenge this script, the twenty-two men, who identify the male discipline script, accept it. No male teacher stated that he thought it was wrong that men were expected to perform the school disciplinarian role and some men openly embraced it. The responses contain a number of gender generalizations; several are based on male physicality:

> Children respond differently to a male. My voice is louder and deeper. My 'get on with it' approach is more direct…I don't take excuses. (New Zealand, eleven years)

There were also Darwinian tones:

> With reference to disciplining children that I often find they can respond differently to a male teacher who will raise their voice to a female. I do not know if this is down to the tone of the voice or natural predisposition; in mammalian mammals males often are found 'in charge' and/or have a level of seniority. (England, NQT)

Again, it is a limitation of this research method that we could not ask this NQT to better explain his rather incoherent statement.

The following excerpt further suggests that male teachers may be 'given' more respect:

> I have found that my approach to behaviour, particular of boys, is quite different to most female teachers, and (I) can usually get to the bottom of most issues. I don't usually have boys showing aggression or belligerence to me whereas the same boys have shown this to female colleagues. (New Zealand, Eight years)

His identification that boys show him less 'aggression' because he is a man mirrors Ken and Neil's interview discussions. However, unlike the two key informants, this man does believe that as a 'male' teacher his 'approach' to behaviour management is 'quite different' and more successful, in particular with boys.

The sending of children to men by female staff in order to 'discipline' even before qualification, recounted by male trainees (see Chapter Two), also featured in this data set. This man was a teaching assistant when sent pupils and he does not:

> … have an issue with this… if people were then to question the sanctions given I would then question why I was asked to discipline. (England, NQT)

Connections with the other male scripts surfaced, for instance; 'there was a perception that the PE teacher can sort the boys out' (England, thirty-three years).

This excerpt demonstrates how the male teacher scripts are inter-related, working to position all 'boys' as potentially disruptive and needing to be 'sorted out' by 'real men'. Experienced teachers (and parents) know that these simplistic gender stereotypes are not only inaccurate, but they can also label children; in these scripts, all boys are assumed to be potentially problematic and in need of 'male' discipline.

One teacher still remembers how in his first year of teaching he was:

> ... sent children to discipline despite female Senior Leadership Team members, with far more years' experience, being available. (England, nine years)

Whilst, another man reflects:

> ... No one said it to me, but I've been given the most challenging class behaviourally compared to the other 3 NQTs at my school ... (England, NQT)

In common with the key informants, there are reports of men being given the older and more 'challenging' classes, but they do not raise any open objections to these practices. Rather, there is a sense of fatalism; 'discipline' is what male teachers are 'expected' to do in schools. It is, as Foucault (1978) would argue, seen as normal, it is a common-sense 'truth' that all men will be naturally better at discipline. Research in Scotland found men entering this occupation are surprised at the gendered beliefs about 'men' they encounter (Hepburn, 2013). The two female teachers in Chapter Nine of this book also express surprise at the gendered beliefs that they can find themselves subject to within this workforce. There are two men who mention that they do not carry out the role of school disciplinarian; they identify another teacher who is already performing the role, in both cases, they are also male.

Conclusion

The male discipline script, in common with the sportsman, role-model and promotion scripts, is concerned with reaffirming a traditional hegemonic masculinity, in this case due to assumed male physical power. It provides a fixed role that 'all' male teachers are meant to perform and this role can be promoted by some female and male staff, parents and pupils who offer male teachers more respect. These male teacher scripts may reflect a wider societal concern that the 'traditional' heterosexual family unit is in decline. In England there are now laws supporting equal pay for women and men; homophobia is illegal; and men may no longer be the family breadwinners. Society has undergone rapid change with people of different genders and sexualities co-habiting; furthermore, there is now no longer a stigma attached to being a divorcee and 'living together' is no longer viewed as a 'sin'. Gender conformity is threatened by these societal moves towards equality and as Connell (2002:143) argues the: 'patriarchal dividend is the main stake in contemporary gender politics. Its scale makes patriarchy worth defending'. Erecting gender barriers is an effective way of ensuring male power is protected.

Today rapid technological advances and unpredictable global markets mean employment opportunities and lifestyles for women and men are being constantly re-negotiated alongside gender (and other) identities. There may be a need, when the world is once again so uncertain and no job is secure, to seek reassurance by attempting to restore an 'imagined' golden age when patriarchy was firmly in charge, homosexuality was illegal and women and men knew and accepted their allotted gender 'roles'.

Martino (2008) sees the present project to recruit male teachers and position them as rescuers of the 'boys'; as a 're-masculinization of schooling'. The data presented in Chapter Four suggests that male teachers themselves are divided over just what sort of mythical version of idealised 'masculinity' they are meant to be representing in schools today (King, 2004). The majority of our key informants reject the discipline script, which they believe can construct them as public 'scare' figures; yet, the majority of our professional peers accept it.

Discussion questions

1. Examine a range of media representations of 'men'. Discuss the legitimate subject positions that are available for men today.

2. Find a photograph of a group of men taken over fifty years ago; what changes can you see in their appearances and what do they signify?

CHAPTER FIVE

Male Role Models

This chapter examines another historical male teacher script drawn from our research data; this is one that is concerned with positioning men as 'role models' for the older boys. In common with the sportsman, discipline and promotion scripts, the male role-model script will work to advantage men in appointment and promotion, providing they perform their patriarchal role. Again issues of hegemonic masculinity are implicated in the constructing and upholding of this male role-model script (Skelton, 2011; Allen Knight and Moore, 2012).

In the 1990s there was a clear resurgence of role-model discourses as concerns over 'boys' took centre stage in policy initiatives in a number of countries (Epstein et al., 1998; Arnot et al., 1999; Martino, 2008). The examination of football initiatives in Chapter Three showed how simplistic, stereotyped notions about young boys' underachievement can devalue their female teachers and downgrade the class and 'race' disadvantages many girls and boys still face today in the English education system (Wright, 1992; Ball, 2003). Johnston et al. (1999:60), researching in Ireland, consider that this persistent concern to appoint male teachers to 'save' the failing boys has become 'akin to a moral stance'. Mills (2001) likewise reports that in Australia one of the main arguments being employed in male teacher recruitment drives concerns boys needing male role models.

These male role-model discourses were laid down over time and they have become embedded within the occupational culture. Prior to examining our informants' responses to this script, we briefly consider the historical campaigns of the National Association of Schoolmasters (NAS) in the 1930s. The campaigns drew heavily on essentialist gender discourses which constructed male teachers as needed role models for boys and denigrated 'spinster teachers'; worked to secure male power, promotion and pay advantage within the occupation.

Union campaigns in the 1930s: Male teachers are the 'healthy' role models for boys

The NAS campaigns of the 1930s employed a set of highly gendered discourses that openly 'attacked' women teachers for taking men's jobs (Limond, 2002). Their propaganda campaign argued that male teachers had unique qualities that ought to be further valued and rewarded. These important male-only qualities were concerned with leadership, discipline and, of course, sportsmanship. Male teachers were credited with providing needed and necessary 'healthy' role models for the older boys. Fear of boys developing a 'deviant' sexuality if taught by 'spinster' women teachers, were part of these pernicious discourses.

Littlewood's (1995) research evidences a widespread public belief that male and female teachers had separate roles to play within the school. The NAS also drew on breadwinner discourses, to argue that male teachers must have a higher salary as they were required to support their wives in the home. The NAS claimed that a woman's true vocation was as a wife and mother and an unmarried woman was clearly 'unnatural' (Limond, 2002). The introduction of the marriage bar for women teachers in the 1920s (which was only formally lifted in 1945) has worked to further cement this belief. The current discourses which attempt to position men who teach young children as sexually deviant (see Chapter Seven) are once again drawing on public fears of 'sexual' abnormality in order to maintain traditional gender regimes in schools (Weaver-Hightower, 2011).

Smedley (2007:380) discusses how during the 1920s and 1930s: 'masculinity and militarism were strongly linked. If boys were to become "real" men, they must be taught by men'. Oram (1989:27) has shown how major structural inequalities were laid down, between male and female teachers, during this period. State policy at both local and national levels intentionally discriminated against women teachers and favoured men's position in the profession. These highly discriminatory campaigns against unmarried female teachers by the NAS continued throughout the 1930s. Boys after the age of seven were 'at risk' if taught by female teachers: 'the castrating effects' of spinsters was one of their key arguments (Littlewood, 1995:51).

In these discourses, single women are the targets, since they are constructed as challenging the patriarchal 'norms', although the marriage bar meant that they were forced to leave teaching if they did conform! This misogyny was overt; the NAS had 'built its reputation as a militant union of male teachers – "the men's movement" it called itself' (Jones, 1985:285). The membership of the NAS rose from 5,000 in 1923 to 10,000 in the mid-1930s demonstrating its increasing popularity with many male teachers.

The NAS belief that boys needed male guidance, helped to further legitimate and fix the separate roles male and female teachers were expected to carry out within schools. The NAS campaigns valorised the public 'patriarchal' family with the rational heterosexual father, good at 'male' sports, providing a role model for his older sons, and clearly in command.

A consideration of the NAS campaigns is useful in demonstrating how social power is carried in gender discourses that work to produce 'common sense truths' such as: young boys must have male teachers as role models. The focus then and again today, when this role-model discourse is once again active, is on boys and male teachers (Allen Knight and Moore, 2012). However, as Foucault (1978) makes clear, no one set of discourses is ever complete and there will always be alternative discursive formations vying for power. Coffey and Delamont (2000:49) discuss how the women-only unions of the 1930s were 'distinctly feminist in their outlook and action'. This resistance was necessary as it was only in 1961 that female and male teachers were given equal pay – a move that the NAS actively argued against. Coffey and Delamont (2000:111) quote from a letter written by a member of the NAS and printed in the T.E.S. in 1957; this man claimed women only became teachers, 'to get a husband…The women's staff room has become a waiting room for the bridal chamber'. The 1975 Sex Discrimination Act made single-sex unions illegal; Coffey and Delamont consider the subsequent lack of a 'feminist' women-only union has helped to reinforce gender differentiation within the occupation (see Chapter Nine). Whilst the sexist view that women only get an education to 'get a husband' is still in circulation, it was propounded by the Mayor of London in 2013, when he 'jokingly' told an international conference, that women only go to university to get a husband (Topping, 2013).

The re-emergence of the 'boys need men' script (Burn, 2002; Hepburn, 2013; Mistry and Sood, 2013) has also found acceptances in circulation, alongside resistances. For example, in 2000 the government, supporting these discourses, called for more male teachers to be recruited as role models for young boys whilst, Durham's Curriculum, Evaluation and Management Centre started to analyse the test results of 8, 978 girls and boys, aged 11 in

413 classrooms (Carrington et al., 2005). The researchers were examining whether children's levels of attainment were higher if they had teachers of the same sex (the role-model script argues it will be for boys). The Durham researchers found that there was no correlation between the gender of the teacher and the pupils' scores. The common assumption carried in the male role-model script that boys will achieve more when taught by men is not supported by these test results. Skelton (2011:10) considers that, now there is:

> ... a substantial body of evidence showing that it makes very little difference to pupils' achievement whether they are taught by a man or woman teacher ...

Carrington et al. (2007), examined interview data, collected from over 300, 7–8-year-olds, in order to examine further whether the gender of the teacher mattered. The results, in common with the larger Durham study, again found that the gender of the teacher was not significant. These two contemporary studies, carried out by male and female researchers, who are experts in the field of gender studies in primary schools, are a very positive addition to the literature.

It is important to carry out both quantitative and qualitative research in order to understand better the validity of the 'claims' made by these male teacher scripts, concerning pupil attainment. In their research, Carrington et al. found: 'it is the teacher's pedagogic and interpersonal skills that are vital in engaging them as learners' (Carrington et al., 2007:412). This research finding supports the emerging pedagogic discourse several of our Reforming key informants are claiming: 'we want to be good teachers, not good male teachers'. This 'good teacher' discourse challenges the gendered belief that all male teachers will have distinctly different (and superior) teaching qualities (Mallozzi and Campbell Galman, 2014). We now discuss our key informants' varied responses to being positioned (or positioning themselves) as needed male role models for boys in school.

Research findings

Interviews with eighteen key informants

Ten out of these eighteen male teachers claimed they were (or aiming to be) 'role models' in schools. Carrington (2002) and Johnston et al. (1999) likewise found that the majority of the student teachers that they researched also saw men as needed role models in schools. However, this male gender script was the most fragmented and contradictory script that emerged from our interview data: only six of these ten role-model men upheld the historical 'role models needed for boys' script, previously employed by the NAS; the other four role-model men proposed they were (or could be) providing different role models for teachers within the occupation. Sargent (2000:418) interviewed twenty-three male teachers and he reports 'the topic of "male role model" arose in every interview'. He likewise found that the male role-model concept was disjointed and 'used as a term that covers a host of unspecified behaviours and attributes associated with a vague image of masculinity' (Sargent 2000:421).

There were three men who rejected the male role-model script, whilst, five did not mention it in their interviews.

Role-model men

Alan, an NQT, teaching in Reception, positions himself, as a much 'needed' male role model. Alan refers to a recent TV programme about single parents:

> they actually raise a point that with there being more single parent families now and the lack of males in primary teaching that (*p*) children are actually growing up (*p*) especially in areas like reading, reading either independently with their peers or with a female …

Alan is uncertain how children are affected by not reading to men, but he does believe 'it's a factor' especially for boys. In this current deficit single parent discourse (Hughes, 2002) the 'parent' is always assumed to be female and deficit (Walkerdine et al., 2001). Mills et al. (2004:361) argue that the idealized 'nuclear family is valorised' in the present call for male role models. In his interview Alan constructs single parents as 'lacking' and argues that the 'feminization' of schools is problematic for boys. Mills et al. (2004:358) discuss how calls for male role models can undervalue women teachers; they point out that a feminized occupation does not mean 'there has been a feminist conspiracy against boys'.

Harry, another NQT, teaching Year Five children, also positions himself as a role model, again especially valuable for older boys from single-parent families. The idea that boys require a 'man' to model themselves on, otherwise their future 'manhood' is endangered, was an important feature of the historical NAS campaigns. Harry is clearly reflecting today's moral panic about boys' academic 'underachievement' which simplistically 'blames' female teachers, alongside single (female) parents for 'failing' boys (Epstein et al., 1998; Arnot et al., 1999; Mills et al., 2004; Skelton, 2011).

Pat, Oliver and Roger, the three Head teachers in our key informants set, all actively endorse the traditional role-model script. Pat, Head of a Nursery school, where the rest of the staff are female, thinks it is 'very important' that children are used to seeing men in schools 'as role models whatever'. Pat is also an Ofsted inspector, who originally trained as a Junior teacher and this is his second Nursery Headship. The interview took place in his office and was very formal; throughout the interview Pat kept repeating 'I'm good at it'. It was only after the recorder was switched off that Pat selected to talk further to Elizabeth about women staff, role models and boys (Burn, 2005:280). Pat believes fathers feel 'more able' to talk to a male teacher and they will tell him things they would not share with a 'big blowsy woman'. He believes that 'the women are turning the boys against men'. Pat's insulting description of his female staff indicates a prejudice against women that can also be held by women teachers against men. In Elizabeth's field diary, a female Head of a Primary school, discussing male teachers, told her: 'I wouldn't have one in the place Elizabeth … they're a waste of space' (Burn, 2005:288).

We wish to make clear, that as practitioners ourselves, who have long been subject to some of the unfair gender practices discussed, we do not condone the biased comments made by these two Head teachers. Yet, as long as gender practice remains it will generate resentment and bad feeling between some male and some female staff (Acker, 1994; Fraser and Yeomans, 1999). Gender binaries operate to divide male and female, offering legitimate male-only and female-only subject positions; the unfair gender practices that can result will attract hostility as well as approval from both male and female teachers (King, 1998; Sumsion, 2000; Jones, 2006).

Oliver, Head of an Infant school, discusses how when he started teaching 'I suddenly had a class of thirty kids and many of them didn't have any male role models.' Oliver is referring to the children of single mothers and he is quite willing to accept the subject position of 'substitute father' for the boys, upholding the familial discourses. Sargent (2000) reports that several of the male teachers he researched also positioned themselves as substitute fathers, especially for single-parent families, again assuming it is the father who is absent.

Roger, Head of a Primary school, likewise believes it is important to provide positive male role models, for boys, due to deficit families. Roger links this script to schools (like his own) in economically impoverished areas:

> from the children's perspective, particularly in an area like this where there is a lot of (p) social problems, where there are not great male role models in all the families, to give them a model to aspire to (p) to see a male. I was in a social service case conference this morning (p) there were ten of us in the room and I was the only male.

These deficit single parents' discourse and 'inadequate' working-class father discourses are part of the present-day role-model script. Martin (1999:110) argues that the '1990s have witnessed a growing emphasis on male disadvantage' in education; these role-model debates continue to focus on boys' needs (Raphael Reed, 1999; Skelton, 2001; Mulholland and Hansen, 2003).

Neil, an Infant Deputy Head, is equally worried about the lack of positive male role models that he believes young children have today due to changes in the family:

The way society's breaking down (p) boys and girls don't seem to have the same constant, stable male role models that they used to have ...

In this particular excerpt, Neil refers to 'boys' and girls'; however, he then provides a long description of the boys' learning needs, with no consideration of the girls' learning needs. Neil describes attending a course about gender difference in learning styles, and he has taken ideas for teaching the boys back to the experienced 'female staff'. Oliver (the Infant head) has also attended a 'gender difference' course where similar research had been presented; also proposing boys have different learning styles.

It is important to recognize that recent work on masculinities has not all been pro-feminist (Skelton, 1989; Martino, 2008). A separatist 'men's movement' has also developed, which again positions women as emasculating boys (similar to the earlier NAS campaigns) and calls for 'male only' work to rectify this problem (Bly, 1990; Biddulph, 1997). This 'men's' movement talks about all 'men and boys' in a narrow unified way and has been criticized by Smedley (2007:370) who argues that when 'men' 'operates as a category, treated unproblematically, individual difference is obscured'.

It is worth noting that both of these male senior managers (Oliver and Neil), working in different LEAs, have attended training sessions about 'boys' learning styles. The focus is firmly on 'failing' boys as Neil argues: 'boys seem to tackle things a lot better through a physical learning approach'. The gender stereotype being that, on the other hand, all girls will happily accept 'passive' learning and will not need a 'physical learning approach'. Once again, all boys, in common with all male teachers of young children are being constructed as a homogenous group. Jones (2006:73) points out that there is 'a general lack of clarity not only about why male teachers should be needed, but also about the characteristics they should exhibit'.

Cushman (2009a:12) interviewed 'Tim' a teacher of 9–11-year-olds, in New Zealand, who claims to be a needed role model for boys: 'a father figure'. Tim enjoys using his physicality with the boys, including 'headlocks' to 'win rapport' (Cushman, 2009a:12). Tim employs the sportsman, discipline and role-model scripts, with the boys in his class. He has recently read the book 'Raising Boys' (Biddulph, 1997), a key text of the separatist 'men's movement' which promotes 'recuperative masculinities' strategies in order to rescue 'boys' from feminization (Martino et al., 2004; Skelton, 2011). Cushman (2005a:335) believes that the: 'qualities of a good primary teacher are largely non-gender specific'.

Reforming role-model men

The imprecision of the term 'role model' means, that as well as constructing the historical father figure, needed for the 'boys', it can also be employed to construct new figures such as: the 'reforming male teacher' and the 'expert male teacher'.

Jeff, who has just been appointed as a deputy head in a new school, positions himself as a 'reforming man' rejecting both the sports and discipline scripts. Jeff positions himself as a potential role model for the male and female teachers in his new school. Quentin, who is already a deputy head, agrees with Jeff; he wants to be a role model for 'teachers not men'. Thomas sees himself as a good role model for future male student teachers, since he moved into Teacher Training two years ago. He believes he can be a positive role model, able to 'encourage' male students who want to teach in primary schools:

> I've done it! Look I'm here and I've dealt with it, and lived to tell the tale (*laughs*) and it's actually quite a good career for a man.

The comment 'I've dealt with it' refers to the gender practices Thomas encountered as a classroom teacher, when he was expected to avoid teaching infants and discipline the older boys. Thomas has challenged both of these gendered assumptions and hopes to encourage future male teachers to do so. It is of interest that Thomas describes teaching as a good career 'for a man' (a discussion of promotion practices is offered in Chapter Six).

Carl, who is supply teaching, also resents being 'expected' to adopt gender-specific roles in school:

> ... that underlying thing that you are different, 'we need a man in the Juniors' but I'm also told 'we need a man in the Infants'. I think people assume, other teachers and parents, especially for the kids who come from one-parent families where there isn't a male, that you can be that male (*p*) but you're not their dad, you're their teacher.

Carl repeats the same phrase 'I'm not their dad, I'm a teacher' several times in his interview. He could be attempting to establish a 'teacher' role-model script which can recruit male and female staff instead of the male-only paternal one. Carl's words have clear resonance with the older familial discourses which cast men as public father figures for boys (Clarke, 1985; Blackmore, 1999). McGrath and Sinclair (2013) also discuss how some parents and staff will construct male teachers as idealized substitute father-figures, whilst others will reject this paternal construction.

Carl's interview demonstrates the complex and contradictory ways we negotiate and take up subject positions in the ongoing attempt to claim acceptable work identities (Giroux, 1992).

Earlier in the same interview, when discussing his initial training, Carl had been quite happy to 'claim' the role of a 'public' father, especially for single-parent families:

> I was a bit of a celebrity 'cause they hadn't had one (*p*) they hadn't had a male teacher there for goodness knows how long (*p*) you're a bit of a novelty aren't you? The kids loved me (*p*) and for a lot of them it was a male in their life.

Raphael Read has criticized the government's continuing campaign to recruit male teachers as role models in schools. She raises questions about what 'type of masculinity is being reproduced by male primary teachers' (Raphael Reed, 1999:102).

Men who reject the role-model script

The three classroom teachers who rejected the script, all identify themselves as 'working-class' and their border-crossing into teaching has been (and continues to be) very problematic. Reay (1998:165) argues that in 'Britain class infuses everyday practices and social interactions'.

In the following extract, Ken, in his second year of teaching, actively derides the stereotypes of male teachers as 'positive role models for boys', good at discipline and ideal for Year Six:

> I was talking in the staff room with the other male teachers (*p*) we were joking with our female deputy head. We said: we should create our own ELITE male supply squad: 'Do you want a good-looking male in Year 6?'(*sing-song voice*).

Ken recognizes that in this gender script the male teacher must be 'good-looking' drawing on the handsome prince discourses, which require a compulsory heterosexuality (Epstein and Johnson, 1998). These male teachers seem well aware of the current role-model discourses; these men know that they are seen as needed for Year Six and in great demand. Ken makes it very clear that he does not actually agree with the male role-model script: 'I don't believe in JUST putting a man in the classroom.' Ken is claiming the emerging pedagogic discourse: 'I want to be a good teacher, not a good male teacher'; he does not want to be reduced by stereotypes to a discipline man, good at sport, acting as a role model for boys and destined for early leadership (Weaver-Hightower, 2011).

Ken returns to mocking further the traditional gender scripts which set out to limit role models to the same sex; he then names a white female teacher as his own role model; describing how she is a 'really brilliant' teacher. Ken certainly enjoys the pedagogic challenge of teaching, but he has clear doubts about continuing in the occupation; these doubts are related to Ken's class background: 'I'm not part of the club, it's a class thing'.

Derek, a black teacher, teaching Infants, strongly resents being positioned as a positive role model for the older black boys. Although he is Early Years trained, Derek found, in his second year of teaching, he was moved into the Juniors by a white female head, to 'deal with' the black boys and provide a role model. Carrington et al. (2007:398) discuss how 'essentialist assumptions about matching by ethnicity' inform many government campaigns to recruit ethnic minority teachers. Derek found he:

> ... was given a year 3 and 4 class. I was the only male with the team (p) I had a disproportionate number of boys with behaviour and emotional problems (p) I had something like 32 children in all with only 9 girls.

After the first week Derek became ill: 'I don't know how they thought I could manage such a large group of boys?' Although he now really enjoys teaching Infants and wants to study for an MA, after six years Derek, like Ken, is 'torn' about staying in the occupation:

> I'm just a token really (p) a black male teacher (p) and I think I don't want to be ANYONE'S token.

Derek finds his 'race' as well his gender and class difference, work to make him subject to multiple excluding practices within the school. Derek is the only male teacher on the staff and he is sometimes mistaken for the caretaker: 'people are surprised that I am the teacher ... they make judgements on what I look like'. Hall (1997:274) argues 'black people have so often been fixed, stereotypically by the racialized gaze'. A 'minority' can always be vulnerable to stereotyping and 'Othering' by the dominant group; a raise of the eye, a subtle sigh, can let us know that we do not belong (Burn, 2000, 2001; Medhurst, 2000). The lived reality of these multiple and seemingly inconsequential petty exclusions, due to 'difference' is cumulative and can have serious 'psychosocial' effects (Walkerdine et al., 2001:15). The pain of exclusion is ongoing and has effects; these three men are the only ones who are considering leaving the occupation, despite their high commitment to, and enjoyment of, teaching itself; as Ken says, 'it's the rest' (referring to his sense of not being accepted).

The third man to reject the role-model script is George, an NQT, who discusses two role models who influenced his decision to enter university. George's role models are Rosa Parks and his uncle, whom he watched, when he was nine, being beaten up by the National Front (British far-right political party): 'they did this for ME, they went through that for ME (p) so I could be here'. As for the idea that boys need male teachers, George refutes this, again drawing on the pedagogic discourse:

> I don't believe in JUST putting a man in the classroom (p) if they're good YES, NOT just because they're a man.

George, who has just qualified, was the only black, male, working-class student in his year group. He had studied for a four years teaching degree, after entering university through the Access route. George is in his mid-thirties, an ex-footballer and a parent, married to a white female primary school teacher. They do not want their child to be subjected to the racism he experienced at school; George was often sent out of lessons to play football and remembers playing Carmen Miranda in a school play with bananas on his head (see Wright, 1992; Connolly, 1998).

George's 'nightmare' training experiences are still very vivid and throughout the interview he is actively trying to 'make sense' of what happened to him. He arrived for interview (with Elizabeth) carrying a briefcase, a full CV and notes, but never refers to them. As the long interview progresses, George moves from an articulate interviewee, into verbal incoherence and becomes visibly upset. At times it seems he is talking to himself and Elizabeth becomes a 'silent' audience aware that she cannot interrupt George's very painful memories of training:

> They think equal opportunities is giving a little black man a job (p) they don't know what EQUAL OPPS [opportunities] is (p) you reach a point where you don't complain anymore and that is wrong ...

George in this excerpt seems to be trying to understand his reactions to the exclusions he experienced, due to his differences. George self-blames, positioning himself as a failure for not being able to 'take it'. Connolly (1998:134) argues that researchers must recognize 'the inherently complex nature of racism and how it can only be understood in relation to other forms of inequality'. George identifies how configurations of class alongside gender and 'race' worked to discriminate against him; in the specific context of a university, George's ability to re-negotiate his position as Other is strait-jacketed by racism, alongside class (Osler, 1997).

George had entered university, confident and financially secure. In his previous career as a professional footballer he had experienced a great deal of racial abuse, being spat at and having bananas thrown at him on the football field. George discusses how over time he developed successful strategies of resistance to these racist practices. George had also felt a sense of occupational inclusion since, as Mills (2001:30) argues, for working-class black and white men, sports can earn 'them a societal respect'. Now he is symbolically challenging the 'legitimate' racial scripts, by entering university as a black working-class man. hooks (2000:33) describing her own traumatic entry into HE, identifies how as a black working-class woman she was a 'stranger' even amongst the black middle class women. The fabric of the university continues to be white, male and middle-class (Bhopal, 1994). George frequently repeats to himself: 'why couldn't I take it ... WHY couldn't I?' He is referring to how he felt 'stereotyped straight off (p) because ... I was dressed neat and tidy (p) just a flash black guy'. George's interview raises issues for recruitment and retention of ethnic minority teachers into an occupation still viewed as white, middle class and female (Carrington and Skelton, 2003). George believes:

> They look at people and think these are the type of people we want to be teachers (*p*) they want white, middle-class people (*p*) I have a strong London accent.

In this excerpt it is his 'race' and class 'difference' that George identifies as the reason for the traumatic exclusions he experienced during training.

The interviews with Derek and George, exemplify how gender scripts are infused with class and 'race' scripts and Osler (1997) argues that we do not have sufficient knowledge about black teachers' experiences of racism (see also Siraj-Blatchford, 1995). Class difference is threaded through these three men's stories. In a similar way, Jenny, a white working-class teacher, also found: 'at university … they basically took the piss … because of your accent' (Burn, 2001:88).

The personal role models selected by Ken and George include a white woman teacher and a black woman who was a civil rights activist; challenging the traditional male role-model script's naïve assumption that role models always have to be an older model of a same 'self'.

Professional peer responses

In contrast to the data collected from our key informants, only one role-model script was identified; the one that constructs male teachers of young children as much needed male role models for children (especially boys) from single parent families. This script has clearly recruited compliant subjects in England, Finland, New Zealand and Canada; thirty-five out of our forty male teachers saw themselves as needed role models. Skelton (2009:43) also found some male teachers who were happy to be public father figures.

One man, discussed how 'young men who would be teachers are fed' this male role-model discourse (England, a university lecturer, taught thirty-three years), but he did not offer his own views and three of the men did not mention it.

The one man who opposed this male role-model script, stated: 'Everyone employed at the school is a role model for everybody else in the school' (England, NQT). This particular male teacher is teaching in a school with six other male teachers on the staff, and in this specific context 'normal' gender practices may not occur, since male teachers are no longer rare and therefore of 'special value' (Sumsion, 2000). Instead, this NQT is claiming the 'teacher role model' script that four of the key informants also subscribe to; a script that is concerned with effective teaching, not symbolical public parenting. The teacher role-model script is concerned with pedagogic practice and as such can be performed by both female and male teachers of young children. In contrast, the male role-model script can only be enacted by male teachers, working to give them high status, due to their unique 'male' traits. One informant revealed that there was an expectation that:

> As a male teacher I was always aware that being in a minority in a primary school, that it was important to act as an exemplary 'role model'...(England, NQT).

His statement shows how we can all be under pressure to internalize prevailing gender beliefs and will 'police' ourselves to ensure conformity to the gender practices of the time. Martino (2008:21) reviewing press calls for more male role models in schools in America reports that there is:

> ... a moral concern about the lack of male role models in elementary schools which is enhanced by what is perceived to be an increase in single-parent families.

His conclusions are fully supported by the commentary provided by our professional peers, who are certain that they are badly 'needed' in schools due to the number of single parent families. These male teachers position themselves (and are also positioned) as public fathers for inadequate single parent families: 'being like a second dad to their kids from solo mums' (New Zealand, twenty-one years teaching).

Several men discuss how they are highly praised by parents, for accepting this 'male' role:

> As some children are bought up by their mothers, many parents think having a male teacher would be beneficial to those children. (England, NQT)
> Male teachers can sometimes be (the) only male role model in (a) child's life because of divorces and different kinds of family situations. (Finland, ten years)

The assumption is that the remaining parent is always female and there are no male relatives, such as grandfathers or uncles in the family. In these excerpts we see how male teachers can willingly accept the responsibility of modelling an approved 'masculinity' to pupils. Many of the informants explain how valued they are for providing this 'male role model' in school:

> I am the only male on the staff and the first ever at the school.
> Male students are put in my class because they need a male role model.
> Being the only male on campus I often feel like I am a bit of a celebrity with the kids.

> I sometimes feel that I am given some leniency from the parents because I am a male.
>
> I am treated with the respect that much more experienced teachers receive. (Canada, three years)

This male teacher is the only man who recognizes his 'advantage' within the occupation due to his gender. He also enjoys his status as the 'only man' on the staff and all the positive attention it brings. His discussion of 'celebrity' status mirrors the comments Carl (one of our key informants) also received from parents, when training in Wales: 'I was a bit of a celebrity'cause they hadn't had one' (Carl). It may well bring career advantage if you are the legitimate white, heterosexual, middle class man, well able to uphold hegemonic masculinity (see Chapter Three). However, for male teachers who actually want to be valued for their teaching expertise, not for their gender, it is both patronizing and insulting to be identified as a 'one' (Carl) and stereotyped qualities applied.

Other male teachers, report finding the 'feminine' workforce of the primary school problematic; for example, despite receiving praise from parents for being a male role model, this man describes how:

> Being a male teacher is quite tricky. It is certainly hard to fit in where it is predominately females. It takes children quite a while to adapt to having a male teacher (mainly because I don't seem as sympathetic at first). Many children are used to the 'cuddled' approach and they find it hard that I am more like their father model than a mother model. (England, two years)

This informant clearly positions himself in the familial role identified by Alexander (1988); a continuation of the Victorian public patriarchal parents construction. In this excerpt, women teachers are described as adopting a 'cuddle' approach, re-affirming the historical 'maternal' discourses (Carrington, 2002) that our two female teachers identify in Chapter Nine. He also describes how he finds it 'tricky' to negotiate the gender barriers he encounters in school.

Some of the men cast themselves as 'heroes' for selecting to enter the world of women; secure in the knowledge that their mere male presence will automatically engage boys in learning. For example, in the following excerpt this young male teacher, who has just completed his first three months teaching in a primary school, willingly performs the 'handsome prince' role identified by Epstein (1997) as well as claiming the male sports script. He has already been told by the parents how:

> ... their child is enjoying school more this year and they think it is down to having a young male teacher. The boys certainly love to tell me about their hobbies and which sports they do, and are always curious to find out what my hobbies are out of school. People are often surprised when I

tell them what I do for a living, other men telling me that they can't think of anything worse and they don't think they would be able to handle it. I do feel a sense of pride that I enjoy doing something that other men would be daunted by. (England, NQT)

Teaching young children is constructed as 'alien' and 'daunting' by his male friends and this NQT is claiming superiority due to being able to 'handle it' in this workforce, where men remain the exception. His views echo the Plowden Report that identified how: 'In infant schools in 1965 there were only ninety-seven brave men out of a total of 33,000 teachers' (CACE, 1967:313–314). The valorisation of 'brave' men for having the 'courage' to teach young children was a feature of our historical trawl of gender practice in the twentieth-century workforce.

There were also comments that were reminiscent of the derisory discourses employed against women teachers in the 1930s campaigns by the NAS (Littlewood, 1995), who suggested that boys are put at risk by women. Several informants clearly identified how they believe that: 'many schools are now female dominated and boys relate better to male teachers' (England, nine years). Mills (2001:139) has examined 'the existence of a backlash politics, which is shaping much of the gender agenda in schools' and boys are seen as being disadvantaged due to female staff. The data shows how parents can support the idea that men are greatly 'needed' as teachers in this sector, especially as role models for the boys:

I think that in today's society being a male teacher in primary schools is praised by many parents and I have personally had parents speak to me about how much their child male or female enjoys having a male teacher and a male role model. Especially the boys within my class. I feel that as a man teaching young children you can connect to the class in a different way to women simply due to the fact that you're a man. (England, NQT)

Several of these men believe that they are 'naturally' more able to communicate with the boys 'in a different way' than women staff. They believe the 'truth' that this male role-model script sets out to establish: male teachers are more valuable in general and for boys in particular they are essential due to their 'natural' masculine traits (which are never defined). There is further evidence that it is not only parents who give men more status, but that young pupils themselves may defer to 'male' teachers and give them more respect. Men reported: 'children respond differently to a man' (New Zealand, eleven years). Whilst, in England, even during initial training this male student records how:

I find harder to reach children respond to me as a male and seem to give me more respect than some female teachers.

This male teacher describes 'children' offering him respect, however the majority of the comments, concerning the role-model script concern boys:

> Comments about 'being a man' from other members of staff are always positive, and usually revolve around it helping certain boys in the class. The general view is that a new experience for these pupils would be useful and that there may (*be*) some sort of breakthrough because the pupil may be more willing to impress me. (England, NQT)

In common with the experiences of some of our key informants, there were descriptions of men being moved to 'certain classes' to provide male role models; however, the men who identified this staffing practice agreed with it, for example:

> I believe that males can be placed within certain classes – especially those with a majority of boys – in order to provide boys with a role model to aspire to, as well as to have a greater connection with…It has been mentioned that I am a role model for the boys (particularly) to look to, and I have had comments from parents/carers that their child has responded to having a male teacher better than when their child has had a female teacher. (England, NQT)

In this excerpt, the male teacher, who has only been teaching for four and a half months, has no problem in accepting the role-model script given by the parents and agrees with the parents' comments that position female teachers as inferior to him. This particular teacher also claims superiority to female teachers when discussing the sports and discipline scripts. These male teacher scripts are working to construct all men as innately 'better than' women and this gender 'truth' is supported by some parents and some women teachers (Acker, 1994; Jones, 2006).

There was no awareness by these men of what their automatic 'value-added factor' might mean for the women teachers who have been teaching for a longer time (in this case). Instead these men state that male teachers (like themselves) are greatly needed in schools as valued role models (especially for boys); this seems to be translating into a great deal of self-belief and work confidence, even when the men have had hardly any actual teaching experience. The question of whether a child requires a 'role model' who is merely an older-self is never raised. Labrinth, a successful black singer and song writer, who himself grew up in inner-London, cites a female teacher, Miss Yusef, as his role model and discusses how good she was at discipline: 'She didn't give up on the naughty kids' but was also interested in the pupils she was teaching: 'That's it, the people. That's what made her stand out' (Labrinth, 2014:29).

The professional peer responses demonstrates how the male role-model script concerned with public fathering seems to be gaining strength as male scarcity continues within the occupation. Jones (2006:69) reports female teachers supporting male teachers as needed role models to provide: 'a positive male influence'.

The 'needed-men' discourses can give male teachers extra status from some parents, pupils and female staff; and upholds the continuation of ongoing gender differentiation in primary schools, which also has curriculum consequences for the children themselves (Burn, 1989).

This particular version of the role-model script with its focus on replacing 'missing' or 'inadequate' fathers' produces the false 'truth' that all men who are teaching young children will have essentially different and superior talents; based on a stereotyped ideal of 'male-hood' which is drawn from the hegemonic masculinity of the time.

Conclusion

The six key informants who uphold the traditional role-model script, are all convinced that 'boys', especially working-class boys from single-parent families (whom they assume to be mothers only) need male teachers to guide them and engage them in learning.

There are indications that gender discourses concerning 'men needed as role models for children of single parents' are increasing. Research from Australia also reports parents agreeing that male teachers are needed as role models for boys and girls (McGrath and Sinclair, 2013). The ongoing stereotyping of solo families as female and deficit, needing 'male' teachers to act as suitable 'fathers', reinforces the public family ideology; equating teaching with parenting, labelling all single mothers as lacking and older boys (in particular) as failing and in need of 'rescue' by male teachers from a damaging feminized environment. Mills et al. (2004:361) argue that the symbolic two parent heterosexual family is being 'valorised' in recruitment drives for male teachers; this argument is well supported by our data.

Attached to this script, there are discourses circulating that propose boys require different pedagogical approaches, based on 'physical learning' that all male teachers will 'naturally' embody; and a belief that there is an urgent need to reaffirm older boys 'masculinity' in the light of feminism which is 'damaging' boys.

Roger's discussion evidences discourses labelling working-class families as inherently deficit, lacking in positive male role models. Bryne (2006:167) has criticized government policy for labelling all economically poor communities as containing 'inadequate people'. The working class continue to be discursively constructed as inferior and Jones (2011:233) argues 'being working class has become increasingly regarded as an identity to leave behind'. Our three key informants who disown all role-model scripts see their working-class heritage as problematic within the class fabric of the teaching workforce (see Burn, 2001).

Data from the key informants shows how the 'term' role model allows for a range of interpretations, with four of our male key informants positioning themselves as role models for other teachers. In contrast three key informants reject being positioned as 'token' role models rather than as teachers and all three of these men are considering leaving the occupation, due to what they believe is their continuing objectification and isolation.

The staffing practices that results from the traditional male role-model script means men may be placed in the Juniors, for the older boys, irrespective of their initial training specialism. So, Derek an Early Years specialist is sent to teach the older boys, against his wishes, by a female head, who positions him as an ideal black male role model. Male and female teachers can both uphold (as well as challenge) this historical script, which works to reinforce hegemonic masculinity, essential for the maintenance of traditional gender regimes in school.

The public acclaim given to 'male teachers', due to their 'special' talents continues to be a feature of the 'boys need male teachers as role models' script; it is a gender belief that works to devalue women staff, affirm traditional patriarchal power relations and maintain present staffing and promotion practices within the workforce.

In contrast, the emerging 'teacher role-model script' that some of our informants claimed, promotes the development of reflexive pedagogical practice and unlike the limiting male role-model script can be performed by female and male teachers, resulting in a welcome focus on teaching and learning rather than on providing substitute father figures for the deficit boys.

The range of role models claimed by the key informants could indicate that the 'role' any teacher is meant to inhabit is increasingly in dispute as the purpose of Education itself continues to be contested (Grace, 1994; Pratt-Adams et al., 2010). It could be that within these contestations a space can be created for discourses concerned with teaching and social justice to gain recruits. In this space, wider society can focus on 'the impact of teaching, the politics of teaching and the hope of teaching' (Edgoose, 2009:121); rather than on making biased assumptions about the qualities of teachers, based on their gender alone.

Discussion questions

1. Consider what (if any) role models you have had in your life. Were they the same gender, ethnicity, class etc.? Did they influence your attitude to education?

2. Which male role models are most valued by children and young people today? Why is this? Do you agree with them? Are they different from past male role models? What alternatives to the current models can you think of?

CHAPTER SIX

Male Teachers and Promotion

In order to unravel the promotion man script, which continues to position male teachers (whether they accept it or not) as destined for early leadership, it is necessary once again to reflect on the historical gender discourses that are still in circulation today (Pepperell and Smedley, 1998; Jones, 2006; Hepburn, 2013). Chapter One traced how this occupation was constructed in Victorian times as a symbolic 'public family', with the nurturing 'mother' teaching the infants and the patriarchal 'father' in charge. The male teacher is to be rewarded for his valued managerial talents; the woman teacher is merely following her inherent motherly vocation (Dillabough, 1999). A consequence of these gendered beliefs is that this occupation has always favoured male teachers in both pay and promotion.

Apple (1988) argues that the existing organizational practices in primary schools remain 'patriarchal' and Blackmore (1999:26) suggests that the development of state education saw the 'characteristics of the father' transferred into senior leadership roles. Skelton (2009:42) reports how male primary teachers are still 'largely occupying management positions, responsible for "masculine" subjects like PE and maths, and often teaching the oldest pupils in the school'. The career experiences of the majority of our key informants support this analysis: highly gendered staffing practices in schools are still working to uphold traditional patriarchal relations.

Patriarchal relations

The concept of 'patriarchy' that literally means 'rule of the father' has long been used in feminist thinking to represent women's subordination in both the private and public spheres (Hearn, 2002:247). Walby (1990:20) defines 'patriarchy' as: 'a system of social structures and practices in which men dominate, oppress and exploit women'. One of the 'social structures' is patriarchal relations in paid work; Cockburn argues that although 'patriarchy itself changes historically', the concept is still useful in signalling 'male dominance' (Cockburn, 1991:8–9).

Hearn (2002:248) discusses how the single term 'patriarchy' has usefully evolved into the recognition of numerous patriarchal structures which are historically specific:

> The concepts of patriarchy, patriarchies and patriarchal relations facilitate a focus on men in terms of not only interpersonal relations but also *structural relations*

Acker (1994:76) suggests that these patriarchal inheritances have been so 'taken for granted' by researchers that the 'sexual division of labour' in primary teaching has been largely ignored. Blackmore (1999:23) discusses how gendered regimes of truth have been established within teaching, that will work to link 'rationality to masculinity in leadership, and thereby emotionality with teaching and femininity'.

Thornton and Bricheno (2000:203), who employed quantitative methods to investigate promotion in English primary schools, concluded that the less male teachers there are, the more they are advantaged; they are: 'a rare breed'. Early feminist research focused on the clear promotion discrimination many female staff face (Evetts, 1989; Acker, 1994); whilst more recent research is largely concerned with the 'masculinities' male teachers are expected to perform. Pulsford (2014) cautions that research into male teachers' masculinities is in danger of reinforcing gender boundaries instead of removing them. Male appointment and promotion advantage within the occupation is no longer being openly challenged and the historical 'failing' boys' discourses are still being employed by teacher recruitment campaigns to affirm men as value-added (Smedley, 2007; Skelton, 2011).

In order to understand better and thus be more able to begin to dismantle unfair promotion practices, we must recognize that female and male teachers are both implicated in affirming, ignoring or reforming this male promotion script. Data collected from our key informants evidences that male promotion advantage can understandably result in female resentment. This hostility is particularly apparent during initial training and we start by examining the experiences of men who felt 'attacked', prior to exploring the key informants' experiences of and responses to the promotion script.

Research findings

Interviews with eighteen key informants

Attacked men

One effect of this script is that men can be 'attacked' whilst training due to their future promotion advantages and for being 'men' (Mulholland and Hansen, 2003). None of the key informants in senior management discuss being 'attacked' as students; this could be because these men have secured institutional power and are no longer vulnerable to open criticism. The promoted men have all been teaching over ten years and they may well have 'negotiated', over time, working relationships with women colleagues where the 'occasional throwaway lines from people' (Roger) do not cause any significant offence.

Ken and Quentin both prefer working with women rather than in their previous all-male employments, since the peer pressure for men to perform 'all that male drink, beer, sexist rubbish' (Quentin) is removed. Cockburn (1991:220) argues: 'men are caught up in the compulsion of patriarchal relations as much as women are'. In a female dominated work place the culture of compulsory hegemonic masculinity is less enforced (Connell, 1987). Nias (1989:204) in her interviews with over a hundred female and male primary teachers found that they: 'tended to see themselves as the "same sorts of people"'. Her findings indicate commonality rather than difference between male and female primary teachers.

However, the majority of men, who are not in senior management, did describe 'attacks' by women students about 'male' promotion advantage and for being 'typical' men. When Alan, an NQT, told the female students how well he was supported in schools during placement, some were angry, believing that it was because Alan was a 'man' that he was given extra support. Alan became used to being asked why he wanted to teach in the Early Years but: 'when they say you're going to get a job because you're a man (*mumbles*) it's outrageous!' Alan avoids acknowledging the career advantage he will still inherit as a man (Jones, 2006).

Alan believes the one-off gender lectures during his training were 'predominately for the women'. Sikes (1991) criticizes single gender lectures and argues training needs to more fully address sexism within society. Alan felt vulnerable:

> things you can't say anymore (*p*) like 'man made' and you're sitting there (*p*)thinking well (*p*) and then you're NOT allowed to say 'man hole' or 'snowman'.

Alan is drawing on a 'politically-correct' discourse (pc) that has been highly influential in devaluing and deriding feminist attempts to challenge sexist practices. Spender (1982:89) reported that when she attempted to talk to male students about gender issues, she was:

> met by responses, which range from bewilderment to hostility, as members of the powerful group explain – from their position and experience of power – that the system is open and fair.

Brian, another NQT, also reports receiving sarcastic comments from female students about male promotion and he believes that this was very unfair since it was not his 'fault'. Brian felt that as the only man in his Early Years group 'you had to watch what you bloody said'. He describes how in sessions: 'you're humiliated (*p*) you keep quiet or tutors and women students would jump down your throat'.

Brian reports keeping 'quiet'; but as Mahony (1985:76), a female tutor within ITT, found, 'even when men are in the minority they can control the conversation'. Brian and the other men who complained about being 'silenced' in sessions, may be measuring their talk time against male norms. These 'norms' work to give men a 'natural' right to talk more in mixed sex groups, whereas women may interpret both the length and manner of male talk in these sessions as dominant and domineering. Brian concluded: 'the more females that there are the more oppressed you feel'.

Derek, after six years teaching in a school where he is the only male teacher, also draws on the 'attacked' man script in his interview:

> It's OK for women to say things about men (*p*) you just like (*p*) you get used to it (*p*) it started from the Access course, it was predominantly women and they were a very strong team and they used to have a go at men sometimes. So there's lots of 'men-bashing' (*p*) and it continues.

Derek describes himself as 'used to it', but Derek's voice and manner betrays a strong sense of unresolved grievance about the comments he still receives about 'men'.

Carl, the supply teacher, receives both positive and sarcastic comments about gender:

> There's this thing that if you stick at it long enough promotion is easier for men (*p*) I've had it said to me by women teachers as well, some have said it positive (*p*) some you know they're being sarcastic

Carl does not consider actual promotion figures within the occupation, although the 'division of labour between women and men within teaching should now be a familiar tale' (Coffey and Acker, 1991:255).

Ken, in his second year of teaching, is from an Irish working-class background and had worked in a factory before training. Issues of 'race' and gender were often discussed in his college sessions and Ken did feel able to speak, despite often being the only man in the class. Ken feels that he 'greatly benefited' from being able to 'think the issues through'. Yet, Ken's account also demonstrates 'the contradictory realities and social restraints under which identity is negotiated' (Acker, 1994:110). Ken believes that wider societal beliefs about 'masculinity' may well deter more men from entering the occupation:

> I think there's cultural issues and class issues, where men are perceived to act in certain roles (*p*) men can't explore their feminine (*p*) they've got to act in a certain way (*p*) so they go into a profession where they feel (*p*) more at home.

So, the male 'home' is not Primary teaching, since it continues to be viewed as 'merely' female work (Walkerdine, 1992). Ken then outlines some of the 'roles' men are meant to perform, drawing on his cultural experiences. In the following excerpt, Ken positions 'men' as defended subjects, having to 'act' in ways that are socially sanctioned:

> I think (*p*) my experience is very much (*p*) men can be quite sexist (*p*) not sexist but macho (*p*) they can't (*p*) they feel they've got to ACT in a way that's totally alien to them (*p*) I think men have a lot of problems anyway in society (*p*) men can't cry (*p*) men can't look after children (*p*) man has to be building things or be tough.

Ken shows that he is a skilled social 'actor', well aware of and often constrained by the 'rules' of public performance (Goffman, 1959). He discusses how it is not only in the workplace that these 'male' scripts are enforced, for instance: 'I don't really drink alcohol much...(*p*) they ask me if I'm a priest'. Ken recognizes that because he is not performing the 'typical' man in public he is vulnerable to both male and female mockery. Ken's disclosures indicate that he understands that the construction of acceptable public masculine identities is ongoing and problematic: they are never certain; they remain fragile, contested, contradictory and fought over (Mills, 2001).

Britton and Baxter (1999:191) suggest that for 'men there are costs in rejecting dominant forms of masculinity' and Ken tells a 'humorous' story to help illustrate the ongoing 'attacks' he still receives over promotion practices:

> I was recently in a restaurant with a woman primary teacher, who is a friend from college, 'all you've got to do to get promotion' she said 'is to show your tackle!'

George, an NQT, in common with Ken, does acknowledge sexism in society:

> Over the years women have been mistreated by men. There's been a lot of sexism. So, this moment in time a lot of men have realised that, that is not the way forward and they're trying to get into jobs with a more caring side.

George is the only interviewee not in senior management to both recognize and challenge male promotion advantage. George considers that promotion practices are 'scandalous' and women teachers 'are disadvantaged SERIOUSLY' but in gender lectures he felt 'attacked'.

> They look at you and seem to be giving you all the stick (*p*) I'm saying just because other people are sexist doesn't mean that I'm going to be sexist. And I don't care what anyone says, because of what we've been exposed to in our life you are going to have some views that need ironing out, that's why we're here (*p*) but you are not going to get every single thing that you've done or bad view that you ever had ironed out in one fell swoop.

hooks (1994), exploring the 'silencing' of students in equity sessions, argues that tutors need to develop pedagogical strategies to improve participation in sessions. Coffey and Acker (1991) identify how women tutors can themselves encounter sexism (from students and colleagues) if they attempt to address sexism in ITT sessions. Leo recalls an 'attack' at college which still bothers him, ten years later:

> We worked in these groups (*p*) and discussed such-and-such and fed back (*p*) after you've done this for about six months you suddenly realised (*p*) there were always the blokes that were doing the feeding back ... and one day I said to the group, I said: 'well I'm not doing it, I'm sorry, I'm really sick and tired of doing it, feeding back all the time, being the spokesperson ...' and one of the girls said 'well, you better get used to it because you're going to make headship before any of the rest of us'. IMPLYING it was because I was a bloke. I KIND OF (*p*) IT WAS LIKE (*amazed voice*) I was APPALLED that someone could think, that's how they saw me. They didn't see me as being someone who's confident and able to report back effectively and someone who is (*p*) they just saw me as a bloke.

Leo is very irate when describing this incident and he mimics the student's views: 'off you go you might as well get used to your role in life, which is to become the head. You'll get to headship before all the rest of us, you're a bloke'. Leo is 'aware' of male promotion patterns:

> You're aware that there are fewer blokes in primary teaching, but you know, there is a far greater chance of those blokes making it to head

ship or senior managerial positions than women. It's a well-known fact. But I didn't see (*p*) myself as being (*p*) a bloke who was (*p*) going to be (*p*) unaffected by it. I saw myself as sort of being (*p*) outside that information. Outside of that fact em (*p*) and I CERTAINLY didn't want other people (*p*) IMAGINE other people's views of YOU! (*angry voice*).

Leo initially recognizes male promotion advantage; Leo then distances himself from this 'well-known fact' by stating he is 'outside that information', although he will benefit from it.

In the complicated and emotional process of identity making and re-assembling, Leo is torn between his socially 'confident and able to report back' self and the inarticulate anger he still feels after being positioned by female students as 'just' a typical 'bloke' who would automatically gain promotion. This is the only time in his interview that Leo becomes noticeably upset as well as somewhat confused in both his speech and actual word usage. The individual actor will always be implicated in the existing gender order; Leo's denial of the patriarchal dividend (and its consequences) does not prevent its operation (Connell, 2002). Leo, unlike George, had no problems with equity sessions: 'we all happily read the books and discussed the issues and fed back (*p*) it was JUST this one incident'. In contrast to George and Ken, Leo did not perceive equal opportunities sessions as constituting an 'attack' on men. Other research also reports mixed reactions from both male and female students to gender sessions during teacher training (Leonard, 1989; Titus, 2000); gender barriers are already in operation.

Jeff had positive training experiences, but:

> when it came down to applying for jobs (*p*) people have always said (*p*) and at that time there was a shortage of jobs in Wales (*p*) people would say you'll get the job because you're a male. I found that really INSULTING EVEN my mother, before this interview (*for deputy headship*) she said to me 'you know you are a male teacher and you're very rare because you've taught year one to year six' but that's what I wanted to do (*p*) I wanted to have that experience, but I found that very INSULTING because (*mumbles*) all the way through my teaching practice I was an A grade student …

Jeff is clearly insulted by the comments, but at no time in the interview does he reflect on why they were made by 'people', even when his own mother, a teacher herself, voices them.

What really annoyed Fred, an NQT, during training sessions was the 'attack' on men by women students. Fred uses very emotive language when discussing the 'strong feminist element' in the course. Fred describes how he felt like a 'war criminal'. He soon retreated, like Alan, Brian and George, into becoming silent; Fred blames feminism and equal opportunities: 'we've got this huge tide of equal [opportunities] that completely ignores men'. Yet, Harry, one of the two men who had 'no problems' with his gender lectures during training, had trained at the same time and in the same institution as Fred.

These two very contradictory responses to the same training sessions, suggest individual male and female student responses to gender equity work can range from acceptance to alienation (Titus, 2000). Thompson (1989:74) reports how a session that had involved male and female students looking at sexism in books had been 'regarded by some students as "offensive". Two male students walked out of the lecture'. Coffey and Acker (1991:256) describe how female as well as male students believed posters showing images of women scientists were biased. Connell (2002:138) argues gender politics 'almost always has this dimension of intimacy' which can result in personal anger. Ord and Quigley (1985:104) recognize how 'anti-sexist education involves change: a long and painful process of changing people ...'. Edley and Wetherell (1995:91) point out that the ongoing 'construction of gender identities is based on the struggle for social power' and gender discussions will at times inevitably cause conflict.

Accepted men

Harry and Eric are the two men not yet in senior management who do not describe being 'attacked' by women students/staff, for their inherited promotion advantage. Eric attended the same training institution as his wife, who was already completing her second year of studying for a B.Ed in Early Years teaching. Eric was the only man in his Early Years group, but unlike Alan, Eric feels 'no different':

> I have never EVER in my life considered myself as this 'male' in a female world, I've just considered 'myself' with other people (p) I don't know why ...

Women are again referred to as 'people' and this strategy of avoiding any discussion of 'gender' power play serves Eric well. Eric had previously worked as a hairdresser, another stereotyped 'female' occupation, which may have helped him acclimatize. Studying and now teaching with his wife may well have contributed to Eric's sense of occupational inclusion; sitting in a staff room with a female partner is very different from Derek's staffroom experience of having to be 'prepared to take what might come flying' about men in general. Eric, who was promoted after one year, is now in a junior managerial post and this may also help to 'protect' him from 'attacks' from female staff. Eric believes that his wife does not mind that he has been promoted before her, despite her longer teaching experience; his wife thinks 'it's normal' and she chose not to apply for the post. Patriarchal relations are affirmed.

Harry, the only NQT who did not feel 'attacked' during training, did receive comments from the 'girls' about his future promotion advantage:

'look at how many women are teaching, but look who's head!' Harry does not believe what they say '... holds a lot of water; people who say that, I wouldn't take a lot of notice of it'. Harry is employing the same strategy as Eric, of taking no 'notice' of the 'people' or their comments. Another interpretation could be that Harry and Eric may not wish to admit to a woman in an interview context that they had actually been 'upset' by these female comments. Kimmel (1994) argues that men are meant to abide by the gender 'rules' which require them not to show vulnerability, especially in the presence of women.

Promotion men

Twelve of our eighteen key informants either ignore their 'inherited' promotion advantage or deny it applies to them. Half of the eighteen men in this sample set have female partners who are teachers; yet, Eric, Stuart, Harry and Alan (who all have teacher wives) do not identify any male promotion advantage. Research involving a postal survey of 2,158 primary and secondary teachers and interviews with 109 primary and secondary teachers (Powney et al., 2003) also found many male teachers do not acknowledge male promotion advantage. Thornton and Bricheno (2000:201) likewise report, in their national questionnaire, that male teachers did not identify 'male sex as an advantage' in promotion, but women teachers did. Thornton and Bricheno (2000:203) report that male primary teachers are part of an occupation where:

> Gender inequalities in power relationships are part of this educational division of labour. Parents, pupils, other teachers, governors and head teachers greet male students and teachers with excitement, awe (or fear), precisely because they are a rare commodity.

Thornton and Bricheno's (2000) research implicates some female teachers as well as some governors, pupils and parents, in subscribing to these 'needed man' discourses, which can and do translate into biased promotion practices. Fred's sense of having no individual power to challenge existing beliefs and promotion practices may be well founded.

If, as we propose, certain male (and female) teacher scripts have become historically embedded within this occupational culture then the removal of these gendered scripts is not only an individual endeavour. Skelton (1991) also reports that men may well feel 'powerless' to confront established gender regimes, which sees them manoeuvred quickly into senior management positions (Acker, 1994; Connell, 2002; Hepburn, 2013).

There is also the issue of self-interest: as Thomas concluded, whatever the reasons for his swift promotions, at the end of the day he benefitted. If men feel they cannot individually challenge these regimes and the promotion script works to advantage them, a strategy could well be to ignore their inherited advantage. Another strategy could be to claim that they are themselves being discriminated against by being 'attacked' by women for this 'well-known fact' (Leo) and move into 'victimhood'. Agnew (1989:84) claims 'leadership is so often linked to stereotypically defined masculine traits'. Bradley (1989:219), in her review of teachers and work practices, discusses how men 'are able to exploit their gender to rise rapidly up the hierarchy to top posts'.

Our data suggests that a more complex set of practices occur: it is not just a case of individual male teachers exploiting their gender, but long established beliefs, staffing and appointment practices which are implicated in continuing male career advantage being given to 'certain' type of men. Quentin easily describes the common stereotype of the head:

> male, 40s, 50s, white, probably wearing glasses, probably wearing some kind of suit (p) wandering around and being very authoritative.

Powney et al. (2003) found some black and ethnic minority teachers (male and female) felt disadvantaged in promotion. The gender stereotype of the head assumes a 'rational' and conforming white man (Blackmore, 1999).

Accepting that you may be promoted because of your inherited gender advantage, rather than due to your teaching talent alone, requires male teachers to look at themselves (and society) critically. Acker (1994:116) also researched female primary teachers who strongly support the construction of senior management along the lines of 'male norms' (Grant, 1989:46).

Al-Khalifa (1989:83) argues 'convergence of masculinity and management roles is in some way accepted at face value by women teachers as well as by men'. Another reading of our informants' responses to the promotion script is that some of them do believe it is 'normal' for men to be given swift promotion due to their 'natural' male talents. Male teachers will not necessarily feel able (or be willing) to disclose this essentialist belief to a women university lecturer in an interview situation. Walford (2001:90) cautions: 'interviewees will only give what they are prepared to reveal about their subjective perceptions of events and opinions'.

Male subject specialisms

The 'masculinist' subjects several of these men specialized in, or were 'given' promoted posts for in schools, could have further worked to reinforce the gender stereotyping of them as 'rational' men, ideally suited for senior management. Alan was promoted after a year to an ICT post, although he had held a PE specialism. The majority of the eleven students in the male support group had chosen ICT and mathematics as their specialisms and these shortage subjects may further advantage future promotion paths (Chapter Two). Hutchings (2002:138) discusses how 'mathematics and IT are seen as "masculine"' and these subject specialisms may serve to reinforce sexist notions of a 'natural' male rationality; hence men may be seen as more able to perform the new management roles in school (Mahony and Hextall, 2000).

Oliver, Neil, Brian, Pat and Harry had all specialized in mathematics when training, whilst Thomas, Leo and Stuart have also been given promoted posts in school for mathematics even though mathematics was not their subject specialism. Leo describes how he was given a science post when he knew 'as much about science as you could write on a postage stamp'! Carl, Quentin and Neil commented on the common practice of head teachers giving men a post for a 'male' subject irrespective of training specialisms; for example, Thomas who had specialized in Religious Education (RE), gained promotions for ICT and mathematics.

There may also be an issue of description and packaging. Quentin disclosed how he had studied a geography specialism during his PGCE, but on his final qualification it states 'science' as the female tutor told him science would have more status as a core subject. What does emerge from the data is how subjects such as mathematics and ICT dominate the men's specialisms. Neil, who was 'given' ICT, discusses how computer courses are 'predominantly male' and 'it's very laddy'; once again gender barriers are reinforcing sex-typed practice.

Alan and Thomas obtained swift promotion for ICT, although they had both specialized in other subjects. Quentin believes men are 'expected' to be 'good at sport and probably IT'.

Thomas reports that in his School of Education, the few male tutors are mainly teaching ICT and mathematics, or they are in senior management. Hutchings (2002:138) identifies that mathematics co-ordinators in primary schools are 'disproportionately male'. Arnot et al. (1999:21) discuss how boys dominate computer studies and the 'dominance of boys in science, technology and mathematics at A-level has also increased'.

The average male teacher may take it for granted that he is likely to take responsibility for an area such as PE, maths or ICT – assumptions that can be upheld by both female and male teachers (Hutchings, 2002).

Male promotion advantage may not only be enhanced by subject specialism choice; Leo describes how none of the applicants for a science post in his school had any subject expertise in science. This book did not set out to 'prove' male teacher advantage in promotion, the statistics are clear, but the extremely swift promotions some of these key informants received may well have been aided further by staffing shortages in London.

Men who identify male promotion advantage

Apart from George (the NQT), the other five men who do recognize their male promotion advantage within this occupation are all in senior management. These promoted men are now in a position to have a fuller understanding of appointment procedures. Several of them are highly critical of Governing Bodies, which they believe seek to recruit a certain 'type' of head teacher and the 'idealized' head teacher they describe is a composite of a conforming 'rational' man who will uphold the status-quo (Agnew, 1989; Blackmore, 1999). Quentin considers that Governing Bodies may also appoint male head teachers' as discipline men:

> If behaviour is an issue and they know it's a tough school and they see some bloke, with a Northern accent, who looks like he's not going to take any rubbish, we're talking about stereotypes here (*p*) I think the point here is some schools think 'oh yeah, we need a man'

In this stereotype, class bias as well as gender practices are working to feed the male discipline and promotion scripts: the 'Northern' tough guy who will not 'take any rubbish'! Quentin, whose female partner is also a deputy head in a primary school, openly challenges male promotion advantage within the occupation:

> if you look at the actual percentage of men in teaching and look at the percentage of male deputy heads or male heads there is a massive imbalance (*p*) if this was the Labour party we wouldn't be allowed to have as many ...

Quentin received a clear message about his future career path whilst a student:

> in my last teaching practice I remember the head (*male*) said 'keep your nose clean son, and you'll be a head in no time'

Roger, whose has held two headships and has been teaching twenty-seven years, also believes that Governing Bodies play a role in perpetuating sexist practices. He links it to his own career:

> why are so many men heads? Unless there are so many things against women (*p*) I think that's why I got this job

Roger describes how men dominated the Governing Body at the time of his present appointment and he felt they 'wanted' him because he was the only male candidate and he still feels 'guilty about this'. Roger also discusses a male teacher he knows that the governors would not have 'wanted' because he wears a pink waistcoat. Roger is well aware of the stereotype of the 'head teacher man' as a conforming, rational man who will conform to and uphold established practices within 'the male-dominated, hegemonic discourse of educational leadership' (Coffey and Delamont, 2000:59). Roger has always noticed the gendered staffing patterns in the occupation:

> It's something that always struck me, in a female dominated area of education the proportion of heads that I know of, that are males (*p*) it's

interesting here in this school I'm the head and the only other male is the deputy.

In his interview Roger describes some of the sexist stereotypes that can be applied to women teachers and their impact on career paths (Al-Khalifa, 1989; Weber and Mitchell, 1995). Roger believes that the 'social fabric', with high childcare costs and some men still thinking domestic issues are female domains, perpetuates the continuation of the belief that women's main concern will always be childcare not career. Roger believes having a break to have children also disadvantages women teachers:

> and even worse (p) the perception of women teachers being a sort of unreliable sort that would not make (p) a good deputy or head

The 'unreliable sort' stereotype, Roger refers to, draws on women's possible maternity breaks and works to uphold the stereotype of the 'exclusive male character of educational leadership' (Al-Khalifa, 1989: 88). Roger finds in the 'many' head teacher meetings he attends, the women have taught 'far longer than the men', and they are 'the better teachers'.

Oliver, the infant head, also identifies how: 'most men are heads'. After one year's teaching his female deputy head became sick and he was offered the acting deputy headship. Oliver, felt that the other (male and female) staff in the school:

> respected the fact that I could control (p) 270 infants in the hall…and I also because I (p) did not have the commitments they had (p) and none of them wanted it

The head teacher then had a car crash and Oliver became the acting head. Oliver decided to find a less demanding position and he started supply teaching in a different area of London. After a term he moved into a reception class, the head teacher became ill and Oliver was again made an acting deputy head. Oliver himself has also felt a 'need' to gain promotion; Oliver believes his class background was implicated in this desire for promotion:

> I had the expectation (p) there was an expectation I felt on me that I couldn't as a MAN be (p) just a class teacher (p) that I had to get up (p) it's hard to unpick (p) it's also wrapped up in class as well.

In this excerpt, Oliver shows how difficult it can be to understand the complex discursive practices that constitute our social behaviours and beliefs. Oliver's working-class background also influences how he constructs his script of occupational success, for Oliver becoming a head teacher is real career success. However, Oliver's friend, a black male head, is viewed by his middle-class family as a 'failure' for 'only' achieving primary headship.

Oliver, who describes himself as 'mixed race', exemplifies how social class and its intersections with other identities, such as 'race', gender and sexuality, are 'simultaneously subjective, structural and about social positioning and everyday practices' (Brah and Phoenix, 2004:75). This idea of 'intersectionality', which is used in postcolonial feminist analysis and diaspora studies, can be extremely useful in allowing us to better understand the tensions of lived difference and Oliver continues to be Other despite promotion to senior management.

In common with Roger, Oliver criticizes Governing Bodies that engage in sexist appointment practices. He also describes the discipline man script and its impact on 'failing' schools:

> An interesting piece of research would be 'who's recruited to failing schools?' (*p*) 'cause Governing Bodies like MALE head teachers (*p*) there's a perception that male head teachers will be tougher and stronger and I think it's completely unjustified.

Again, early promotion is also influenced by supply and demand, Thomas discloses that prior to his move into HE, he was 'offered 3 headships' by the LEA, before they were advertised:

> The expectation was (*p*) they needed someone desperately to take on tough schools. I like to think it was because I was good (*p*) but I don't know what their agenda was really (*p*) I also think they were desperate.

On qualifying Thomas had moved back to London and he 'was snapped up like that' in contrast to his fellow students who were applying for jobs in the North of England. After a year Thomas was offered an ICT support post out of the classroom, although his specialism was RE. A year later Thomas moved to another school and after three years became a deputy head, with responsibility for mathematics. Thomas did not think at the time 'it's a lot easier for men' but he now thinks he was appointed 'probably' because of his gender:

> The ten years I was in that school, I actually took on a lot of the stereotypical male jobs, running the sports, and I was often the year 6 or year 5 teacher.

Thomas easily lists the 'typical' subject positions that can be given to male teachers (sport, mathematics, science and ICT). Thomas was 'quite young' when gaining deputy headship and he feels there was some resentment from the older female staff.

Neil, an infant deputy head, thinks it is 'implied' that he will receive better promotion as a man and he does believe that he is 'advantaged' in promotion as a male teacher within this feminized occupation. He certainly found this as a middle class, Asian man when he applied for a PGCE course and the white middle class tutor 'took one look at him' and:

> she went 'hold on a minute' and picked up the phone and she went 'we've got another one and oh! oh! Wait till he gets down'

Neil felt 'another one' meant a 'man' and his ethnicity also helped; Neil had 'no formal interview, that was it'.

Neil's female partner is an acting deputy head teacher in a primary school and Neil is well aware of and tries not to perpetuate the 'sexist stereotypes' he finds within the occupation.

Men who argue that gender did not influence their promotion

Pat, the nursery head, is the only promoted man who does not discuss male advantage in promotion or raise issues of Governing Body bias. Pat's previous headship was also of a Nursery school and when inspected, Pat was given 'excellent' for management:

> The inspectors were all women and they were so positive, so positive about me (p) I don't think it's because (p) if I've got anything going for me it's because I'm me and I happen to be a man.

Three years later Pat moved into his second headship, of a larger school and he is now a trained Ofsted Inspector. He denies any male promotion advantage within the occupation.

Stuart believes male teacher promotion advantage did not 'work for me', he is now teaching ICT in HE, and he did not achieve early promotion. Stuart taught for twenty-four years in six Outer London schools before gaining a temporary deputy headship. After several unsuccessful interviews female staff advised Stuart to 'shave his beard off' and he feels he did not 'conform' to the 'normal' promotion man script. He thinks he was 'too kind, too nice, in interviews (p) not macho enough (*laughs*)'.

Stuart's non-conventional 'appearance' could also have been a factor; Epstein and Johnson (1998:128) discuss how the 'matrix of heterosexuality' in primary schools requires male conformity. Stuart enjoys country dancing and dresses casually, sometimes in flowery waistcoats; he does not conform to the traditional 'male manager in a formal suit' stereotype identified by several of these promoted men (Quentin, Roger, Neil and Thomas). However, Stuart does support the traditional 'breadwinner' discourse (Arnot et al., 1999:127). He believes that primary teaching is still only a second income for many women:

> Perhaps for women it's a second job and their husband is the main breadwinner (p) he is going to go for the higher paid job ...

Stepping off the promotion ladder

Four out of the six non-management men in this sample set (who were not NQTs) have stepped off the expected male teacher career ladder, in order to better develop their pedagogic practice.

Carl, Derek, Jeff and Leo all subscribe to the emerging pedagogic discourse of 'I want to be a good teacher'; and they believe this requires significant classroom experience and further academic study.

Leo, who has been teaching for ten years, had first received a promoted post 'for swanning around, not doing very much'. Leo then became a deputy head in another school; he subsequently gave the post up as he disagreed with the female head's teaching philosophy. Since the interview, Leo has completed his MA and moved into advisory work as he wants to 'help children learn'; again, he is espousing the pedagogic discourse.

Derek, who has been teaching six years, decided not to apply for the permanent literacy co-ordinator role, even though he already is the temporary literacy co-ordinator and literacy was his training specialism. He cites gender and 'race' difference from the rest of the senior management team as one reason for his decision. Derek is also highly critical of what he considers a 'totally white euro-centric curriculum' that excludes black pupils and black teachers like himself. Since his interview, Derek has been offered promotion at another school; he has turned it down and is now supply teaching and studying for an MA.

Carl, who has also been teaching for six years, is now supply teaching and strongly rejects the 'stereotypical' male roles he has been given in the past: such as, boys' sport. Carl has given up several promoted posts and is unhappy that he is often positioned as 'needed' for the older boys, 'we talk about equal [opportunities] for the children but it doesn't seem to apply to staff'.

Jeff, has been teaching for eight years and after initially teaching in Wales moved to London, where after a year teaching Year Six he was given a post for RE, his training specialism. After teaching Year Four for two years, Jeff then made a decision to develop his teaching expertise:

> Then I decided that I didn't want to go for promotion. That what I wanted to do was to concentrate on my professional ability as a teacher and I asked if I could move for Key Stage One experience.

Jeff received a number of very negative comments from some of the women teachers: 'a lot of people were watching for me to fail' and told him he did not 'understand key stage one'. Jeff then decided to 'prove to them, my degree is 3–11' and after gaining successful infant teaching experience, he moved to another school. Here is an example of women claiming inherent superiority in teaching the youngest children, which parallels men claiming to be better at teaching the older pupils. Jeff then returned to junior teaching, with a management point for humanities, and he has recently gained a deputy headship in a new school, where he intends to openly challenge gender barriers in staffing allocation.

These four men want to become good teachers, rather than zoom up the male promotion ladder. Hepburn (2013) reports research which also found male students: 'were "troubled" by the idea that they would be promoted quickly'. The research suggests male teachers are expected to aim for early promotion; men who select to remain classroom teachers are made to feel that there is 'something wrong' with them (Hepburn, 2013). They disturb the 'natural' gender order as they are not conforming to the promotion script. When men actually enjoy teaching young children, which is still equated with 'mothering' then they are challenging the gender belief that men cannot nurture; and their refusal to become instant 'management men' also means patriarchy itself may be weakened. Gender practices that seek to move male teachers away from the classroom as quickly as possible, into early management, need further investigation.

Professional peer responses

The responses further confirms the continued circulation of the male promotion script, alongside the sports, discipline and role-model scripts previously examined. Although twenty-one men identified the promotion script, no man acknowledged that male teachers might expect to receive career advantage in this gendered occupation. These research findings replicate Thornton and Bricheno's (2000) national questionnaire findings, where again male teachers denied or ignored any male career advantage. In contrast, a third of our key informants did discuss and challenge 'scandalous' promotion practices that can discriminate against women teachers (George, NQT).

Many of the key informants report being told by women staff about their male 'promotion advantage' and this practice was also highlighted by our professional peers. This trainee teacher has already been told this many times:

> ... mainly by female teachers who have not yet progressed in their careers beyond subject co-ordinators. There seems to be an assumption that it is my wish to be promoted and that I cannot possibly simply want to *teach* children. (England, trainee)

There is an indication in this comment, that this new entrant, irrespective of his wishes, is already being inducted into the accepted gender order, which, requires men to move into senior management as soon as possible, reaffirming the patriarchal order (Apple, 1988). Gendered promotion practices are so embedded within this occupational culture, that they become seen as 'normal'. One NQT even reports being told at university about 'his' enhanced career opportunities:

> I heard this lot from my university and I felt it was setting up our hopes as young men entering the profession. Especially as some of us may not want headship and if we don't get a headship in our careers then our hopes that were raised at university have been dashed. (England, NQT)

Whereas some of our key informants and the trainee teachers in Chapter Two felt attacked by these comments, there is a sense that the lure of early promotion is being used as 'bait' to attract more men into the occupation. However, as with the ineffectual recruitment campaigns critiqued by Skelton (2009), this approach may well back-fire.

There were a few comments that indicated some resistance:

> On more than one occasion I have been told that I should have no problem finding a job being a man. I find this uncomfortable, as I would expect schools to select the best candidates regardless of gender. (England, trainee)

There was further evidence that men were being offered early promotion for subjects that are constructed as 'male', regardless of their actual specialisms. This man who has been teaching in England, for 'just over one year' was:

> ... offered head of maths at my school. This was because I was judged to be an outstanding teacher in a school that was deemed inadequate. I turned the position down as I felt it was too much for the second year of teaching.

The specialisms this man lists are, English/ICT, not mathematics, yet, that was the post he was offered. In common with Oliver, one of our key informants, he believes that he needs more classroom experience prior to promotion. So, although none of the men recognize that there is any gender bias in appointment and promotion, there is an emerging discourse challenging the promotion script's insistence that all male teachers will 'naturally' want to claim their 'rightful' place in senior management as soon as possible.

Again male resentment of promotion 'comments' surfaced:

> It was most unwelcome when comments had been passed that I got a job due to being a man. Majority of staff treat me as a 'woman'. I am not disadvantaged in any way. (New Zealand, eleven years)

Whilst, this English NQT, justifies why he will receive early promotion:

> as I would not miss months on maternity leave in the future and that
> women often leave the profession to become mothers.

A man, who has been teaching in England for eleven years, discusses how:

> I have progressed quickly within my school but this is largely due to
> pushing myself and being proactive rather than waiting for jobs to be
> given to me or waiting to be shown how to do a job.

He could be suggesting that being 'proactive' is a male characteristic and
accounts for his swift promotion in the school. This teacher also reports
how:

> Some female staff definitely feel that being a male primary teacher
> does have benefits; parents perception, children's behaviour and career
> progression.

The key informants and the professional peers comments support the
women teachers' assessment.

Conclusion

The promotion script has worked to control male advantage in appointment
and promotion practices since the establishment of the occupation. Wider
societal changes are evidenced in the research findings that indicate some
men are both resisting and subsequently selecting to step off the accelerated
paternal promotion ladder. These 'pedagogical men' intend to learn their
craft and study for high degrees, prior to seeking promotion to senior
management.

There is evidence from the 'attacked' men that some women teachers are
resentful of these male promotion patterns, whilst, other women teachers
will uphold them. Overall, the vast majority of the men either ignore male
career advantage or deny that it applies to them; by doing so they are
absolved from challenging it.

Stuart believes male teachers need promotion since they are the
'breadwinners'; however, there has been a significant gender shift in respect
to who stays at home to care for young children. In the last fifteen years,
there has been an 80 per cent rise in households where it is women who are
the breadwinners in the UK. And two million working mothers are now the
main breadwinners (Boffey, 2013). These figures indicate that more men
(and their partners) are challenging the historical strait-jacket of hegemonic
masculinity, which requires men to swiftly rise up the 'promotion ladder',

leaving any childcare to the women at home. By doing so, these non-traditional households are subverting and destabilizing the same traditional patriarchal beliefs that permeate the gendered promotion practices within primary teaching. The more legitimate 'versions' of masculinity (and femininity) that there are in circulation, the sooner this outdated paternal promotion script will start to unravel.

Discussion questions

1. Has your gender had any impact on your own educational/employment choices?
2. Some of the key informants felt men in society were being 'attacked' by women: what effects do you feel the feminist movement has had in breaking down gender barriers?

CHAPTER SEVEN

Moral Panics

The previous four chapters have examined historical male teacher scripts that are still working to position male teachers of young children as: sportsmen, strict disciplinarians, male role models and senior managers, especially needed for boys. These particular constructions can advantage male teachers in both initial appointment and fast track promotion, provided they 'play the game' and do not cross the gender barriers. In stark contrast, Chapter Seven focuses on the circulation of a present-day gender discourse that is highly detrimental to all men who select to enter this occupation. This negative discourse is working to label men who select to teach very young children as 'potential sexual deviants' (Martino, 2008: 25).

The silent discourse

We begin by examining the painful stories told by our key informants; stories that evidence how pervasive and damaging these current discourses can be for men who select to teach young children. This ongoing male 'fear' of false accusation was discussed in the male student support group (see Chapter Two) and features in research findings in Scotland (Hepburn, 2013) and in other countries (Parr and Gosse, 2011). The chapter also offers a consideration of how homophobia and the defence of patriarchy itself may well be implicated in fuelling these damaging 'truths' that mean 'society still views males in the EY/primary school settings as suspicious' (Mistry and Sood, 2013:2). This gender barrier is even more powerful when it remains 'unspoken' but 'understood' and greatly feared by the male teachers themselves.

Research findings

Interviews with eighteen key informants

The present widespread 'moral panic' about men working with young children was discussed by fourteen out of the eighteen men interviewed. Connell (2000:192) comments:

> It is distressing to see how a rare sexual disorder has been exaggerated into a state of public fear where parents are made constantly anxious, and gay men, schoolteachers, and child-care workers are under constant threat of accusation.

Our key informants discussed accusations of child abuse as a 'fear' with which they had to live. This 'fear' of false accusations is reported by other research studies (Pepperell and Smedley 1998, Lewis 2001; Weaver-Hightower, 2011). Sargent (2000:417) has described how 'the ever-present cautionary tales keep the men teachers both invisible and condemned'. Sargent further argues that male teachers of young children are always being scrutinized; the data from our key informants indicates a degree of self-surveillance, with men consciously avoiding any physical contact with pupils. This agrees with Foucault's identification that we consciously or unconsciously 'police' ourselves in order to conform to the dominant discourses of the time. Skelton (1994:90) describes how male teachers of young children may adopt individual 'strategies' in order to protect themselves. The perceived need to keep a physical distance from young pupils can further reinforce the stereotype of men as not caring, and therefore unsuited for Early Years teaching. Cameron et al. (1999:150) have likewise identified 'a discourse of risk around men as childcare workers'.

The discussions with our key informants were marked by a sense of disclosure, and the interview context itself may have provided a safe opportunity for these men to talk through, with an experienced female teacher, mainly 'unspoken' issues (Skelton, 1994; King, 2004).

Derek, Alan, Carl and Brian, who all have Early Years specialisms, openly discussed their worries about the current moral panic (Cushman, 2009a). Weaver-Hightower (2011:10) describes how one of his informants in the United States changed his specialism during training, in order to avoid teaching the youngest pupils:

> By giving up on teaching younger children, he performed for everyone that he really does not have sexual intentions towards children. The price to prove his sexuality – giving up his intended career – was high indeed.

This 'fear' is working to ensure that male teachers avoid any contact with young children; all men are being positioned as potential sexual predators and gender barriers are erected. Carl senses often that 'behind' people's shock when they find out he is an Infant teacher, there is an unvoiced suspicion:

> there's something wrong with you if you want to teach young children (p) you've got to be a pervert (p) well it's true (p) you rarely get a female warned not to be on her own with young lads.

Carl had been told by a male head not to be on his own with a disruptive female pupil who had made allegations against male staff in the past. Carl recounts two stories. When taking pupils swimming, Carl describes a notice in the male changing rooms saying a 'female teacher' may enter for supervisory purposes; he believes that 'no way on earth' could a male teacher enter a female changing room. Carl feels it is the same when supervising pupils changing for PE in school, where he will never put himself at risk of accusations: 'it's an unwritten rule, you just DON'T do it!' Elizabeth has always felt able to enter the boys' changing rooms to ensure good behaviour when teaching pupils to swim; but Simon, in common with Carl, always felt unable to check the girls' behaviours in their changing room due to the fear of false accusation. These gender barriers create real problems for men who know that they must take responsibility for ensuring adequate supervision of all pupils during sports lessons.

The second 'story' Carl tells concerns two other male teachers:

> a friend of mine was accused (p) and it got into the paper (p) he'd gone in and seen the girls getting changed and a mum came up and went absolutely CRAZY (p) the head calmed her down but she also went to the press.

The male teacher was new to the school and he had opened the door to tell the girls to 'hurry up and stop making a fuss'. Elizabeth always was legitimated as 'the class teacher'; while, this 'male' teacher is viewed as potentially suspect and maybe a paedophile. The issue of how men safely supervise girls and boys when they are changing for PE without being 'at risk' was also raised in the male student support group (Chapter Two). The students had similar worries about supervising pupils during PE in case they were open to potential allegations of abuse. The other male primary teacher Carl talked about was:

> A guy I trained with was dragged out of bed at three o'clock in the morning, because he'd been in the swimming pool and he saw a female pupil get in, he got out straight away as soon as he saw her and she made an accusation (*p*) I go to (*a local pool*) and if I EVER see kids from the school I get out the pool (*p*) it's not worth it!

Carl believes that as a male teacher: 'you're always only one or two steps away from being dragged out of bed by the police'. So, even when not at school, Carl 'polices' himself due to the power of child abuse discourses that can be applied to male teachers (Mills et al., 2004). Carl returns to this fear of being 'accused' of child abuse three times during the rest of the interview. It is an emotive and fearful issue for him: 'you're always looking over your shoulder (*p*) you're always treading on egg shells'.

The present moral panic about men and young children was the major reason Alan gave for male avoidance of teaching young children. Alan believes that men who select to teach older pupils get 'less hassle' about abuse than Early Years men.

Alan's viewpoint is supported by the gendered staffing patterns discussed in the previous chapter; male teachers who affirm the legitimate male promotion script are assumed to be 'naturally' interested in teaching the oldest pupils. A man who chooses to teach in the Early Years is transgressing, as this sector is especially deemed low-level 'women's work' (Miller, 1996). Alan was told both in schools and by a female tutor at university not to cuddle young children or take them to the toilet. He angrily challenges this assumption as shown in the following excerpt:

> It makes you feel awkward (*p*) If a male has gone through 4 years of studying (*p*) there'd be lots of easier ways of becoming a paedophile than doing four years writing assignments and sitting exams.

Derek agrees with Alan that men who teach in the Early Years can be more vulnerable to accusations of abuse:

> For a long time I was very scared about entering into Early Years (*p*) you know there's all that stigma about males working with the Early Years because of the abuse and it's a real shame (*p*) and I think sod it!

Derek is showing agency and resistance, by crossing the gender barriers, regardless of the possible sanctions; we applaud his stance and wish to make clear that despite the strait-jacket of the male teacher scripts, several of the key informants were attempting to challenge them.

Brian, when on his teaching practices, felt that some of the parents were rather 'suspicious' of a man teaching young children. This issue of parents' perceptions also surfaced when we examined the male discipline and role-model scripts and one of the key informants described how men can be positioned as 'cruel monsters' by parents (Chapter Four). This moral panic is contributing to the negative construction of all 'male teachers' as potentially dangerous and as such, young children are not safe in their care. It is a very effective exclusionary discourse.

Balchin (2002:28), himself a teacher, asks why men need to 'make themselves susceptible to potentially harmful allegations by seeking to work in primary schools'. These gender barriers are particularly effective in maintaining a feminized workforce since, at the present time, women teachers do not face the same fear of false allegations.

Research into men who select to teach young children (King, 1998; Johnston et al., 1999; Sargent, 2000; Carrington, 2002) also found that their informants felt vulnerable to being labelled potential child abusers. Eric, the only Early Year teacher in the sample who did not mention this fear of being labelled 'a pervert' in his interview, teaches in the same school as his wife. This fact may serve to 'legitimate' Eric as a 'proper heterosexual man' and work to protect him from being subject to the potential paedophile discourse that many male teachers of young children are subject to today (Lewis and Weston, 2002; Gosse, 2011).

Four out of the six male primary teachers discussed current discourses that can label men who work with young children as potential paedophiles (see also Skelton, 1994; Mills et al., 2004). Harry feels 'there's that thing (p) why do YOU want to work with young children? There's that stigma'. Fred describes an unspoken but powerful sense of apprehension:

I think it's just something that's there (p) it's like a sort of cloud (p) it's THERE. You're VERY aware, especially men in the Early Years.

Like Carl, Fred felt very vulnerable during PE lessons. On his final Junior school practice, Fred had 'found it very awkward' when the pupils changed for PE and he would 'turn round and stare at the blackboard'. George and Fred remember being shown by male teachers during school practices how to avoid risks. Fred speaks with gratitude about a male tutor who passed on his own 'survival notes'; we suggest whole-school policies are needed to provide some safeguard for these vulnerable men who teach young children. Also the provision of suitable facilities to ensure privacy for girls and boys when changing for PE needs to be seen as a priority in primary schools (see Chapter Ten).

Jeff was warned during teacher training that as a man 'you should never be alone with children' and that if you need to talk to a child 'you must have the door open' and have another teacher present. Jeff feels these unwritten rules are 'quite horrid' and that it 'feeds a culture where men are paedophiles'. Jeff continually polices himself.

George like Jeff and Fred is very 'careful' in school, but he understands why there is so much public anxiety about men working with young children:

> I'm very, very, very careful (*p*) because of what has happened with men abusing children, its society's way of saying 'let's be safe, not sorry'.

Lewis (2001) also reports male student teachers as fearful of being accused of paedophilia. Ken believes that the stigma surrounding men who work with young children is 'getting worse'. Yet, when Ken had told his male friends in the factory about his career choice, he had received joking comments that did not offend him:

> Child molester, paedophile (*laughs*) a lot of it is just in jest (*p*) because I'm educated, people will give me wise cracks (*p*) but it's like the world over (*p*) working-class people (*p*) cracking jokes (*p*) deep down I know they respect me.

Within this particular social context, the men in the factory are able to transform this normally powerful and censorious discourse. It is made visible, defused and transformed by humour into harmless 'wise cracks' that do not offend Ken. Goffman (1959) argues that jokes and jibes can be key props in helping to ameliorate potential embarrassment in social situations. The public mocking of gender stereotypes may reduce some of their painful effects; it can also allow for women and men to enter into a dialogue, since we are all subject to these dominant societal discourses which will vary over time and in specific contexts (Foucault, 1978). Once the 'unspoken' discourses are made visible and their generalizations ridiculed, their disciplinary power is reduced. Ken's work colleagues' warned him of the costs he may encounter by crossing the gender barriers, enabling him to develop strategies to survive them rather than be controlled by them.

The context-specific aspect of gender practice is evidenced in Leo's account of his own occupational experiences. Leo does not mention any fear of being accused of inappropriate behaviour, and the four schools Leo has taught in have all had 'lots of men' : this may have helped to legitimate Leo as a teacher rather than as 'an oddity' (Carl) and as such a potential threat to children. The more men there are in a school, the more 'normal' they will appear; they will be seen just as 'teachers' rather than be gender labelled as the rare 'male' teacher. Several of the key informants who had periods of supply teaching, identified how they were less subject to being labelled as 'oddities' in the schools where there already were a number of men on the staff; they describe how they felt accepted as teachers and their gender was not seen as suspect. Also, the age range men teach can help legitimate their position and protect them from accusations of deviancy. The male teacher of the oldest children can be viewed as fulfilling the legitimate male teacher scripts, soon on his way to headship, while, the man who moves into Infant and Nursery teaching can be viewed as not a 'normal' man since he does not obey the male teacher scripts and the pervert discourses can be applied.

Pat, the Nursery head, also believes the fear of being accused of child abuse is a barrier to male recruitment. King (1998:10) discusses how male teachers can be associated with the 'negative, low-prestige features' of femininity, homosexuality and child abuse. Pat himself is:

> horrified that anyone would think that of me, horrified, that's a purely private thing (*p*) I'm equally horrified as what happened to me the other night when a woman whom I'm walking behind stops and looks at me (*p*) I'm equally as horrified (*p*)I think that says something about society.

Pat is again identifying how men may be constructed as potentially dangerous and actually 'frightening' to women and children – a construction that is also part of the male discipline script.

Stuart, who is now in HE, also describes how men wanting to teach young children are often seen as 'a bit funny', again evidencing the many insidious ways male primary teachers can be publicly and effectively stigmatized for their career choice. Once again, the suggestion is that they are not 'normal' men and their masculinity/sexuality is suspect. Jones (2006:72) reports female teachers referring to male Infant teachers as 'being "wet" or "wimpy"'. Stuart has read an article about this 'issue'and like Ken, he feels the moral panic is getting worse:

> Parents not trusting their children with men (*p*) I feel very awkward putting my arms round a child and I suddenly realise I shouldn't be doing that (*p*) and I can't and I don't (*p*) in the past if a child needed a cuddle it was alright.

Quentin, the deputy head, in common with Carl, tells several 'stories' about his male teacher friends and accusations of child abuse. One friend was a male primary teacher who had used the boys' playground toilets when playing football after school. This male teacher has now left teaching altogether due to an ensuing 'rumour'. Whispering and rumour spreading can be extremely effective ways of developing and reinforcing moral panics and are virtually impossible to confront. Quentin also recounts the experiences of his 21-year-old friend who had taught in a Sixth Form College (an educational institution where students aged 16–19 study for advanced school-level qualifications) for a short period: 'can you imagine? He had no chance!' Quentin is referring to another unspoken discourse that concerns the sexualization of girls. He then discusses his own fear of accusation and as a consequence monitors himself in class: 'I've taught year

6 girls who have been very aware of their sexuality (*p*) and …it's terrible…'. Mahony (1985:84) has also reported Junior girls making 'subtle attempts to get physically close' to a male teacher. Thomas, now working in HE, finds that when he is teaching all-female groups, he can be 'teased', and he focuses on teaching, leaving the 'other agenda alone'. The other 'agenda' is concerned with male and female sexuality, an official taboo subject in classrooms (Epstein and Johnson, 1998).

Quentin agrees with George and Stuart, that it is more of a worry now: 'it's tragic but its modern life'. He discusses the importance of protecting pupils:

> if you're a female teacher and you're seen hugging a kid it's no issue at all. If I'm seen hugging a kid on playground duty suddenly it's alarm bells (*p*) so many kids need TLC (Tender Loving Care) (*p*) but then again let's be honest, evidence suggests that people who are paedophiles (*p*) put themselves in positions where they can access kids.

When Roger, the Primary head, first started teaching in a Middle school, he had no problems as they had separate PE changing rooms for girls and boys. Roger then moved into Junior teaching and the 'problem' of men supervising girls changing for PE became clear to him. Again, the actual provision of separate changing room facilities rather than expecting pupils to change in the classroom could help prevent some of the painful dilemmas faced by many male teachers during PE lessons.

Most of the key informants did identify feeling particularly vulnerable when pupils change for PE. Neil, the infant deputy, discusses this one reason why he has avoided teaching older pupils where he would feel more at risk; yet, Derek and Pat think it is Early Years men who are more at risk. So, whether teaching the oldest or youngest children in primary schools, these male teachers clearly know that they are open to accusations of perversion because they are men selecting to teach young children.

Other research in the field likewise reports male teachers of young children are fearful of being seen as potential abusers, even during initial teacher training. Thornton (1999:46) reports that during teacher training some of the male students 'expressed concern that they might be seen as perverts, or potential child abusers'. Sargent (2000:417) suggests for 'men, nurturing children is dangerously close to molesting them' and the stressful experiences our key informants live, demonstrates how these particular gender discourses are in widespread circulation and they are causing a great deal of distress. The majority of the key informants argue that these unspoken 'suspicions' are getting worse and may actually be preventing some men from entering the occupation in the first place. None of the professional peers recorded this pernicious gender script; and it could be one of the limitations of inviting short responses that such sensitive issues do not surface.

One could argue that as currently the traditional family structure is becoming fragmented and new family groupings are emerging, the maintenance of patriarchal relations is under threat. More men are becoming involved in caring for their young children and today domestic duties are not only performed by women. The present-day pervert discourses could be attempting to restore childcare (including the teaching of young children) to a female-only occupation. Certainly these male teachers are being made to feel uncomfortable and 'at risk' due to being in daily contact with young pupils; and hints of homophobia are also implicated.

Homophobia and the reaffirming of patriarchal relations

It is difficult to believe that 200 years ago when Robert Owen opened the first Infant School and Samuel Wilderspin led the Infant school movement in England (see Chapter One), it was men who were seen as the 'natural' moral guardians and teachers of the youngest children. Today, as the key informants evidence, it is no longer the case; men who teach this age range can be viewed as 'unnatural' and even deviant (King, 2004; Gosse, 2011).

However, what these two highly contrasting gender constructions of male infant teachers do starkly demonstrate is the way gender beliefs can significantly shift over time in order to best maintain male power. At the start of the nineteenth century, patriarchy was secure and men were in charge; at the start of the twenty-first century, women are now able to hold senior positions in society and it is no longer automatically accepted that only men have the moral qualities necessary for holding public office. This dramatic change is a serious challenge to male institutional power and as Connell (2002) reminds us, the continuing unequal gender order will be well defended.

Men who demonstrate a wish to enter work, that is now defined (by some) as merely an extension of the female domestic role, are symbolically crossing the established gender barriers and will face censure. A moral panic is a powerful and effective way of controlling behaviour and as our key informants show, its beliefs can quickly become internalized and result in self 'policing'. It is worth considering that Pickering (2001:190) has suggested that moral panics themselves can be a response to new social behaviours, working to 'create the need to put things back in their place'. We traced in Chapter One how as the teaching of young children became constructed as female-only work, its status within society declined; and it became viewed as an occupation that only 'failed' men would enter (Widdowson, 1980). This is an effect of a society that is still organized to give men advantage in the public sphere, providing they are prepared to uphold the legitimate male teacher scripts. Ken (one of our key informants) insightfully identified that the 'young handsome prince' willing to discipline the older boys is still very much in demand! His sexuality will always be heterosexual, he will always be white and he will follow the male teacher scripts without question, soon reaping the reward of early promotion into senior management. Epstein and Johnson (1998) suggest that all schools will knowingly or unknowingly be engaged in reinforcing existing hegemonic masculinities that are needed for the maintenance of wider patriarchal relations. It is imperative that young children see that it is men who lead and women who carry out the 'nurturing' of the youngest children, which is still given low status by many and classed as 'not really teaching'(see Chapter Nine for a discussion of the devaluation of Early Years teachers).

King (1998) believes that if men do transgress by entering into female 'caring' work, they are symbolically challenging the patriarchal norms and sanctions will be applied. The public linking of child abuse, homosexuality and male primary teachers could almost be designed to force men to abandon any caring (and therefore female) work, and by doing so, gender regimes are symbolically restored and the patriarchal family upheld. According to gender stereotypes, 'real' men are supposed to be inherently aggressive and clearly heterosexual and if they enter into women's work then their 'masculinity' will be put at risk. Charlie, a student teacher, interviewed by Lewis and Weston (2002:9) disclosed how: 'when I tell people I want to be a teacher, they either call me a paedophile or gay'.

Sargent (2000: 417) also argues that male homosexuality has been 'conflated with paedophilia' as a mechanism of social control. Real men are meant to uphold a hegemonic masculinity, which will require a rejection of both homosexual masculinity and femininity (Connell, 2000). The data collected from the key informants and student support group well supports this thesis and the present fear of being labelled a 'pervert' is proving a powerful deterrent in limiting male entry into this 'female' occupation. The homophobic alignment of homosexuality with paedophilia is intended to reaffirm hegemonic heterosexuality, an essential requisite of patriarchy and as Connell (2002:54) points out: 'we are not free to enact gender however we like. In reality, gender practice is powerfully constrained'.

In the previous chapters, we have shown how the male teacher scripts work to construct school as an idealized Victorian public family with the heterosexual father in charge (Alexander, 1988) and this requires a certain 'type of man'. The desirable man will be a role model for the older boys, reinforcing muscular discipline, engaging in male sports, a leader in waiting. He has no wish to engage in any activity that could be seen as 'female' or damage his hegemonic 'masculinity'; due to his male rationality, he is 'naturally' suited for early promotion, especially needed for mathematics, computers and science posts, irrespective of his actual training specialism. There is no room in this biased construction for a 'caring' man who wants to teach the youngest children and, by doing so, symbolically disown the virulent heterosexuality which rejects any traits labelled 'female' in the traditional gender order.

Men who teach young children can find themselves both vulnerable and valuable in this workforce; they are 'needed' in schools (as the four historical scripts attest) yet they now can also find themselves viewed with a deal of 'suspicion' due to their gender. What is so difficult about the sexual accusations discussed in this chapter is that they often remain unsaid but as the stories of our informants show, they are certainly understood and their effects are cumulative. Gay men can be particularly targeted due to homophobia and men who select to teach the very youngest children may attract the most suspicion due to their clearer transgression of the legitimate male scripts.

Conclusion

This chapter has discussed how today men who seek to cross gender barriers by entering into so-called 'women's work' (teaching young children) may be subject to charges of sexual 'deviancy'. These pernicious discourses could be compared to the NAS campaigns in the 1930s which applied discourses of sexual 'perversion' to single women teachers in order to consolidate male power. The present-day malicious discourses about male teachers and child abuse, which are in widespread public circulation, are very effective in censoring gender non-conformity and they need to be opened up to further scrutiny. Once again, we wish to state that safeguarding for pupils in our schools is already firmly in place, but the safeguarding of their male teachers, who can find themselves extremely vulnerable due to their career choice, has to be put on the educational agenda. The particular vilification of gay teachers, which is a consistent feature of these perversion discourses, needs to be both recognized and challenged.

Discussion questions

1. Examine media images featuring young children and adults; what 'messages' do they give and how many of them feature men as well as women?
2. Do you agree that 'unspoken' suspicions surrounding all men and young children are getting worse? How can these discourses be tackled?

CHAPTER EIGHT

International Experiences and Perspectives

This chapter draws on a number of international research studies, concerning men who teach children aged 3–11 years. We begin with a short review of international research. We then focus on three educational systems across three continents in order to examine the gender barriers that men may experience due to their choice of occupation. Finally, we explore a number of international initiatives aimed at increasing male entry into the workforce.

The number of male teachers of young children has fallen in many countries. For instance, in Sweden the number of male teachers in primary schools had fallen from 32 per cent in 1985 to 25 per cent in 2010 (Lofgren, 2012) and in many countries it is below 20 per cent (Cushman, 2009b) with secondary schools only slightly better. Many schools – from head teacher, classroom teachers and administrators to caretaking staff – are now places of a single (female) gender.

The three countries that have been chosen for close scrutiny are Canada, Finland and New Zealand. We recognize that gender practices will not be experienced by all men teaching in these countries or indeed elsewhere. As in the UK, the recruitment of men to teach very young children has remained low in these three focus countries and, as in England, there are frequent calls for there to be more male teachers in classrooms before they become a thing of the past (Mills et al., 2004). For instance, an OECD report in 2005 identified the shortage of men teachers as a long-term concern. There is a general recognition of the need to recruit and retain more male teachers of young children to address the gender imbalance in the workforce plus a consideration of what 'male' teachers can specifically bring to the school environment (Martino, 2008). We begin by identifying the main issues that have been internationally researched, as concern about gender-imbalance in the workforce grows.

A review of international literature on men teaching 3–11-year-olds

There has been a range of studies investigating the shortage of male teachers and the supposed 'impact' of this shortage on the education of boys. The literature focuses on the following areas:

- Scarcity and decline in numbers of male primary school teachers, problem of minority representation, recruitment and retention issues (Farquhar, 1997; Cunningham and Watson, 2002).

- Reasons for crisis in low numbers of male primary school teachers, such as the stigma attached to working with young children, unattractive career choice – low salary in some countries, low social status due to the high number of females working in what is seen as women's occupation as an extension of mothering; conversely countries with higher salaries have less problem attracting men to apply to become teachers (Allen, 1997).

- The motivations of men to choose to teach primary school children (De Corse and Vogtle, 1997; Cruikshank, 2012).

- Strategies for recruitment and retention including positive discrimination, incentives and hiring policies (Nelson, 2008; Robinson, 2010; Lett, 2013).

- Gender balance/equity in teaching and questioning whether the gender of the teacher important in teaching young children (Arreman and Weiner, 2007; Carrington et al., 2007; Cushman, 2010; Szwed, 2010).

- Issues and concerns that male primary school teachers face, namely physical contact, accusations of child abuse and paedophilia (Cushman, 2005b, 2009a).

- Men working in caring professions as stereotypical women's work (Friedus, 1992; Simpson, 2009; Mallozzi and Campbell Galman, 2014).

- Male role models and issues around forms of masculinity (Martino, 2008; McGrath and Sinclair, 2013).

US research by Oyler et al. (2001) explores the experience of one male student teacher who did choose to train as a first grade primary school teacher following a career in the armed forces. The research aimed to explore how gender is deployed uncritically in the classroom, using an oral history inquiry approach to gather data about the male students' school experiences and noting *critical incidents* that reflected key events or ideas. Their findings highlighted what these researchers termed the 'silenced male gender' (2001:373). The researchers were troubled to note that the teacher education programme that the student had enrolled upon remained silent regarding particular differences males encounter when they cross gender borders into the feminized 'world' of the primary classroom.

Hakan Lofgren (2012) explores whether more male teachers acting as positive male role models is the answer to *problems* with boys in Swedish schools at a time when attempts are being made to counteract traditional masculine roles. Lofgren found that there are different narratives concerning male role models in schools, depending on the context and who is telling the story; acknowledging that some assumptions draw on stereotypical views of men.

In terms of policy issues, the work of Martin Mills et al. (2004) in Australia closely resonates with our own research arguments concerning feminism and masculinities. In particular, as educationalists ourselves, we support their challenging of the simplistic 'belief' that all boys are failing in non-masculine environments and that the quick-fix strategy of having more male role models in schools, to act as surrogate father figures, will lead to 'all boys' improved educational attainment. To continue to perpetuate this deficit historical belief means female teachers will continue to be positioned as the 'problem' and male teachers will become the stereotyped 'solution' (Burn, 2002). The research findings indicate that 'needed and necessary' discourses are still being applied to male teachers in Australia, accompanied by deficit notions of absent or inadequate fathers.

Mills, Martino and Lingard, researching in Australia as well as Canada, are also concerned to challenge the notion of the male, hegemonic disciplinarian and other essentialist, patriarchal arguments for having more male teachers of young children simply because they are 'male'. They assert that gendered beliefs are damaging to men and women and boys and girls as they limit the multiplicity of masculine (and feminine) performances that are permitted for male teachers and pupils and maintain gendered power relationships. In common with these international researchers, we wish to encourage more talented men to enter the teaching profession, particularly in non-traditional areas where they have an important role to play in challenging the stereotyped, homogenized forms of 'male' teacher that is sometimes expected of them.

Martino (2008) provides a fascinating analysis of the male teachers as role models script, drawing on work from a number of countries. He argues current role-model discourses are part of the recuperative masculinity or re-masculinization backlash against feminism. Once again, men are being cast as 'heroes', saving boys' essential masculinity from the feminization of primary schools.

Cruikshank in Australia (2012) examines a range of relevant international literature regarding the recruitment and retention of men teaching children 3–11 years and the reasons that have motivated men to enter in occupation. Furthermore, he identified strategies in the literature that have been put forward to improve recruitment and retention, namely making a difference to childrens' lives by doing something worthwhile, the targeting of fathers who may be less affected by negative issues associated with physical contact with children, the advantages in employment and promotion through positive discrimination and being more valued because of their minority status as male teachers.

The work of Prevost (2011) offers a North American perspective; his research focus is on the shortage of male teachers and the effect of this imbalance on pupils, in particular on disengaged boys. The research critically considers a range of viewpoints, including that the sex of the teacher does not matter as long as they are good teachers; diverse role models are needed; and including the presence of male teachers that will help all learners achieve their full potentials.

One solution suggested is to introduce affirmative action programmes similar to that which has been used to address minority representation elsewhere such as the shortage of girls on maths and science courses. Other solutions suggested are public information campaigns to address misrepresentation of male primary school teachers and finally male only scholarships as a financial motivation.

In some countries, such as Sweden, there is a contradiction that some men experience in terms of, on the one hand, supporting gender equality discourses that counter traditional gender roles and attempting to address gender discrimination; and on the other hand, continuing to believe that men and women are different and encouraging male teachers to serve as male role models for boys in schools using stereotypical, culturally conditioned masculine characteristics (Cushman, 2009b). As Lofgren (2012:73) comments in the context of managing expectations of men: 'It is necessary to discuss what dimensions men were supposed to bring as role models in school and how traditional gender roles are (re)shaped.'

Cushman who has investigated male teachers in several countries found conflicting messages about some men maintaining traditional masculinities while others followed gender equality policies that challenge these stereotypes (Cushman, 2009a). The findings mirror the ambivalence shown by many of our English Key Informants; for instance, some men reject the male discipline script while still claiming the male sports script. We have argued that the ongoing claiming and rejecting of the available subject positions is problematic and contradictory, as male teachers attempt to navigate the gender barriers, and Cushman's findings clearly evidence this tension. It seems male teachers are required to both claim and disown a range of highly stereotyped 'masculine' dispositions alongside developing their teaching practices.

There is clear pressure in many countries to increase the number of male teachers in this age range. However, the research indicates a range of reasons why men may choose not to become teachers of young children; including the fear of accusations of paedophilia being rife and stirred up by the media (Chapter Seven). This also affects the practices of qualified teachers in the classroom where they become confused about how they should interact with children (Cushman, 2009b).

The 'primary' education system and the training of teachers in Canada, Finland and New Zealand

In this section, we provide background details of the schooling systems in order to aid clarification.

Canada

In Canada, primary school (also known as elementary school) usually begins at the ages of 4–6, starting with either Kindergarten or grade 1 and lasts until grade 6 (ages 10–12). In general, teachers in Canada require a Bachelor of Education (B.Ed) or equivalent degree; and since education is regulated provincially, they also require a teacher's certificate from the province in which they wish to teach. Elementary school teachers in Canada have to be well versed in all subject areas, since they cover them all. To gain a teaching certificate, they will normally need an undergraduate degree and one year of teacher education. Only once a trainee has completed their education and received the appropriate provincial certification can they apply for a teaching position.

A further historical and political overview of men teaching pupils 3–11 has been provided by a number of academics from Canada. The work of Coulter and Greig (2008) has enlightened us regarding the ongoing debates in the Canadian education system about the place of men in classrooms in relation to boys' underachievement. Their research traces the emergence of the, at times, uneasy feminization of teaching since the end of the nineteenth century, identifying how low financial, professional and natural child rearing status drivers encouraged women into the workforce and discouraged men from entering this occupation. The story replicates the historical development of the teaching workforce in England that we examined in Chapter One. Since that time in Canada, there have been concerns about the dearth of men from teaching as it is no longer seen as a *real* profession. The authors ask what this means for the education of (underachieving) boys in terms of reconstituting hegemonic forms of masculinity and the disciplining of 'bad' boys (see Chapter Four).

Male teachers are again being required to fulfil the role of substitute father role models in an overly feminized school environment, where women are being constructed as not capable of managing boy's 'natural' masculine ways. The argument being put forward by the gender discourses is that students and teachers of the same sex are better placed to work together as they have innate similarities. This 'anti-women' argument, which the authors point out and which is still in circulation today, reflects the continuation of the legitimate male teacher scripts which we have identified from our own English research data.

Finland

In Finland, 9 years of primary school (Peruskoulu) are compulsory. Kindergarten from 6 to 7 years is optional, then follow 1st grade: 7–8 years to 5th grade: 11–12 years. Teachers working at all levels of education receive 5 years of training and are required to complete a rigorous Master's degree as well as an assessed yearly teaching practice. Teachers are highly respected and teaching is a popular occupation in Finland, which makes it possible to select the only best students to train as teachers. University-based teacher education programmes in Finland are very popular and tough to enter. In 2010 over 6,600 applicants competed for 660 available places in primary school preparation programmes in the eight universities that educate teachers. The Master's degree is studied for without financial cost since Finland funds education from preschool through to graduate education.

Finland offers no other route into teaching; and admission to a teacher preparation programme includes a national entrance exam and a personal interview, which allows the country to ensure consistency from programme to programme. Preparation to become a teacher differs in respect of which grades teachers want to teach. Primary school teachers major in education and minor in various subject areas; whilst training they study educational theories and research in university and quickly practice applying what they've learned in designated placement schools following university coursework. By graduation, a student has completed at least 120 supervised teaching lessons, all in conjunction with a supervising teacher. Successful completion of the degree constitutes the licence to enter teaching.

The ethnographic research by Elina Lahelma (2000) with school students in Finland found that the gender of their teachers was not significant for students when talking about what they valued in teachers. Furthermore, discourses concerning the lack of male teachers were not supported by the students nor did they need men to be acting as male role models. Lahelma (2000) concludes that the gender of the teacher seems to be more problematic for adults than for school students.

New Zealand

In New Zealand, children may start school at age 5 and the majority do so, although schooling is not compulsory until 6 years of age. Primary education starts at Year One and continues until Year Eight when children are in their twelfth year with Years Seven and Eight mostly offered at either a primary or a separate intermediate school.

In order to become a primary school teacher, a person needs to have: a three-year Diploma of Teaching; or a three-year Bachelor of Education (Teaching); or a Bachelor's degree and a one-year Graduate Diploma of Teaching. Alternatively, they can complete a four-year dual degree, such as a BA/BTeach or BSc/BTeach, which combines study in teaching subjects with teacher training. This degree means they can teach both primary and secondary students. Teachers also need to be registered with the New Zealand Teachers Council and have a current practising certificate, which is renewable every three years.

The valuable research of Penni Cushman has been important in helping academics and educational researchers develop their thinking about this subject area. Cushman has been studying the experience of men teaching young children for many years, analysing their attitudes towards primary school teaching and the issues they face. She is based in New Zealand, where the majority of her early research was carried out; however, Cushman has also researched men teaching in other Western countries (Cushman, 2007).

In agreement with Skelton's academic argument in England (Skelton, 2011), Cushman also criticizes how many recruitment initiatives highlight the stereotyped 'benefits' of having more men as role models in the classroom to address underachievement rather than on the quality and merit of the applicants as talented and effective teachers (the pedagogic script).

Cushman (2005a) points out it is not that men have difficulty entering the profession but that they choose not to do so for a range of complex factors and this pattern seems to be growing. Cushman's study of male teachers in England, Sweden and New Zealand concentrated on male fear of being accused of child abuse and the impact of this on recruitment. She argues that issues of male recruitment need to be addressed by long-term, multifaceted policies that take social justice and equality seriously alongside developing greater awareness of gender issues in teacher education programmes, since differences about acceptable and non-acceptable male and female behaviours are still deeply embedded in societal expectations in a number of countries.

In Canada and New Zealand (as well as the UK), there have been widespread calls for more men teachers relating to concerns about boys academic underachievement and behaviour and the need for male role models in classrooms (Carrington, 2002; Mills et al., 2004; Cushman, 2007). However, such an approach can infer that female teachers are in some way deficit: 'Women are seen as the problem and men as the solution' (Mills et al., 2004:361). The belief is also held by some that because boys and girls learn differently, female teachers do not relate well to the males in their class but there really is no evidence to support females not being able to teach males (Lett, 2013). Indeed, it is more the case that all children learn differently and teachers need to have a range of approaches to work with the different needs in a classroom.

Status of the teaching profession in each country

Teaching young children remains gender segregated in the three focus countries with few men choosing primary teaching as a career. The percentage of female teachers versus male teachers is similar across the three countries. In Finland, 21 per cent of teachers are men (World Bank, 2011); in New Zealand, 17 per cent are men (World Bank, 2011); and in Canada, just 16 per cent are men (2013 statistics Canada www.statcan.gc.ca).

There is significant difference in terms of the status afforded the teaching profession in each of the three focus countries. In Finland, the quality of the teachers is seen as the hallmark of its education system and one of the main reasons for Finland's recent success as one of the top scoring nations on the international PISA assessments (OECD, 2012). Morally, rather than materialistically, teaching is considered Finland's most respected and prestigious profession as offering a service to Finnish society. Primary school teaching is one of the most sought-after and competitive careers. This status is supported in terms of teachers being highly respected and trusted in schools rather than being subject to rigorous inspection regimes and media criticism (Sahlberg, 2010).

In many countries, men still do not select to teach pupils 3–11 years of age as it lacks prestige. Lett (2013) argues this lack of male teachers means that from an early age boys don't see this as a suitable profession for them, which results in a general lack of interest among men. Conversely, it can still be seen as an attractive career for women with its gendered association with nurturing and childcare, maintaining gender segregation in the workforce.

Teaching is not generally considered a high status occupation in New Zealand; however, this lack of status does not appear to make teaching unattractive, as a teaching career and teachers are respected and the profession is seen as honourable. People understand the nature of teaching and the relative advantages and disadvantages of entering the occupation. There is a focus on 'making a difference' to society, the diversity of the work, the pleasure of working with children to prepare them for their futures, despite the relatively low salary and cases of poor pupil behaviour.

A joint research project by Hall and Langton (2006) was undertaken between 2003 and 2006 for the New Zealand Teachers Council and the Ministry of Education inquiring into the publics' perceptions of teachers and teaching in New Zealand – particularly teacher status –and implications for recruitment, retention and professionalization of teachers. Teaching was not seen as a high status profession according to the indicators of providing fame and fortune. However, teaching was still seen as a desirable career choice and well respected by most people as making a difference to society, although the research found teachers were themselves negative about the profession. Another report (Kane and Mallon, 2006) came to several similar conclusions about providing an important service to society but in terms of status and respect found that males held higher status.

As in Finland, teachers in Canada have a higher status and are paid fairly well compared to other workers and the vast majority have high job satisfaction. Teaching in Canada does present challenges including large class sizes, diversity issues and with about half the teachers citing pupil behaviour issues as significantly challenging as found in the Canadian Teachers' Federation Survey (2011). However, in many parts of Canada there are more teachers than there are positions, resulting in unemployment, particularly for those teachers who have recently completed their training. In order to gain more experience in teaching to help them gain positions in the domestic market, many resort to working in international schools abroad (Sagan, 2013). A culture of equality is broadly embedded in the public education system in Canada although women still account for the majority of the teaching workforce.

Initiatives to attract men into teaching

The current concern about the shortage a male primary teachers has resulted in a number of countries devising specific initiatives to attract more men into the teaching profession. Policies and practices have been introduced to address some of the barriers that deter men from selecting to teach children aged 3–11 years of age. Policymakers in various countries including Australia, Canada and England have been concerned about the low numbers of male teachers. For instance, the State of Queensland in Australia produced a policy document that raised concern about the lack of recruitment and retention of male teachers into the education system who could act as role models for boys in an increasingly feminized profession, an argument critiqued by Mills et al. (2004).

In order to address the moral panic surrounding men, which we discussed in Chapter Seven, New Zealand introduced a 'hands off' national policy restricting physical contact in order to safeguard all teachers (Cushman, 2005c) which was amended in 2006 to allow physical contact in some situations. Other countries have not been bound by such formal guidelines or policies to address gender discourses surrounding male teachers in this sector. Cushman (2010) reports that in New Zealand men who demonstrate the more traditional masculine traits are more in demand and the students in our support group (see Chapter Two) were concerned about being seen as deviant if they didn't uphold typically masculine traits.

Another approach involves addressing the shortage of men through positive discrimination to address the gender imbalance – arguably one of the few occupations where men can be both advantaged and disadvantaged, despite their clear appointment and promotion advantages (Jones, 2006). There have been proposals for quota systems and financial incentives rather than formal policies: for instance, the Finnish ministry of education was considering offering incentives that encouraged males (Nelson, 2008). Yet as Cushman (2007) points out, this could imply that men have difficulty getting places on teacher training courses, which does not appear to be the case as the 'needed role model man' discourse continues to circulate in numerous countries (Skelton, 2011; McGrath and Sinclair, 2013).

In Toronto, 77 per cent of all primary school teachers are women, and now, the largest school board in Canada is trying to address the gender imbalance in this occupation. The Toronto District School Board has considered giving preference in its recruiting of qualified male teachers (Tremonti, 2013). The proponents argue that it is important to have positive male role models at an early age and that the education system should try to reflect the society it serves. Not surprisingly, there has been some negative reaction from those who argue that teachers should be recruited and appointed on ability rather than in order to achieve gender quotas and that such affirmative action is unfair.

Cushman (2007) noted that Australia did propose a scholarship scheme for men to encourage them to enter teaching programmes but there was an outcry over this and the proposals did not go forward. Extra financial incentives for male teachers have also been called for in New Zealand (Russell, 2013). The focus remains firmly on the 'men' and the impact of these 'male-affirmative' proposals on women teachers is not even on the patriarchal agenda.

We suggest that in the light of English research findings, schools and teacher training colleges may already carry out favouritism towards men in order to increase their male quotas (Raphael Reed, 1999; Thornton and Bricheno, 2000). The dominant male role-model script in particular, with its negative views on single parent families, means that there may be a greater tendency to recruit more men rather than recruit according to quality. The establishment of these male-affirmative policies in countries remains highly contentious; yet Sweden has already gone some way towards this as part of gender equality initiatives to challenge stereotypes of what counts as men's and women's work (Cushman, 2007). Furthermore, it needs to be remembered that the recruitment of more male teachers will result in the recruitment of fewer female teachers to a finite allocation.

There have been suggestions to teach male trainees in single sex groups to encourage 'a more "masculine" – "male friendly"– environment' (Mills et al., 2004). This suggests that present environments are not and the male student group we set up in England evidenced this unease, with male students reporting attacks from both female students and staff, due to being 'men' (Chapter Two). However, such proposals would be limiting in a number of ways: not preparing men for working in predominantly co-educational schools; working with female colleagues; and continuing to valorize hegemonic masculine groups, as their 'male' student group would be smaller allowing for more tutor support. Yet, as we ourselves found, there may be some benefit to provide informal men's support groups as part of initiative to support all students in danger of course failure.

High profile advertising and recruitment campaigns focusing on attracting more men into teaching have been attempted internationally for many years. One example comes from the United States and is known as 'Call Me MISTER (4)' – the acronym for Mentors Instructing Students Toward Effective Role Models – provides tuition assistance and leadership training to male African American students pursuing teacher education degrees (Jones and Jenkins, 2012). In Germany, the Ministry of Family Affairs started the initiative 'More men for kindergarten' (Hamann, 2013). Posters were displayed around cities to encourage young men to become kindergarten teachers –'Musician, magician, mediator, philosopher, goalkeeper, baker – be all, become a kindergarten teacher!' was the advertising slogan. Not all of these initiatives have succeeded and we address this issue further in Chapter Ten.

Conclusion

Chapter Eight has found surprisingly similar gender discourses are still circulating in a number of countries, concerning men who teach children 3–11 years of age. Comparable gender beliefs and practices to those identified by international research are also written into the English male teacher scripts that Elizabeth wrote from her interview data (Chapters Three to Seven). So, as in England, internationally men are being publicly constructed as 'needed and necessary', as well as 'suspect' due to their career choice. A number of these international men, in common with several of our English informants, continue to uphold and promote these stereotyped male teacher scripts (especially the role-model one) whilst others refute them. Again, there are 'typical' gender practices rather than 'typical' men.

International recruitment drives have included several suggestions of positive discrimination in training and appointment, in order to achieve a more gender-balanced workforce. These measures have been criticized for their inherent unfairness to women teachers, who continue to face promotion barriers, as 'rare and valuable' male teachers will often receive advantaged promotion, provided they play the game (Jones, 2006). Yet, despite such enticements, as in England, these gender-specific campaigns have failed to develop a more balanced workforce.

In short, the gender practices our key informants have identified in English primary schools are alive and well internationally. Respected female and male researchers, such as Penni Cushman and Wayne Martino, whose international research findings we have drawn on extensively in this book, have argued that a damaging hegemonic masculinity is being upheld by these male teacher scripts. This conclusion is also in agreement with the substantial research carried out by Christine Skelton in England, which we have also benefited from in this book. Cushman, Martino, and Skelton further point out that these male teacher scripts are implicated in the devaluing of women teachers. In the next chapter (Chapter Nine), we offer three women teachers' voices, which evidence how the gender scripts can also cause anger and distress to them as 'women' who have selected to teach primary school children.

Discussion questions

1. Several countries (such as Finland) have considered the usage of 'positive discrimination' for men in both initial recruitment and appointment, in order to address the present gender imbalance in the workforce. Consider the advantages and disadvantages of this strategy.

2. Discuss why, despite extensive campaigns and initiatives in a number of countries, so few men select to enter this workforce.

CHAPTER NINE

Women Teachers Talking

This chapter draws on feminist research that explores how women who teach children 3–11 years of age negotiate their work identities within these gender regimes that are still operating within this occupation. In the light of the historical origins of the gender scripts, we begin by reflecting on the positioning of women within the Victorian construction of teachers as public patriarchal parents for children of the poor. Then, after a short discussion of feminist research itself, Elizabeth provides a re-analysis of face-to-face interviews she carried out with two women primary teachers, when (like our key informants) they were teaching in London inner-city schools. Informed by further insights into the female gender scripts, identified by Penny and Prue, we consider how this ongoing gender stereotyping of teachers has serious consequences for both male and female staff. We conclude this chapter by considering the implications of these maternal and paternal teacher scripts for teacher recruitment drives.

Establishing the 'mother' teacher

Jones (1990:75) has drawn on Foucault's ideas to suggest that the transformation of the female urban teacher into 'a good and nurturing mother' by the end of the nineteenth century provided 'a moral exemplar' for inadequate parents in the 'urban abyss'. The 'strictly relational character of power relationships' (Foucault, 1978:95) means that if women teachers were positioned as 'mothers', then the only legitimate subject positions available for male teachers were as 'substitute' fathers. In the 'Western gender order', women are expected to receive their status from their domestic work: whilst men are still expected to achieve status from their success in the public sphere (Connell, 2002:61). Hence, the woman teacher is constructed as merely attending to her 'maternal duties' within this occupation. As Burgess (1989:85), who was herself a primary teacher for fourteen years, argues 'the history of women in teaching is closely linked to the familial aspect of primary schooling equating the class teacher with a mother'. In the light of this positioning, ideas of career and promotion are not on the agenda, since women are 'merely' using their 'natural' maternal instincts.

Martino (2008:8), in his comprehensive historical review of how women teachers in Canada and the United States have also been demeaned and devalued over the years, argues: 'by the early 19th century, teaching came to be constituted as an extension of the domestic duties deemed appropriate for women'. The labelling of the occupation as 'women's work' has meant that it attracts little public status – it is merely what women are 'born to do'.

Steedman (1992:61) remembers, when she became a primary teacher, 'I was unknowingly, covertly, expected to become their mother, and I unknowingly became one.' In this excerpt, Steedman captures the 'covert' way we can all become subject to dominant discourses and resistance to them, as Elizabeth's interviews with Penny and Prue demonstrate, will be problematic.

Elizabeth's commitment to 'feminist' research

In this section, Elizabeth revisits two of the interviews she has carried out with London male and female primary teachers since her entry into Teacher Education in the early 1990s. Elizabeth re-interprets her original analysis of Penny and Prue's face-to-face interviews and draws up female teacher scripts in the same way as data collected from our key informants' interviews generated male teacher scripts. Elizabeth begins by outlining her feminist research principles, selecting to use her personal voice. In re-reading the interviews with Penny and Prue, Elizabeth overtly draws on her own occupational experiences of gender barriers, as research interpretations will always include the biography of the researcher (Skeggs, 1997), and when acknowledged, it can be used productively (Weiner, 1994).

My long, personal and political commitment to feminism as 'a movement to end sexist oppression' (hooks, 1984:31) has been central to my research activities throughout my long teaching career (I qualified in 1970). Coffey and Delamont (2000:136), discussing feminism, research and women teachers, argue that:

> How social actors understand, view and 'do' gender needs to be a central part of all research endeavours.

My ongoing construction of myself as a feminist teacher strongly influenced my decision to start investigating gender issues within the teaching occupation, as Lather (1995:294) also argues 'to do feminist research is to put the social construction of gender at the center of one's inquiry'. Weiner (1994:24) discusses how there are an increasing number of 'feminisms' as 'different social and economic formations emerge' – this is helpful in allowing for a number of perspectives. It also parallels the move to 'masculinities' that we discussed in Chapter Three, as poststructuralist theorizing has seen essentialist ideas of 'male' and 'female' begin to unravel, allowing the complex, contradictory and context-specific ways in which our gender identities are being 'negotiated' (alongside other identities) to be better understood.

Kirsch (1999:5) identifies specific feminist principles to be included when carrying out feminist research. The principles she selects are concerned with researcher recognition of ethical issues, researcher reflectivity and an obligation to challenge social inequalities. However, Acker (1994:58) warns of the real danger of drawing up legitimate 'feminist' research 'rules', which may themselves erect hierarchies and create new 'gatekeepers'.

Jayaratne and Stewart (1995:230) have also criticized some of the literature on feminist methodology as being unrealistic, and difficult to access and implement in practice. Lees (1993:12) argues that all feminist research will be 'subversive' since it:

> challenges the separation between the public and the private, between reason and emotion, between masculinity and femininity.

My previous gender research opportunities have required me to reflect carefully on the many debates surrounding feminist perspectives (Lown, 1995). Flax (1995:144), for example, has argued that feminist theory needs to be accompanied by feminist political actions. I now recognize the value of drawing on 'the analytic tools of feminisms' (Coffey and Delamont, 2000:13). My feminist research 'principles', at present, are:

1. My research should be concerned with the social construction of gender and its effects, alongside other social relations, such as 'race' and class (see Lather, 1995).

2. My research should have a potential to contribute to challenging sexist practice and other social injustices (see Ramazanoglu and Holland, 2002:147).

3. All stages of my research should be reflexive, acknowledging my own researcher power and bias (see Delamont, 2003:69). Hence I recognize I am also 'implicated' in my research design, data analysis and findings.

4. My research recognizes that within the social sciences 'knowledge' has been mainly presented by men as 'objective'. I do not accept the claim that science is value free; rather theories of 'knowledge' will be partial and culturally specific, and as such, 'open to criticism' and re-interpretation (Weiner, 1994:63).

5. There is not a particular research 'method' that is 'feminist'; both qualitative and quantitative methods can be used (Jayaratne and Stewart, 1995).

6. Since gender practice involves both women and men, both need to be involved in researching and dismantling its effects (hooks, 1984:81).

I recognize, as Acker argues, it is: 'impossible to find a definition of feminism that pleases everyone' (Acker, 1994:43). Weiner (1994:51), who was herself a primary teacher in London, provides a useful review of the multiplicity of 'feminisms' and how they have impacted on educational research and practice.

Luke and Gore (1992:7) are critical of emancipatory discourses that aim to 'empower' the researched, instead: 'poststructuralist feminism… remains critical of its own complicity in writing gender and writing others'.

After carrying out many interviews over the years, I am well aware of Griffiths' (1998:97) identification that there: 'is no hope of doing perfect research'. Yet, despite the limitations, I continued to interview male and female teachers in order to understand better gender practice within an occupation that I had invested a 'substantial' self in Nias (1989) and Burn (1989, 2005).

I now present my re-interpretation of Penny and Prue's told stories and, in doing so, I am following Wieler and Middleton's (1999) call for the reclaiming of women teachers' lives.

Interviews with two female primary school teachers

Penny

Penny is a white, female primary teacher in her early thirties, who has been teaching in London for 9 years. She has taught full time in three schools;

after 3 years in her first school, Penny spent 2 years supply teaching and also completed her MA which was concerned with reading development. At the time of her interview, Penny was teaching 8–9-year-olds in a primary school where 97 per cent of the pupils were Bengali. She holds a responsibility for mathematics and in her previous school held a post for literacy.

Penny left school at 16, for financial reasons and studied A levels at evening classes. At the age of 20, Penny began a full time B.Ed Hons degree and found the 'white middle-class tutors' problematic due to her working class background (see Maguire, 1997; Reay, 2003).

> It was disgusting actually... one of the lecturers'... a guy... said to me 'well if you want to be a teacher you'll have to drop the working class cockney accent'!

Penny did not accept this:

> It made me rebel actually... I said 'NO WAY'... a little bit of this, a little bit of that!
> It doesn't really affect me now because I know what I'm talking about... it doesn't matter what accent I use. That's what you do... sort of 'feed them with it'.

In this excerpt, Penny is displaying a similar sense of agency and resistance as the teachers Munro (1998) interviewed; these women were also actively negotiating their workplace identities. The classed discourse Penny is challenging works to construct all teachers as 'middle-class', and another white working-class female teacher I have interviewed also found that her class background has worked to Other her (Burn, 2001).

Penny discusses further her 'difference' within teaching; this continual class displacement is also clearly present in the interviews of our three working-class key informants (see Chapter Five).

In the same way as some of our male informants described their unease and isolation in the staffroom, due to gender difference, Penny, as a female teacher who does not uphold the legitimate 'class' scripts, also finds herself positioned as an 'oddity' by other teachers in the school. Although I too, have maintained my working-class voice, I did not have Penny's painful experiences of staffroom interrogations; largely due to my childcare commitments, I spent most dinner breaks in my classroom working to complete my marking and future planning, so I did not have to carry lots of paper work home on public transport. However, in common with Penny, I was well aware that my own working-class background marked me as Other and I was not the 'norm' in the middle-class world of teaching.

Penny finds her 'class' isolation in the staffroom is compounded by her position as a single woman without children. Penny is often asked, by women staff, about her plans to have children. The maternal scripts women teachers are subject to, work to define all women as being mainly concerned with having children and as such not suitable for (or interested in) moving into senior management. I have certainly heard many of these intrusive 'maternal' interrogations, but, unlike Penny, I had 'proven' myself by having three children and I was never myself given such interrogation. However, it is also important to avoid 'demonizing' all women teachers'; I found in my first three all-female Infant schools, it was 'education' that was on the agenda, not my domestic arrangements. However, once I entered gender-segregated primary schools (with men as leaders), women teachers did make comments about why as a married woman I was working outside the home. These examples show that just as all men do not play the patriarchal power games that will gain them fast promotion, not all women engage in upholding gender barriers, but some will and Penny's testimony is evidence of this practice. Men and women can both be implicated in reinforcing gender barriers within this occupation, and both need to be involved in dismantling them.

Powney et al. (2003) report 98 per cent of male heads have a partner yet 32 per cent of female heads live alone. Acker (1994:119) found that several of the women primary classroom teachers she interviewed were working 'triple' shifts, juggling the demands of work, home and childcare. My own experience of these shifts is etched on my memory and as I was also studying part-time with the open university; often when I arrived at school I had already 'done a day's work'.

Penny finds that she is increasingly positioned as a woman who should be 'settling down':

> God... they say it all the time... 'when are you going to get married, when are you going to have children?'

Penny argues that this maternal construction also impacts on curriculum practices and the level of intellectual challenge offered to young children, especially in the area of reading:

> We need more reading in Reception... sometimes the intellectual is undermined because of the nurturing role.

Penny tells me that the older women teachers tend to talk about 'MY class, MY children', again evidencing the historical public mother reconstructed within the 'domestic and maternal world' of teaching (Oyler et al., 2001:374). I support Penny's identification of how 'the intellectual is undermined' by this 'public mother' construction, laid down in Victorian times. So, just as gender stereotypes can work to position men who teach the youngest pupils as potential deviants (Chapter Seven), women who teach the youngest pupils can be constructed as 'carers' rather than as educators. Early Years teaching is very challenging and intellectually demanding; yet, these gender scripts are working to devalue women Early Years teachers and stigmatize male Early Years teachers.

In her interview, Penny clearly identifies the legitimate male promotion and discipline scripts:

> Without a shadow of a doubt men ARE favoured and they are perceived to be the authoritarian figures within the school... children are sent to the males...

Acker (1994:116) in her ethnographic study of two English primary schools reports that when interviews for a new head teacher were being held, the candidates were three men and one woman. The consensus in the female-dominated staffroom was they did not mind who was appointed as long as it was not 'The Woman, as she was termed.' This reminded me of numerous conversations I held whilst researching gender practice in four schools, as part of a teacher fellowship at Newcastle University (Burn, 1989). Although many women staff applauded the move to challenge gender practice, many told me they 'preferred to work for a man'. In the same way as some of our male key informants still claim patriarchal scripts, some women teachers will also uphold maternal scripts, once again reproducing symbolic public parents with the authoritarian 'father' clearly in charge.

Penny, in agreement with several of our male informants, believes male teachers are given 'more respect' and she also identifies how some women teachers support these biased gender practices:

> there was a female head in my previous school... she always sent the children to a male and she was the head teacher!!!

This gender practice, produced by the male discipline script, was also challenged by many of the key male informants, although three still claimed it (Chapter Four). Several of the 'professional peers' also report being 'given more respect' by both pupils and parents. The 'respected and needed man' discourse translates yet again into mirror constructions of the 'inadequate woman' who does not deserve public respect as she is merely carrying her maternal duties (which are also widely devalued) in the public sphere.

Penny wants a more balanced workforce, but she is concerned about where men are placed and their unfair promotion advantage – two practical effects of the male promotion script:

> there should be more male primary teachers rather than them being in positions of power and deputy headships and heads as opposed to being in Reception or Infant classes... You do not see many males in school at all, often it's the caretaker... and also it's... seen as women's work.

I recall how Lucy, a white female middle-class teacher, that I had also interviewed, told me that during her training, Early Years students were mocked by the Primary students and this sector was called 'the easy years' (Burn, 2000). Numerous entries in my research diaries also evidence this devaluation of teachers who select to specialize and teach the Early Years. The day I interviewed Penny at my university, I had received an email from a female BA student enquiring about the PGCE course, as she knew I was the maths tutor: 'not Early Years. I want to teach maths'. A male Upper Primary maths student had previously informed me that the Early Years was: 'not really teaching, Elizabeth, it's only play'. He assumed, that as I was a maths tutor I was not an Early Years tutor; as did Quentin, the key informant, to whom I had been introduced (by a student) as a maths tutor, when he confided to me that he was now considering going into Nursery teaching 'because it's easier' (Burn, 2005:197). Fred, Harry and Stuart, three of our key informants, also support this damaging maternal script that works to construct Early Years teaching as female-only work; it is akin to 'mothering'.

Penny has many tales to tell of how the younger the children you teach the less intelligent you are assumed to be within the primary school community:

> There's an undercurrent that you can go and take the Early Years and Reception because you can 'cope' with the child wetting themselves and you need to tie their laces, it's 'Penny you go and deal with the child that's just fallen over' (*said in a sing song voice*).

The false gender dichotomy between maternal/intellectual is once again affirmed, and teaching the youngest children is constructed as public mothering and therefore non-work, with no public status (King, 1998; Dillabough, 1999; Sargent, 2000).

I had met Penny, when final-year students had told me how supportive she had been during their teaching practice and how knowledgeable she was about literacy. I interviewed her after I had visited her in school, observed her practice and thanked her for her support. I was a Year Tutor at the time, and I invited Penny to offer a literacy session at our university; I then interviewed Penny in my office about her occupational experiences as a primary school teacher. I still consider her opening statement: 'I am fed up with being the Elastoplast lady' one of the most succinct descriptions of the negative effects of the maternal discourses that I have yet heard or read in the literature.

Penny is clearly angry at being positioned as 'the Elastoplast lady' rather than as a skilled primary teacher. In common with the male informants who claim the pedagogic script, Penny actively challenges these 'patriarchal parents' scripts that work to construct her as a public 'mother' rather than as a teacher. What is clear from the anger in her voice, is that it is not only male teachers who may be alienated by these gender practices, but women teachers like Penny and myself are also displaced in an occupational culture that judges us on our gender rather than on our teaching competences. Penny's stressful work experiences, due to her non acceptance of the maternal scripts, reminds us that the present gender barriers are disadvantageous to female as well as male teachers who do not agree with unfair gender stereotypes. This shared experience of gender discrimination means helpful alliances across the gender barriers can be made by teachers who prefer the pedagogic script.

Penny has now returned to Junior teaching: 'you're actually seen as a proper teacher', and my own career well evidences this belief. When I was teaching in a Primary school I was promoted to the Nursery, managing two other teachers and two nursery nurses, yet parents pitied me: 'is this where they have put you now Mrs Burn?' They assumed I had been demoted. The female Early Years Advisor told me 'you will be alright Elizabeth you have children of you own'. I strongly contested this devaluation of Early Years (and mothers) and the LEA subsequently agreed to fund my studies for a part-time DAES in Early Childhood Play.

In contrast, when I was appointed to a Year Six class, mid-year, in a very 'challenging' Junior school (i.e. an area of high economic poverty) as their male teacher had had a nervous break-down and left; I was given a great deal of applause and status from the parents (and staff). They all assumed I must be very intelligent to be a woman teaching the oldest children. I also recall a male NQT I had interviewed being told by his friends: 'now you are qualified you can move up to Secondary'. The gender message is clear: the younger the children you teach the 'dimmer' you are (Miller, 1996); this is non-acceptable.

Throughout her interview, Penny totally rejects the maternal teacher script that has worked to construct her as a public 'mother' and a 'mother-in-waiting'; instead she claims a pedagogic one that also emerged from interviews with our key informants:

> I've never fitted in... I don't see my role as giving children medicine... I'm a teacher, an educator.

Two years after I interviewed Penny, she decided to give up her permanent teaching post and return to supply teaching; she really enjoys teaching, but 'it's the rest'. After reflecting on Penny's story, I am reminded of Derek's interview (one of our black, working-class, key informants) – these are two experienced London teachers, who have both studied part time for higher degrees in order to improve their teaching practice. They have now both given up permanent posts and started supply teaching as they could no longer accept being positioned as Other within their staffrooms. For Derek it was his 'race', class and gender differences that isolated him; whilst, for Penny it was her class difference alongside her refusal to accept the required maternal script (personally and professionally), which has soured her work experiences within this gender-saturated occupation.

After re-interpreting Penny's account, I examined a research diary that I had kept when I returned for a short period to classroom teaching in London to refresh my practice. No longer an Advisor or University lecturer, I was once again a primary teacher, comfortable in a world that I have lived in for most of my working life. My diary entries record lots of 'maternal' chat in the staffroom, supporting Penny's analysis. For example, one day the only male teacher complained: 'all you ever talk about in this staffroom is babies!' I had also noted the embarrassing way some of the older women had attempted to 'mother' this young male teacher. Researchers in Scotland, in 2013, likewise report that several of the male students that they interviewed complained about being 'mothered' by older women teachers whilst on school practice (Hepburn, 2013).

The maternal script works to exclude pedagogical talk because if the focus is on 'teaching' rather than 'public parenting' then the sex of the teacher becomes irrelevant. Penny was also criticized by some female staff for completing her MA: 'well... you should go and work in a college or university'; again evidencing the rejection of the intellectual in order to maintain this maternal script. Penny links her work experiences to her social class and age as well as her gender:

> having a M.A. coming from a working class background... and being... successful... and being young is not liked... and wanting to do a PhD
> ... and when students come in I take an interest... they don't like it.

Once again, the many complexities of social practice are evidenced and the denial of the 'intellectual' demonstrated.

Prue

The second interview I re-visit is with Prue, another primary teacher. Unlike Penny, she has 'legitimated' herself by having children; yet, like Penny, Prue also identifies and challenges the maternal script that she now finds herself subject to whilst teaching in the Early Years. These two women teachers do not know each other; they trained at different times and at different universities, and I interviewed Prue a year after listening to Penny's teacher story.

Prue is a white female Early Years teacher, from the North of England, in her late forties, who has taught in one London Primary school, since qualifying 4 years ago; she holds posts for Maths and Computer Science/ ICT and is at present the Nursery teacher. Again, it was student teachers who had recommended her to me due to her excellent classroom practice and student placement support.

I interviewed Prue at her school, again asking: 'can you tell me what it's like to be a primary teacher?' Prue had decided to study for a teaching degree after her children had grown up. Prue's memories of her own schooling influenced her decision to teach in the Early Years:

I really felt from an early age I had missed out… Father in a cotton factory, mother also a cotton factory worker and there was no expectation… I think the teachers were like… middle or upper class and we were the working class and it was so obvious… there was class distinction all the time…

Reay (1998) argues that working-class pupils can be marginalized at school and Plummer (2000:187) reflecting on her working-class upbringing, describes how schools taught her 'at an early age that I belonged to a group of people who were perceived as inferior'. Prue's words remind me that to look at 'gender' practice alone is artificial and other social relations will also entwine and impact on how we are positioned and how we position ourselves. Walkerdine et al. (2001), examining the educational experiences of working-class and middle-class girls, found that 'social class, in all its confusions and contradictions' worked alongside gender and 'race' in the subjective experiences of the girls. Oliver, a 'mixed race' key informant told me: 'you can't divorce class or race from gender relations' (Burn, 2005:222). The intersections of these relations mean that simplistic statements, concerning 'all women' or 'all men', only serve to fuel stereotypes rather than dismantle them, and need to be avoided when seeking to examine how social power operates to exclude or advantage (Connell, 1995; hooks, 2000).

At the age of 20, Prue married a vicar and moved into a middle-class world:

I never actually felt it until I was in my forties and I suddenly thought… I'd never classed myself as being middle class and… probably… still don't…

Prue's own two children were very successful academically and 'I felt I hadn't had the education I wanted', so she decided to train as a nursery nurse. Prue found that when she was in placement schools the women teachers told her 'you must become a teacher'; this is an example of women teachers supporting other women, rather than criticizing them. Prue studied for further academic qualifications and became a mature student on a teacher training course. Prue still acknowledges the support these women teachers gave her and how her 'whole being was changed'. Prue relished her teacher training and she found the women students and tutors inspiring:

I really felt it was somebody opening a big door and it was all this knowledge… I HAD to attend every lecture, I HAD to know… I couldn't get enough of things about… education… about art… it was just MARVELLOUS… and the books…

There were three men on her course and: 'I never really got to know them… it was as though they didn't have a voice.' Prue's observation supports the

Attacked Men discourse that we discuss in Chapter Two, when the few male students on the course felt 'silenced' in sessions.

Prue started teaching in the Reception class and felt that the children could have been more intellectually challenged when they were in the Nursery, so after two years she moved into the Nursery and found, like Penny 'I became a parent!' Prue really resents this maternal teaching construction and discusses how even the parents view her as a 'mother':

> They feel I am there to be... a surrogate mother... I would say 60% is being a mother and 40% is teaching. The thing that I love, teaching, is a small part of my working day... that is frustrating, totally frustrating...

Prue (like Penny) intends to return to teaching older pupils so that she can 'become a teacher again'. Once again, like Penny and myself, Prue is claiming a pedagogic script, informed by her knowledge concerning effective teaching and learning, not child-bearing.

Prue (like Penny) also supports more men entering the workforce, and she identifies how images of 'masculinity' may work to exclude them from the 'maternal' domain:

> I think for lots of men... they don't want to show that they have feelings... the man's got to be strong... he's got to show he is in control... they associate it with childcare not teaching...

Prue's words echo the same gender discourses that Ken (one of the key informants) used to mock the way hegemonic masculinity seeks to ensure all men conform to public gender scripts (see Chapter Six). Prue likewise refutes this patriarchal construction and she discusses a male teacher on the staff:

> The Year One teacher is excellent... he motivates the children, but at the same time he has that gentleness and understanding.

Here is an example of a women teacher praising a male colleague, not as a 'role model for boys' or as the stereotypical 'sports man', but because of his exemplary classroom practice.

In Prue's school there are two other male teachers on the staff, but they are class teachers in the Infants and Juniors and both the head and deputy are female. This school does not fulfil gender stereotypes in staffing; gender practice is context-specific. In my first three Infant schools the teachers were all women; teaching roles, such as discipline, sport, senior management, caring roles, etc., were carried out by 'teachers' who just happened to be women. It was only after career breaks that I worked with a few male teachers in Junior and Primary schools: all were either Head teachers, Deputies or Year Six teachers. I saw experienced women teachers, many particularly skilled at teaching reading, passed over for promotion if a male teacher was available for appointment; like Acker's (1994:120) women teachers, most of these experienced women teachers had adopted a 'fatalism' to these gender practices. If I had not by this time become committed to teaching, I would not have continued in an occupation where women (especially women with children) were so openly discriminated against in promotion. When I did gain a deputy headship it was in an Infant school in London, and once again all the staff and all of the candidates were female, the focus of the interview was once again on my teaching ability not on my gender and childcare commitments.

I subsequently moved into teaching in a university school of education, and within my first month of appointment, I listened to female tutors commenting on the teaching practices of student teachers; gender practice was clearly evident. The ten male students in the year group of 125 student teachers' were given either an 'A' or an 'E'; they were described in highly subjective ways as either 'he's a lovely young man' or 'he's lazy and incompetent'. In marked contrast, the 115 female students were graded from A to E and the comments made about them referred to their classroom competencies: such as their ability to plan effectively, teach, and manage a class. I was so surprised at this open gender bias that I asked my male colleague (who also taught mathematics) if this was 'normal'. 'Oh, yes' he replied, 'the men are always A's or E's'. That is one reason I continued to explore gender practices within the teaching occupation. I was a Year Tutor for 7 years and monitored the high male student drop-out rate (repeated nationally); I then set up a male support group and invited a male colleague, Simon, who was also researching gender practices, to join me (see Chapter Two).

Women teachers, men teachers and the gender 'barriers'

We now offer a brief consideration of the female and male teachers who do not wish to conform to the gender scripts. This is deliberate, since we argue that when teacher alliances are formed, across the gender barriers, we can start to better identify and unpick the practices that mean many dedicated teachers of young children still do not receive equal opportunities within this workforce. It is also why we decided to include this particular chapter in the book; to research only one side of the gender seesaw (Thorne, 1993) is to misread the complex and contradictory ways gender practices will be working to both advantage and disadvantage female and male teachers in specific contexts. For example, gender barriers can work to stop men teaching in the Early Years (accusations of child abuse); whilst, women teachers can be discriminated against in promotion (women being defined by the womb, not teaching ability). Both of these unfair gender barriers need dismantling and only by women and men working together can effective dismantling begin. In the 1980s and 1990s, a number of feminist researchers carried out research into the discriminations women teachers can face in this feminized but certainly not feminist occupation (Evetts, 1989; Windass, 1989; Acker, 1994; Wieler, 1999); whilst, for the past few decades the focus has been firmly on male primary teachers (Thornton and Bricheno, 2000; Smedley, 2007; Pulsford, 2014). In the light of both our male informants telling stories and the voices of Penny and Prue in this chapter, it is clear that gender barriers can impact on both female and male teachers. We now need to synthesize past research findings in order to make progress in developing a less discriminatory environment for all practitioners and the children they teach.

Gender practices are both institutional and personal; they can be upheld by female and male teachers and they can be challenged by female and male teachers, but often at a personal cost. It could well be argued that we ourselves are 'transgressing' by collaborating on this book. What is clear is that female and male teachers need to start discussing these gender practices: why are some women sending men boys to discipline and why are some men claiming superior talents as role models and sportsmen? Why are some male teachers given more respect than women teachers by pupils and parents? Why are some women teachers 'attacking' male teachers for being 'men'? This chapter, mainly written in female teacher 'voice', exemplifies how we are all implicated in these so-called 'insignificant' everyday gender practices and beliefs. Elizabeth recalls how when she was appointed to her first teaching post, the female head informed her that she did not 'believe women with young children should be working' and if she was ever late she would be dismissed. In contrast, all of the other all-female staff were extremely supportive of her. Once again we note that gender practice can be carried out by male and female staff; it can also be resisted by male and female staff. If we were writing a book about the gender practices that women teachers of young children experience, we would also include a chapter presenting male teacher 'voice'. This alliance strategy can help prevent a descent into the easy gender stereotypes that produce comments such as 'all men are useless' or ' women are best at Early Years teaching as it's like mothering' (comments taken from Elizabeth's field notes). It allows us to recognize that whilst it is unacceptable to 'attack' new male entrants for long-established male promotion patterns; it is equally unacceptable for men to either ignore their career advantage or deny it exists (see Chapters Two and Six).

In our own case, we both recognize that at times we have been advantaged or disadvantaged in schools due to our gender. Elizabeth has never had to worry that when she was teaching the youngest pupils she might be accused of being a child abuser (see Chapter Seven); Simon has never been cross-examined in an interview about his childcare commitments. We both resent these gender practices and we agree with Prue, Penny and key informants like Carl and Quentin, who all reject these biased male and female gender scripts and instead claim the 'pedagogic script'. We are well aware that this equality stance may lead to isolation from the rest of the staff group. Penny describes how she is fed up with constantly receiving questions in the staffroom about when she is going to 'conform' to the maternal script, get married and have children. Several of the male informants also report receiving upsetting comments in the staffroom, this time due to being 'male'; both practices are wrong:

> many times in the staffroom, if I have ever made a mistake, I often get, 'what do you expect from a man'. I have found staffrooms very sexist. (England, trainee teacher).

Yet, once again we must avoid generalizing, not all female and male teachers face staffroom censure due to their gender. Several key informants and professional peers do report actually enjoying the gender 'banters' between male and female staff, as this male teacher identifies:

> saying how useless we are as a species! It's always said in a jovial manner, and I always give my best back! (England, NQT)

Whilst, this man has:

> lots of fun bantering with female teachers – I give it back just as hard. (New Zealand, 23 years)

We have already discussed how Goffman (1959) argues that humour can be a very effective way of debunking these ridiculous stereotypes; and staff 'joking' about the strait-jacket of gender conformity may well be very effective in allowing male and female teachers to come together and finally evict these damaging gender beliefs and practices from the occupation. However, we would also argue that 'making the joke' can itself further justify and in fact reinforce stereotyping.

Conclusion

In Chapter Nine, the voices of Penny, Prue and Elizabeth evidence that female teachers of children 3–11 years of age can also be subject to unfair gender beliefs and practices in schools. Maternal discourses are in circulation and these are working to produce public heterosexual 'mothers' rather than skilled teachers. The two women teachers Elizabeth interviewed strongly object to the gender practices that they are subjected to and are implicated in; instead, in common with some of the male key informants, they claim the pedagogic script. This pedagogic script works to construct teachers who are concerned with quality teaching; not with constructing public 'mummies' for the Early Years and public 'daddies' to discipline and manage the school.

In agreement with Skelton (2009), we question the recruitment campaigns for 'male' primary teachers in England and elsewhere, which are not working (see Chapter Eight). We agree with Skelton (2009:49) who argues that campaigns should 'eliminate the obvious targeting of particular groups'. The focus on 'gender' alone can inadvertently uphold the damaging gender stereotypes that work to exclude men who do not wish to be positioned as the 'token' male. We also support Miller's (1996) earlier criticism of a government recruitment campaign at that time, which focused on 'women'. The advert offered an image of a pregnant woman next to a small child (a boy of course) and it reinforces maternal scripts that, as Penny and Prue identify, are working to construct teaching as 'merely' mothering and the intellectual is downplayed (Miller, 1996:11).

We ask, are these recruitment campaigns concerned with attracting good teachers into the occupation, who are able to teach girls and boys aged 3–11 years; or, are they recruiting public symbolic 'parents' in order to affirm patriarchal relations in the public sphere?

In England, the recent Government initiative of setting up a panel of 'male' primary teachers (Adams, 2013) again works to merely reaffirm damaging gender binaries. The 'male-only' panel approach further supports the segregation of primary teachers along gender lines, replicating some of the failed international recruitment strategies (Chapter Eight). We recommend the involvement of both male and female teachers in future recruitment campaigns and we discuss this gender-inclusive' approach further in Chapter Ten.

At the present time, the fast changing composition of the primary teaching workforce in England is a cause for concern. England has the youngest primary teachers in Europe, with a third of teachers being 32 years or younger (Adams, 2013). Several of our experienced informants have now decided to leave teaching; they are no longer prepared to accept being labelled as 'a bloke in a tracksuit' or 'an Elastoplast lady'. These inner-city male and female teachers want to be identified as committed teachers needed to educate pupils between 3 and 11 years of age; not positioned as stereotyped gender puppets, dancing to the patriarchal tune.

Discussion question

1. Discuss what sort of recruitment posters/campaigns would attract both men and women into teaching children 3–11, avoiding gender and race stereotypes.

CHAPTER TEN

Removing Gender Barriers

In Chapters Eight and Nine, we concluded that future recruitment drives need to stop focusing on 'gender' alone as this well-used recruitment strategy has failed in numerous countries and may even work to reaffirm gender bias itself. Certainly, several of our English male teacher informants, who have recently entered the occupation, seem to believe that they are already superior to women teachers, purely because they are male. It could be argued that this inflated opinion of unproven classroom talents is an effect of the 'needed man campaigns' long promoted in England and other countries (Chapter Eight). In fact, it is worth considering if these inexperienced male recruits are actually being set up to fail: since the teaching of young pupils is about rather more than 'bantering about football' with the boys, or using male voices as 'weapons' in the nursery to obtain discipline. Our research data shows that parents and governors may also be unwittingly reinforcing this prejudiced belief that 'male' teachers are 'naturally' more valuable due to being a 'rarity' in the workforce. However, we were heartened to find that the majority of the experienced English teachers in our data sample reject this simplistic idea and like (Penny and Prue in Chapter Nine) are claiming instead the pedagogic script. The pedagogic script is concerned with teaching and learning rather than with upholding outdated gender stereotypes and it is the teacher script that we also subscribe to, as former primary practitioners ourselves.

It is a feature of our data collection that our key informants were interviewed at different stages of their career paths; other research studies in this field have focused on male students or classroom practitioners. The wiser voices of long experienced and successful male teachers, such as Roger who has been teaching for twenty-seven years and twice held headships, stand in clear contrast to the views of the newer male entrants; some of whom seem to have swallowed the current media view that they are public heroes who are somehow 'saving the boys' and reasserting an imagined hegemonic 'masculinity' just by entering a classroom (Burn, 2005; Martino, 2008). As Alan, an NQT, told Elizabeth 'they're crying out for male teachers…the government was going to bring in a bonus scheme' (Burn, 2005:138).

We suggest that as all these affirmative male-only recruitment initiatives have failed to make the workforce more representative of society, a new approach is needed based on evidenced-based research rather than merely repeating already failed, ill-thought out, piecemeal ideas. Teachers of young children may find such recruitment campaigns offensive and demeaning; nobody enjoys being reduced to a stereotype. Policy makers instead of asking 'how can we recruit more men' should reframe the question to ask: 'how can we recruit more good teachers of young children' and this will include men and other under-represented groups. The book has explored how complex and contradictory gender discourses are still working (consciously and unconsciously) to maintain the present gender order within this occupation, with unfair work consequences for both male and female teachers. The few men who are being recruited into the workforce are often expected to gain early promotion into senior management, well away from the 'dim mothers', in order to symbolically represent public patriarchal fathers, good at discipline and male sport.

The wide range of research scrutinized in this book clearly evidences that female as well as male teachers are implicated in upholding or challenging present gender barriers, so both need to become actively involved in dismantling them – this includes joint participation in future recruitment campaigns. In the light of this, Chapter Ten provides a number of specific strategies that can be employed by all concerned with recruiting and retaining committed teachers of children 3–11 years of age. We avoid offering simplistic tick-lists; gender segregation within this workforce has been maintained for centuries and will not be fully removed quickly. However, unlike some of our key informants who believe it will 'not happen in my life time Elizabeth' (Derek), we are encouraged. This book has demonstrated how highly respected international academics have now provided a substantial body of evidence concerning gender practice in this workforce. These rigorous research studies have in the past focused mainly on female teachers; whilst in the past two decades the researcher gaze has moved to researching men teaching in this occupation. We intend this book to start to blend these valuable research findings into male and female teachers and all of our recommendations in this chapter are informed by them, as well as by our own research data.

We are well aware that not all of our recommendations will be applicable to all school communities or to all countries; as our own data has demonstrated, gender practices will vary and are context-specific over time. However, we believe many of our recommendations will provide productive food for thought, and they can be adapted to best meet the needs of a particular school in a particular country. They also can be usefully employed for teacher training and teachers' continuing development sessions (including governor training). Once people (including parents) realize that the so-called 'minor' gender practices and beliefs that exist within this occupational culture may actually be limiting the potential of pupils as well as of the practitioners who teach them, further progress should be made (see Conclusion). We begin our strategies for change by concentrating on the everyday school practices that our informants identified, and that are also evidenced in other research findings. As we argued at the start of this book, it is these seemingly 'minor' comments and behaviours that are the ones to unpick first, in order to begin the process of effectively dismantling gender barriers within this workforce. One of the world's greatest educators', who was also a primary teacher, reminds us:

> The possibility of transformation dwells precisely in changing what is possible to change today with the aim of achieving in the future what seems impossible today. (Freire, 1995:11)

Recommendations for dismantling gender barriers

The school environment

Staffing

The Early Years/Junior divide was a feature of the data collected from our key informants, who were all teaching in inner-city English schools and nurseries (see Appendix 1). Several men identified the low-esteem Early Years teaching was held in by their school community. It was often constructed as 'mother's work' and as such, non-intellectual. Some men felt they were excluded from Early Years teaching and describe being 'sent' to the Juniors (7–11 years) in order to 'discipline the boys' by male and female head teachers. Men with specific Early Years training were still 'moved' into the Juniors. Men reported higher status being given to the teachers of older pupils by the school community. The teachers of 10- to 11-year-olds

(Year 6) were given most acclaim for their 'intellectual' talents. Our data indicated the placement of men in certain classes was sometimes linked to sex stereotyping, rather than to effective staff deployment.

Recommendation 1
Staffing policies and practices in schools need to reflect the age range specialisms of all teachers whilst ensuring all staff are offered equal access to developing their teaching experiences across the age range trained for, with appropriate CPD.

Subject specialisms

A number of the men in sample sets one and two were quickly 'given' promoted posts for Computer Science/ICT, Mathematics and Physical Education (PE) irrespective of their actual subject specialisms. Some men resented these practices; others accepted the financial rewards. Leo, for instance, knew 'as much about science as you can write on a postage stamp'. This identification of certain subjects as requiring 'male' leadership, even when the male teacher is newly qualified with a specialism in a different subject area is wrong; it impacts on the quality of teaching offered to pupils, and the curriculum support available for other teachers in the school, as well as perpetuating gender stereotypes that certain subjects (like mathematics and science) are male.

Recommendation 2
Quantitative research needs to be undertaken into the profile of subject co-coordinators, in order to determine and rectify gender bias in present subject appointment procedures. Governors and school inspectors (in England) need to examine the subject knowledge of mathematics and science coordinators; these two subjects require teachers who have advanced subject expertise so they can best support other colleagues in the school.

Discipline

The majority of our male teacher informants described how they had experienced being 'sent' boys to discipline from other classes; because they were 'men'. In our student support group, this issue also surfaced and the black students reported that they were 'expected' to discipline black boys in particular. This discipline script was also reported in numerous international research studies and again whilst some men resented being constructed as 'discipline dads' others willingly claimed this gendered role. This specific gender practice is one that can result in women staff being given less respect (especially by boys) and yet, it were women (including a female head) who were sending boys to men, perpetuating this gender practice, reinforcing stereotypes. There were also indications from the professional peer responses that, as more classroom assistants are being recruited into English schools, the few male classroom assistants appointed are likewise being either 'given' or 'claiming' the male discipline script, further reinforcing outdated gender stereotypes that construct all men as potentially violent.

Recommendation 3
School policies need to establish fair and equitable practices and procedures in order to prevent certain teachers, students in training or classroom assistants being allocated extra discipline responsibilities, ensuring discipline practices do not perpetuate stereotypes of aggressive men who rule through fear of their physical power. Again, governors and senior management need to monitor the effectiveness of whole school discipline policies. If it is identified that female staff are given less respect by pupils than male staff, then the head teacher needs to plan a whole-school programme of work to address this serious issue and this needs to be regularly evaluated after its implementation. Parents could also become involved by ensuring that they do not unwittingly endorse the sexist view that 'men are better at discipline' by their off-the-cuff remarks.

Sport

A key script that many male teachers of young children seem to be expected to follow is one of male-only sports (in particular football). Whilst, some of our key informants, like Thomas, whose subject specialism was Religious Education (RE), accepted this male sports role willingly due to their out-of-work interests; other male teachers strongly resented being cast as 'a bloke in a track-suit'. Our research data also indicated that men were being given (or claiming) the male sports role as some female staff did not have knowledge of the rules of the game. In England, teacher training is being reformed and shortened and the opportunities for all trainee teachers to receive sufficient sports training in order to teach the subject well, is declining. So, if men already have an interest in and knowledge of a specific sport (such as football), their male 'expertise' will be further valued and the focus on boys, men and sport increased. This is unfair and a clear matter of concern when issues of childhood obesity are increasingly being raised in England. When Elizabeth trained in the late 1960s, PE was comprehensively taught to all student teachers and gymnastics, dance and other sports (such as rounders) were on the official curriculum for all pupils. So, there was not an issue of women teachers having insufficient subject knowledge in order to teach PE and games. All male and female teachers had in-depth sports training; and all children received an hour's PE a day, including swimming, if pool access was available; with out-of-school sports clubs being run for boys and girls. In English schools today, far less official curriculum time is spent on PE and men are entering the occupation and being expected to, or offering to, teach boys sport.

These gender practices may work to marginalize girls and female teachers and they also work to stereotype male teachers as needed sportsmen. There are suggestions in our research data that some women teachers are helping some men to avoid this male sports script by offering to teach football themselves. This is encouraging, the more men and women teachers work together, the sooner these gender practices can be dismantled and the focus will once again be firmly on enjoyable PE for all pupils; not only male teachers, boys and football.

Recommendation 4
Schools and training providers must ensure that all male and female teachers have adequate training in order to be able to confidently teach a wide range of sport to both girls and boys. A school audit needs to be carried out to see who is participating in out-of-school sports clubs, and governors must ensure that girls and boys have equal access to a wide range of sports as part of a broad and balanced PE curriculum. This is essential to ensure pupil health and well-being, and sports needs to be seen as an important subject to teach rather than being reduced to a 'male-only' discipline strategy to engage potentially disruptive working-class boys. Governors must also identify teachers (of either gender) who need to acquire more subject knowledge in order to teach all sports effectively and CPD offered to these staff.

Safe-guarding

A serious issue, raised by both our male trainees and key informants, was concerned with male teacher vulnerability, especially when supervising pupils changing during PE. There is an urgent need to publicly address this issue in schools and in nurseries when, for example, young children may need taking to the toilet. Women teachers do not seem to be considered 'suspect', and Elizabeth never thought twice when entering boys' changing rooms or boys' toilets to ensure discipline. Teachers have a duty of care, so do employers, and no teacher should live 'in fear' (as Carl said) of carrying out their teaching duties due to their gender. There were indications that the younger the pupils, the more vulnerable male teachers become; the sooner these men move away from classroom teaching into headship the sooner these often unspoken 'suspicions' about men and young children are diminished. We once again express our thanks to our male informants who discussed their present experiences and 'fears' of accusation; unless we do address these issues this pernicious script will continue to circulate, promoting the idea that 'any man who teaches young children is a pervert' (Brian).

Recommendation 5
School governing bodies and teacher trainers must develop a clear code of practice to safeguard all teachers as well as upholding the existing ones

for children, and this code of practice must be regularly monitored and assessed for effectiveness. In particular, Physical Education facilities ought to be developed to ensure male and female staff, as well as pupils, are given adequate privacy. All staff must be given opportunities to ask for advice and talk in confidence to a mentor or safeguarding officer if any issues arise either in the classroom or outside in the playground. The current media panic about child abuse is impacting particularly on men who select to teach young children; this needs to be better acknowledged within the occupation and explicit procedures for the safeguarding of all staff, in particular, men, put in place in schools and training establishments as a matter of urgency.

Appointment and promotion

Several experienced key informants, now in senior management, identified governing body bias as one reason why so many men gained early promotion to headships. One male deputy head teacher reported being 'offered' three headships, prior to the posts being advertised. These unfair appointment practices, not only break employment laws but they also indicate that the 'hidden agenda' where men are 'approached and coached' is still in operation. We remain grateful to our key informants who disclosed these unfair practices, which can advantage men whilst causing resentment from some female staff (and students); thus strengthening gender barriers. It also means that even long experienced male teachers, such as Roger, still 'feels guilty' over his career promotions and finds the female head teachers he meets 'are far more experienced and capable'. One senior male teacher identified and rejected the survival of sexist ideas about women, child-care and their lack of suitability for promotion; other men upheld the belief that men better deserve promotion as they are the chief 'bread-winners'. There was evidence that male teachers may receive early 'sponsorship' for promotion from male heads and a man who does not receive rapid promotion may be at risk of being labelled a failure. Women staff as well as men can collude to maintain male promotion advantage; and current male recruitment drives may be further fuelling unfair appointment practices. Being a 'rarity' in the occupation can work to advantage men in interviews, as the 'needed man' discourses continue to circulate; some men recognize and employ their 'rarity' for career advantage, whilst other men reject this and attempt to become good classroom teachers before obtaining promotion. Most of our male informants either deny male career advantage within the occupation, or ignore it, even though they will still benefit from it.

Recommendation 6
Better scrutiny of present appointment and promotion practices within this occupation needs to be carried out, in order to remove gender bias and ensure equity for all applicants. Further statistics need to be collated concerning

length of service and promotions achieved, with a gender, age and ethnicity breakdown, in order to gather materials that can be employed for ongoing governor training to remove unfair appointment and promotion practices. Not all men are seen as 'suitable' for early headship, as Stuart found with his beard and flowery waistcoat. Alongside this necessary quantitative research, qualitative research into the actual interview experiences of a range of teachers (male and female) should also be carried out, focusing on access issues; enabling the 'hidden curriculum' with all its gendered assumptions to be both identified and removed. No teacher of children aged 3–11 years, should be offered a job before it is even advertised purely because of their gender or 'race'; as long as these biased practices continue, gender resentment within the occupation will continue and any male teacher who receives promotion is open to the accusation that he was appointed 'only' because he was a man.

Recommendation 7

We also recommend that a career path be developed for both male and female teachers who want to remain in the classroom and not pursue the present promotion track into senior management. Instead, these primary teachers could select to develop their pedagogy through substantial reflective classroom practice involving further academic study, with the aim of becoming 'expert' practitioners, able to advise other staff (and students) on teaching; and be financially rewarded for this choice. Once again, protocols to prevent gender bias need to be put in place to ensure this career route is open to both female and male staff.

Teacher training

We are well aware as we write this book, that the way English primary teachers are being 'trained' is under-going significant change; the ramifications of which are yet to be known. In the light of this major restructuring the recommendations below will need to be adapted to meet future training paths. However, irrespective of these changes, the training experiences of primary teachers, whether in schools or in universities, must include work on identifying and resisting the gender barriers entrants into this workforce may face.

Equity training

Our male informants had varied experiences of lectures concerned with gender equity during their initial training; a few men said they had benefitted from these sessions; however, the majority of newer male entrants felt 'attacked' and many blamed feminism itself. This is worrying and demonstrates how examining gender relations can be fractious and sessions aimed at breaking down gender barriers can actually work to reinforce them. Our research data also evidenced the intersectionality of gender with other relations such as racism, homophobia and social class bias, and there is still a real shortage of research into minority ethnic student experience during initial training (Crozier and Menter, 1993; Osler, 1997).

The two working-class African Caribbean teachers interviewed by Elizabeth (George and Derek), both described very painful and excluding experiences in Initial Teacher Training (ITT). Neil, the Asian middle-class teacher in contrast felt his ethnicity (alongside his gender) advantaged him at all stages of his training (Neil had been accepted onto his training course without even an interview). Equity work was both infrequent and problematic for most of the male NQTs interviewed and all of the men in our student support group. No male tutors were involved in any of the gender lectures discussed. Gender regimes operate in teacher education as well as primary schools; where once again, despite their gender minority, men in schools of education, tend to move swiftly into senior management positions. Well-qualified women tutors are left to do what can be still stereotyped as low-level 'housekeeping', such as interviewing and face-to-face teaching; especially the teaching of equity work (Burn, 2000; Dillabough, 2000). Elizabeth has been asked many times if is she is 'one of those feminist man-hater types' (a woman teacher); whilst, Simon has never been subject to these 'backlash against feminism' (Faludi, 1992) discourses in his teaching career.

The cumulative effects of homophobia often surfaced in our student support group. After receiving numerous comments in school about his 'voice', Colin (a gay student) had shaved all his hair off and arrived at Elizabeth's office with the question 'why have I done this Elizabeth... is it about being a man'?

Several men reported a sense of isolation during their initial training; as well as on school placement, where some men were positioned by women staff as 'handsome young princes' and others received 'typical men' comments.

Recommendation 8

Further research is required into interview procedures, placement practices and gender equity work during ITT and where possible, male and female tutors need to co-teach these equity sessions. A female and male tutor teaching together can better explore the way gender practice affects males and females, thus avoiding the simplistic 'it's a war against men' male student response when inherited patriarchal advantage is unpicked (hooks, 1989; Connell, 2002).

Other inequalities faced by student teachers, due to racism, homophobia and class bias, for example, need to be identified and tackled by all training providers, and this includes the monitoring of students' experiences whilst on school placements. This 'hidden curriculum' is just as important as the overt one; and no student teacher should be subject to so-called 'harmless comments' about their 'difference' whilst on school placement, or whilst in training sessions, due to their career choice.

We set up our male student support group as these students were at risk; they faced a higher than average drop-out and failure rate. We recommend that all students who are in danger of non-completion (which may be male and female black students, or other under-represented groups) are given targeted support during training to rectify the extra barriers they may face due to their minority status. So, the questions should be 'who is under-achieving and what strategies can trainers develop to better support these students and ensure that equal opportunities applies to all trainee teachers as well as to the pupils that they are learning to teach?' Equal opportunities are synonymous with good practice.

Recruitment and retention

Research evidence suggests that there is no point in encouraging men (and other under-represented groups) to enter an occupation where gender practices are still flourishing and, in England, the lack of long-term retention of both male and female primary teachers is now a serious issue. Recruitment schemes such as 'teach first' replicate American initiatives that expect new graduates to spend a few years in classrooms; Apple (2013), whilst praising their individual commitment, rightly criticizes the lack of time these 'temporary teachers' spend in learning the complex craft of teaching, before moving on. In England, the increased workloads, inspections and general de-valuation of teachers continues to impact. Teachers, who were once considered as respected professionals, have now been recast as managers of learning to be inspected and graded (Mahony and Hextall, 2000).

In short, prior to repeating more of the failed 'we need men' recruitment campaigns, policy makers need to take stock of what sort of primary teachers they are seeking to recruit. Do they wish to recruit 'managers of learning' obsessed with meeting externally set 'targets'; or are they attempting to recruit well-educated men (and women) who desire to become skilled practitioners by developing exemplary pedagogical practice over years of scholarly service?

Several of our more experienced key informants claimed the pedagogic script, as did the two female teachers interviewed in Chapter Nine. The intrinsic satisfaction of 'making a difference' to pupils' lives by teaching them to want to learn, as well as to achieve across the curriculum is what committed teachers are attempting to accomplish; and this needs to be considered further before any more 'quick-fix' male-only recruitment initiatives are rolled out. Ken, a reflective practitioner who actively challenges many of the male teacher scripts he himself is subject to as a young male teacher, astutely points out: 'it's no use just putting a bloke in a classroom'.

Recommendation 9

Policy makers should examine research evidence from internationally respected academics, such as Professor Skelton, who herself was a primary teacher, which indicates that in order to better attract under-represented groups, recruitment campaigns need to stop merely show-casing 'token' black and white men. In the light of both our own research findings and other research reviewed, we support Professor Skelton's recruitment recommendations (Skelton, 2009). We also recommend that practitioners themselves (male and female) are invited to contribute to these future recruitment campaigns which will not only be concerned with achieving a more representative workforce, but also with restoring this under-valued occupation to the respected profession it was when we ourselves were successfully recruited.

Teachers and research

Paulo Freire (2007), one of the world's most respected educators, has long argued that teachers need research just as a fish needs water. In the 1980s, when Elizabeth was a primary school teacher in the North East of England, she had two periods of full-time academic research study at Newcastle University, fully funded, in order to carry out classroom-based research designed to improve curriculum practice in primary schools (Burn, 1989). This model of teacher-action-research, where experienced and successful practitioners are supported by their employers to engage in research aimed at improving the educational achievements of pupils, needs to return. At that time, Elizabeth was being publicly constructed as a reflective teacher concerned with developing pedagogical practice (a pedagogy script) not as a 'dim mother' substituting for inadequate working-class parenting. The majority of our teacher informants also claim this teaching script, and several were already studying part-time for a higher degree. However, none of our informants have had access to periods of full-time research and academic study. If we intend all children to become young successful learners, then the ongoing intellectual development of the teachers who teach them needs to be attended to once again; especially in the light of technological developments which are providing both new teaching resources and challenges. Instead of being mocked in the staffroom, Penny, who had already studied for her Masters, needs to be offered respect not criticism and governing bodies must work to establish and promote an educational culture in schools, rather than a domestic one based on gender practice.

Recommendation 10

A policy decision is made by the government to support and fund both qualitative and quantitative research projects involving experienced primary teachers in order to improve equal opportunities for both primary teachers themselves and for the pupils that they teach. The data these research projects generate can then provide a resource (including statistics and case studies of teacher's stories) that can be employed for future CPD work with students, teachers and teacher trainers (very useful for equity work). So 'theory' is informed by practice and practice is informed by theory. We offer an example of this usage of research data, by providing Gareth's teacher story as a training 'resource' at the end of this chapter.

All primary school teachers should be required to engage in further academic study as part of their career development and access made available for this study by school governors and government policy directives. Classroom assistants need also to be required to continue their academic studies in order to better ensure the development of a vibrant 'learning community' with a clear focus on education rather than on recreating public patriarchal parents (complete with nurse-maids) needed for the care and control of economically poor pupils.

Conclusion

We were engaged in our final edit of this book at the end of 2014, when Elizabeth met an inner-city male primary teacher working in England, who in common with most of our key informants is teaching in an inner city primary school with a very high percentage of working class pupils (93 per cent are in receipt of Free School Meals). However, in contrast to our key informants, he is not teaching in London; Gareth's school is located in the North East of England. We are indebted to Gareth for writing his teacher story, and we conclude this chapter by offering his story (plus discussion questions) in the spirit of recommendation 10.

Gareth's story: a recent male teacher voice

Gareth has taught in one inner-city primary school in the North East of England, since qualifying 5 years ago after a previous career. He is the only male teacher in the school:

> Because of the recession my own career was at risk. I was volunteering at the local sports club to "put something back". When I applied I am sure I would not have got on the course if I was a woman. They all had far more experience than me; many had been classroom assistants for a number of years.
>
> In both my placement schools the heads were male and there was one other male teacher.
>
> I used being a man to my advantage. Perhaps this is one of the only scenarios where being a man over 30 is in fact a factor to exploit.

Gareth is now studying for a senior leadership qualification:

I was a senior manager in my previous career so am looking to have more influence as I progress within education.

I think men are more career driven. A number of fantastic women teachers, part of our senior management team, have said they do not want to take the final step to be heads. I think females contemplating managing a team of predominately females can find it very daunting.

Gareth is well aware of the gender stereotypes applied to primary teachers:

Many men think of primary teachers as being middle-aged women who have different coloured pens for different jobs and woe betide someone who gets them mixed up.

Gareth is used to lots of staffroom banter about 'men':

I make the same comments regarding 'women'. I have great colleagues who have lots of experience. I am the only man on the staff, but in many ways I enjoy this and exploit it to my advantage.

Gareth receives many positive comments about his latest career choice:

All of my friends are very envious. I work in a school with lots of socio-economic problems and the main response is admiration.

Gareth also reflects on his influence on pupils:

I think boys in school like the fact they can talk to me about football.

For lots of my kids me enjoying sports etc. but at the same time appreciating arts, music etc. is an alien concept, because they have never come across a male who thinks like that. For example I enjoy singing in music lessons and I feel some boys who might want to but feel embarrassed, do take part because they see me doing it.

Lots of our 'tougher boys' see me talking about football with them etc... So when I say I have enjoyed reading a book or poem, I do think they give that thought a bit extra credence because of our previous connection. I make them think twice about a subject they may have received no encouragement or negative comments (*about*) such as reading and writing at home.

Gareth has been teaching lower KS2 since qualifying (7–9 years), and he holds posts for Physical Education and ICT:

I would love to be a Reception teacher, and did this during my placement.

All our Senior Leadership Team (SLT) are female and they are better than me at discipline.

As with any job surely we should have a 50:50 split. This is what society is and why should primary schools be any different?

I know this is a generalization... I think lots of men don't work well having to follow instructions to the letter. We enjoy being more off the cuff (*spontaneous*). Teaching is becoming more and more restrictive and I think this puts lots of people off.

Discussion questions

1. Discuss how Gareth is positioning himself as a man teaching pupils 3–11 years.

2. Identify and discuss the male teacher scripts that Gareth claims and rejects.

3. Which of the male teacher scripts are not visible in Gareth's told story?

4. What are Gareth's views on women teachers and female pupils?

5. What reasons does Gareth offer for the lack of men in the occupation?

6. Is the social-class background of Gareth's pupils of any consequence for his work identity constructions?

7. How does Gareth view his position as a minority in this workforce? Does he feel disadvantaged or advantaged by being a 'man'?

Conclusion

This book has presented the work stories of a number of men teaching 3- to 11-year-olds in English inner-city schools and nurseries situated in areas of high economic poverty. We also invited professional peer commentary and employed Elizabeth's data from participant observation of a male student teacher support group; together with scrutiny of a range of international research to strengthen our understanding of gender practices (Appendix 1). The legitimate male teacher 'scripts' that have emerged remain surprisingly similar over time and place; English and international male teacher recruitment drives have also not changed the gender imbalance in this workforce.

One could argue that on the surface, these male teachers have very little to complain about. They may receive a few negative comments from some female colleagues (mainly during training) about male career advantage and about 'men' in general, but they are also 'a bit of a celebratory' in school, often applauded by parents and female staff. They are increasingly being viewed (and can view themselves) as valued 'male' role models, replacing missing or deficit working-class fathers and naturally able to engage boys, in particular, in learning. The continuing rarity of male teachers in this sector helps maintain their swift promotion paths as long as they abide by the 'rules' and do not cross the long-established gender barriers.

What does it matter if men are: being sent extra boys to discipline, even during initial training; given boys' sport to teach; offered promotion for 'male' labelled subjects (such as mathematics and science) even if their actual specialisms are religious education or art; being expected to teach 10- to 11-year-olds, even if they trained Early Years (3–7 years)? Soon all these 'trivial' gender practices will be left behind as they claim their reserved place in Senior Management. They will be 'in charge' of the women (some of whom may prefer to work for a man), a symbolic head of the public patriarchal family, dredged up from highly romanticized notions of the Victorian home, where women and men happily performed specific sex-typed roles and all was well! These unfair gender practices in schools and their intersections with 'race' and class and homophobic practices (Apple, 2013:19) are working to consistently reaffirm a familial model in staffing that is totally inappropriate for the twenty-first century.

Is it a case of 'get the man out of the classroom' well away from the actual teaching of young children and the unspoken 'suspicion' that any man who chooses to spend time with young children might be a child abuser? This is a powerful current discourse that many of our key informants live in daily fear of, due to their choice of career. Why else would men choose to enter into 'women's work' and disturb the established gender order? The same 'work' was once actually constructed as important 'men's work', when the male Infant School Movement was set up in England in the early nineteenth century.

Whether male teachers accept it or not, they are still being positioned by many in the school community as 'natural' disciplinarians and leaders; given more respect by parents and even by pupils themselves due to their 'innate' male qualities. Men may enter the occupation safe in the knowledge that they will quickly 'rescue' the failing boys, improve academic results and inherit their well-deserved patriarchal dividend: early promotion. Our own data, staffing patterns and promotion statistics confirm this 'typical' career path for male teachers of young children. In the UK, government recruitment drives continue to draw on 'needed male role-model' discourses, helping to further establish the male 'value-added factor', irrespective of actual teaching talents.

We know that there are many excellent male and female teachers of young children, whom we have the greatest respect for; unfortunately, we also know that there are incompetent male and female teachers of young children. To consider that the effective teaching of young children can be assured by merely 'putting a man in a classroom' (Ken) is an insult to both female and male primary teachers who have spent years learning their difficult craft. Teachers who, irrespective of their sex (or any other physical characteristic), spend long hours reflecting critically on their teaching, in order to give all of the children (not just boys, or just girls) opportunities to learn across the curriculum. A 'good' teacher does not base their assessments of a child's learning needs on what sort of family background the child comes from, or whether the child is male or female. Yet, many talented teachers of young children are being devalued by the continuation of these gender stereotypes that construct them as 'discipline dads' or 'dim mothers', rather than as well qualified teachers who have an expert knowledge of teaching and learning (and this is not a male-only or female-only quality).

Whatever our personal beliefs are about men and women (and we are entitled to have them) as teachers, we should leave these beliefs at the classroom door and concentrate on teaching all children, not just to enjoy learning, but also to succeed in doing so. We strongly support our key informants who identify that it is pedagogical practice that matters, not the gender of the teacher, and this 'truth' is also evidenced by the actual test results of pupils (Carrington et al., 2005). For readers of this book who may be parents, governors, policy makers and students, rather than teachers, we now provide a very short overview of what is understood as good primary pedagogical practice; and it does not include the ability to shout, play football or perform a stereotypical 'male' role-model script.

Effective pedagogical practice

The male teacher scripts we identified argue that men are needed to teach the older children and only women should be teaching the youngest pupils. In the light of this, let us first consider what we know about the effective teaching of the youngest pupils. Margaret Donaldson (1978) in her seminal book 'Children's Minds' discussed how teaching young children to become fluent readers is one of the most important roles of primary education. Crucial in the development of early literacy is ensuring there are opportunities for children to listen to stories and discuss them further with a skilled teacher. What happens if that wolf decides not to eat the grandma and wants to be friends, or the dragon is scared? Donaldson clearly identifies how it is high cognitive challenge in 'meaningful contexts' that is vital for young children's intellectual growth. When children are being told or read a good story they become totally engrossed; the gender of the story-teller is not important, rather it is the quality of the storyline; the ability to take a child into imagined worlds rich and strange. This pedagogical thoughtfulness where teachers and pupils explore new ideas and generate new meanings (Pollard, 2010) is an integral part of research into best practice (Alexander, 2010). To argue that 'only' women can carry out this important aspect of pedagogical practice is ridiculous.

Let us now look at the effective teaching of another essential subject, Mathematics. Research has consistently shown that children need to explain their mathematical thinking and by doing so start to self-correct their misconceptions if they are to succeed in this subject (Drews, 2005; Sutherland, 2007). Teachers have a key role to play by engaging in subtle tutorials, enabling the pupils through skilled dialogue to justify and improve their methods and develop mathematical thinking (Anghileri, 2001; Lees,

2006). To argue that it is 'only' male teachers who can engage in this 'dialogic' teaching is also ridiculous (Alexander, 2006).

In summary, it is skilled teaching that teachers of children 3–11 must become experts in: what do the children already know, how can I move these children on to the next stage of their learning journey in a meaningful and respectful way? It is not 'banter' about football with the older boys that develops early literacy and sound mathematical understanding: it is quality teaching by female and male practitioners.

Paulo Freire reminds us that teaching is an intellectual act, irrespective of the age of the pupils taught (Pratt-Adams et al., 2010). This internationally applauded teacher, scholar and political activist, who recognized that no education is neutral, also argues that teachers should continue with their own intellectual study (Freire, 1996). It is worth noting that in Finland where young children achieve high academic results, all teachers are expected to study for higher degrees. A major European longitudinal study, researching effective Early Years pedagogy, has found that highly qualified staff: 'were the most effective in their interactions with the children, using the most sustained shared thinking interactions' (Siraj-Blatchford et al., 2002:11). The world famous Reggio Emilia Early Years programme also requires staff to continue their educational studies (Giardiello, 2014). There is no research evidence to support the sexist hypothesis that it is 'gender' rather than intelligence that makes a 'good' primary teacher.

Male teachers who challenge gender practice

A re-reading of the data and research findings presented in this book attracts the thought: What is it like for men who do not board the quick promotion train, or select to step off it?

The costs for men who actually want to stay in the classroom and receive the real satisfaction of helping all young children to 'read, write and add-up' are considerable as long as these gender barriers remain. The male teachers who select to do so, may be viewed (and view themselves) as failures; rather than as succeeding in the difficult art of teaching young children to develop a 'love of learning'. Teaching a young child not only to read but also to want to read, for example, is very rewarding and this highly pleasurable aspect of teaching young children needs to be both researched and disseminated further if government recruitment drives want to attract potentially 'good' teachers, not just a number of token 'male teachers' to 'ensure that boys' masculinity remains intact' (Martino, 2008:7). The 'objectification' of men is no more acceptable than the 'objectification' of women.

One of our key informants reports that even his own mother (who was also a primary teacher) expected her son just to accept swift promotion, rather than gain more classroom experience in order to develop his teaching expertise; and he was understandably annoyed. This male teacher, alongside a few other key informants, did decide to step off the rapid male promotion ladder; these men wanted to learn to become 'good teachers' (Carl) by gaining wider classroom experience teaching across age ranges; four of them were also studying for higher degrees. Then there was Stuart, the male teacher who did not receive the 'expected' early promotion that gender practice demands. Stuart was even told by the female teachers on his staff to 'conform' if he wanted to achieve the 'expected' male promotion! Obviously, only certain 'types' of men are allowed to board the male promotion train, and they are the ones who uphold the hegemonic norm. Our key informants also included men who felt they were merely the 'token' black teachers and two of them have now left the occupation.

Male teachers, who are willing and able to comply with the male teacher scripts and accept early promotion, become vulnerable to accusations of only achieving the promotion because they are 'men'. They rightly resent this, but until these men, when they have gained institutional power, actually start to both publicly acknowledge and challenge the unfair gender practices they have benefitted from, the accusations will remain valid. Our data did evidence some men being offered jobs, or being recruited into training, even before (or without) an interview because they 'wanted a man'. We thank the male teachers who revealed these unfair procedures and hope that other male and female teachers will also start to openly challenge unfair gender practices during initial recruitment and appointment.

The present reality is that male teachers who do refuse, or who do not hold the 'legitimate' masculinity required to play the gender game, risk isolation and disapproval; both from other staff who do uphold these gender practices, governors who appoint 'men' for gender reasons and from parents who expect male role models who will be willing to perform stereotypical 'male' behaviours, such as being 'a bloke in a track-suit'.

It is reassuring to find that the majority of our key informants wanted to see gender reform, and we were delighted that this book has been commissioned at a time when this under-valued and under-researched occupation is undergoing substantial restructuring. All change can provide opportunities to interrupt established regimes and anyone concerned with providing all young children with effective teachers needs to be aware that present gender practices may undermine primary teachers. Teachers who want to 'teach' not merely represent ludicrous stereotyped models of supposed 'male' and 'female' behaviours. There is also a concern that the current reorganization of teacher training in England is impacting negatively on recruitment. The Director of the Institute of Education in London believes that the shift to school-based teacher training: 'Simply does not work' (Exley, 2014:1).

The interview data collected by Elizabeth also found a pedagogic script in circulation, working to affirm the 'truth' that teachers of young children are primarily concerned with the intellectual, physical, social and emotional growth of their pupils, not with providing substitute public 'parents' for deficit working-class families. We recommended in Chapter Ten that future recruitment campaigns need to start highlighting the intrinsic satisfaction male and female teachers can gain when young children learn. Several of our key informants expressed the wish to 'make a difference', and it is important to remember that the economically poor pupils that these men are teaching, remain educationally disadvantaged in the English school system today (Garner, 2014).

An article in the leading newspaper for teachers in England (TES) demonstrates that some primary teachers are already openly identifying and challenging several of these male teacher scripts:

> the one that expects us to sort out badly behaved boys, instil a much needed sense of discipline into the classroom and manage the school football team (Eddison, 2014).

This particular article is written by a male primary teacher and he is clearly calling for other men to resist these gender stereotypes. We would go further than Eddison and recommend that male and female teachers need to work together in this pursuit, since our data indicates that they can both be targets of (or bearers of) gender practice within this occupation. This book is an example of such alliance-work between educators.

The educational consequences of gender practice

A shadow has stalked this book; it is the possible educational consequence of gender practice within this occupation. We reiterate that it is not possible to generalize from the testimony of eighteen key informants teaching in economically disadvantaged London schools and peer commentary. Unfortunately, other research studies carried out at different times and in different countries also confirm the continuation of these historic male teacher scripts.

In the 'male role-model script' in particular, the notion of deficit families (especially single mothers) surfaced as a key motif. It was common, for the men to claim that they were compensating for, or substituting for, the inadequate 'fathers'. We tentatively suggest that there may not be such a 'need' to construct public parents for the 'deficit children of the poor' in more middle-class areas, where parents may not be viewed as educationally deficit and instead the focus is firmly fixed on pupils' academic achievements (Ball, 2003). In the light of our findings, we would encourage other educational researchers (and teacher/researchers) to start to examine what gender scripts are operating for teachers in schools that are situated in affluent areas; where parents have the economic means to pay fees or buy expensive property, ensuring that they have access to 'good' schools, that is, schools with low numbers of pupils on Free School Meals. In these economically advantaged schools, will the patriarchal gender scripts still dominate or will it be the pedagogic script that is in ascendance? In advantaged schools, parents may have the confidence to demand that their children succeed academically, and this target is what all teachers are under pressure to achieve (Ball, 2003). The focus is on teaching and learning rather than on rectifying assumed deficit parenting; teachers' expectations of pupils' potentials continue to be influenced by a persistent class bias against the poor in England (Reay, 1998).

What is the impact on the quality of the curriculum offered when some male teachers of young children are insultingly constructed as 'natural' disciplinarians, needed for 'naughty' boys, male sports, maths, Computer Science/ICT and fast promotion; rather than being allowed to employ their training specialisms and therefore contribute to further curriculum development, instead of being given 'male' subjects that they may not have any expertise in?

Good teachers (male and female) need to learn their craft (Apple, 2013) and the focus must be on reflective teaching, allowing all primary teachers to gain successful teaching experience across age ranges, prior to promotion, or be rewarded for becoming 'pedagogical experts' staying in the classroom. We maintain that primary teaching needs to be constructed as principally concerned with pupils' intellectual growth, regardless of their social-class background, not with mothering or bullying the pupils of economically poor families.

Oliver, one of the head teachers in our sample, strongly criticizes the way some teachers position the pupils in his inner-city school: 'Its low expectation (p) it's that missionary zeal, which I really hate and deplore!' Oliver's description is highly reminiscent of the discourses of charity and control that circulated in the nineteenth-century London Board schools (Jones, 1990; Copelman, 1996; Davin, 1996). If teachers 'of the poor' today are still constructing themselves (or being constructed) as substitute patriarchal parents, as these gender scripts are working to achieve, then the focus on quality teaching and learning is reduced.

In summary, we posit that the historical construction of teachers of young children as public patriarchal parents rather than as educators may still be having educational consequences for children from economically disadvantaged homes, as well as impacting on initial recruitment, retention and promotion practices. Carl, one of our key informants, strongly criticizes this ongoing configuration of Early Years teaching as 'merely' public mothering:

> That's an insult to every teacher and to every male... cause (*sing-song voice*) 'women can do it'... it's like that nurture thing... it's NOT education!

Jeff, another key informant, also argues that 'education' ought to be the focus:

> I want to be appointed because I'm the right teacher for the school; I have the right qualifications NOT because of my gender!

The anger in Jeff's voice reflects our own, and we echo his words. We need good teachers of young children, and the gender, class, sexuality or ethnicity of these teachers should not be their defining characteristic: it ought to be their teaching ability that is paramount. We hope this book will encourage other female and male teachers/researchers to work together to help dismantle the numerous unfair and damaging gender barriers that still exist within this occupation – barriers that have consequences both for the teachers themselves and for the young children that they teach.

APPENDIX 1

Male student support group

Students	Study year	Ethnicity	Age	Class	Sexuality	Main subject	Sessions attended
1. Adam	2	White	Young	w.c.	Hetero.	Maths	7
2. Bill	2	Black	Mature	w.c.	Hetero.	ICT	6
3. Colin	2	White	Mature	w.c.	Gay	ICT	7
4. Mike	2	White	Young	m.c.	Hetero.	Maths	6
5. Dave	2	White	Mature	w.c.	Hetero.	Maths	7
6. Frank	2	Black	Mature	w.c.	Hetero.	Maths	5
7. Gavin	2	White	Young	w.c.	Hetero.	History	1
8. Henry	3	White	Mature	w.c.	Gay	ICT	2
9. Ian	3	White	Young	m.c.	Hetero.	Geog.	4
10. John	3	Black	Mature	w.c.	Hetero.	ICT	4
11. Kevin	3	White	Mature	w.c.	Gay	Maths	2

Young, under 24 years of age; Mature, over 24 years of age and non-traditional entry to Higher Education.

Eighteen Key Informants

Name	Length of service	Ethnic group	Age	Trained	Schools worked in	Present post	Training specialism
1. Alan	NQT	White	23	B.Ed London	1	Reception	EY
2. Brian	NQT	White	32	B.Ed London	0	Not teaching	EY
3. Carl	6 yrs	White	36	PGCE Wales	Supply	Yr 5 Supply	EY
4. Derek	6 yrs	Black	30	B.Ed London	1	Yr 2	EY
5. Eric	6 yrs	White	41	B.Ed London	3	EY co-ordinator	EY
6. Fred	NQT	White	30	B.Ed London	1	Yr 6	Primary
7. George	NQT	Black	36	B.Ed London	0	Not teaching	Primary
8. Harry	NQT	White	31	B.Ed London	1	Yr 5	Primary
9. Jeff	8 yrs	White	32	B.Ed Wales	3	Yr 5 Senior teacher	Primary
10. Ken	2 yrs	White	28	B.Ed Midlands	1	Yr 5	Primary
11. Leo	10 yrs	White	37	B.Ed South West	4	Yr 6 Senior teacher	Primary
12. Neil	11 yrs	Asian	35	PGCE London	1	Infant Deputy	EY
13. Oliver	17 yrs	Mixed 'Race'	39	B.Ed West Sussex	3+	Infant Head	EY
14. Pat	26 yrs	White	48	B.Ed North of England	5	Nursery Head (2nd Headship)	Junior (EY converted)
15. Quentin	10 yrs	White	37	PGCE North of England	3	Primary Deputy	EY

Name	Length of service	Ethnic group	Age	Trained	Schools worked in	Present post	Training specialism
16. Roger	27 yrs	White	49	B.Ed South East	7	Primary Head (2nd Headship)	Junior/Sec
17. Stuart	27 yrs	White	48	Cert of Ed. West London	6	Lecturer in HE	Junior/Sec
18. Thomas	12 yrs	White	36	PGCE North of England	2	Lecturer in HE	Primary

- 8 of these 18 male teachers are Early Years; 10 are Junior/Primary.

- 5 of these men are NQTs; 6 are class teachers; 7 are in senior management.

- 14 are White; 1 is Asian; 1 is Mixed 'Race'; and 2 are African Caribbean.

- 2 men are gay; the rest do not disclose their sexualities.

- 9 of these men are from London.

- 12 of these 18 men qualified when they were older than 23 years of age (a typical pattern).

- 9 of the men interviewed have female partners who are also teachers.

- 10 of the men interviewed are parents.

Details of Professional Peers, collected 2014

Nationality	
England	31
Canada	3
Finland	3
New Zealand	3

Number of years teaching	
Trainee teacher	6
Newly qualified teacher	14
2–10 years teaching	10
Over 10 years teaching	10

Note half of the professional respondents (20) are either NQTs or have been teaching less than 2 years.

GLOSSARY

B.Ed	Bachelor of Education (teaching qualification, England)
BP	Block Practice
CPD	Continuing Professional Development
DAES	Diploma in Advanced Educational Studies (Post Graduate Studies)
DfE	Department for Education
DfEE	Department for Education and Employment
EY	Early Years. Children below 5 years old (England)

Elementary School 1870–1944 provided education for children aged between 5 and 14 in England

HE	Higher Education (England)
Infants	5–7 years (England)
ICT	Information and Communication Technology
IT	Information Technology
ITE	Initial Teacher Education
ITT	Initial Teacher Training

Juniors 8–11 years (England)

KS1	Key Stage 1. Ages 5–7 years (England)
KS2	Key Stage 2. Ages 8–11 years (England)
LEA	Local Education Authority (England)
MA	Master of Arts (Post Graduate Studies)
NAS	National Association of School Masters (England)
NQT	Newly Qualified Teacher

Nursery 3–4 years (England)

NUT	National Union of Teachers (England)
OECD	Organisation for Economic Co-operation and Development
Ofsted	Office for Standards in Education (England)
PE	Physical Education
PGCE	Post-Graduate Certificate in Education (Teaching qualification, England)
PhD	Doctor of Philosophy (Post Graduate Studies)

Primary 3–11 years or 5–11 years (England)

PISA	Programme for International Student Assessment
Reception	5-year-old children (England)

Supply Teachers	Also known as substitute teachers – temporary work in one or more schools
TES	Times Educational Supplement (England)
TTA	Teacher Training Agency (England) became the Training and Development Agency for Schools on 1 September 2005. From 1 April 2012 it was replaced by the Teaching Agency. On 1 April 2013 the Teaching Agency merged with the National College for School Leadership and became the National College for Teaching and Leadership (NCTL).
Year 1	6-year-olds (England)
Year 2	7-year-olds (England)
Year 3	8-year-olds (England)
Year 4	9-year-olds (England)
Year 5	10-year-olds (England)
Year 6	11-year-olds (England)

BIBLIOGRAPHY

Acker, S. (1989) 'Rethinking teachers' careers', in S. Acker (ed.) *Teachers Gender and Careers*. Lewes, Falmer Press.

Acker, S. (1994) *Gendered Education*. Buckingham, Open University Press.

Adams, R. (2013) 'UK primary school teachers youngest in OECD'. *The Education Guardian*, 25 June, London.

Agnew, D. (1989) 'A world of women – an approach to personal and career development for women teachers in primary schools', in H. De Lyon and F. Widdowson Migniuolo (eds) *Women Teachers: Issues and Experiences*. Milton Keynes, Open University Press.

Ainley, P. (1994) *Degrees of Difference*. London, Lawrence Wishart.

Alexander, R.J. (1988) *Primary Teaching*. London, Cassell.

Alexander, R. (2006) *Towards Dialogic Teaching: Rethinking Classroom Talk*. York, Dialogos Press.

Alexander, R. (ed.) (2010) *Children, Their World Their Education. Final Report and Recommendations of the Cambridge Primary Review*. London, Routledge.

Alexander, S. (1983) *Women's Work in Nineteenth-Century London: A Study of the Years 1820–50*. London, Journeyman Press and the London History Workshop Centre.

Al-Khalifa, E. (1989) 'Management by halves: women teachers and school management', in H. De Lyon and F. Widdowson Migniuolo (eds) *Women Teachers: Issues and Experiences*. Milton Keynes, Open University Press.

Allan, J. (1993) 'Male elementary teachers: experiences and perspectives', in C. Williams (ed.) *Doing Women's Work*. London, Sage.

Allan, J. (1997) 'The persistent fewness of men elementary teachers: hypotheses from their own experiences'. Paper presented at the annual meeting of the Midwest Sociological Society. *(ERIC Document Reproduction Service No.ED418064)* http://files.eric.ed.gov/fulltext/ED418064.pdf (1 October 2014)

Allen, S. (1994) 'Race, ethnicity and nationality', in M. Maynard and H. Afsher (eds) *The Dynamics of 'Race' and Gender*. London, Taylor & Francis Ltd.

Allen Knight, B. and Moore, T. (2012) Supporting beginning male teachers as they transform to skilled professionals. *Improving Schools*. Vol. 15, No. 1, pp 61–72.

Alvesson, M. and Due Billing, Y. (1997) *Understanding Gender and Organizations*. London, Sage.

Anghileri, J. (2001) *Principles and Practice in Arithmetic Teaching*. Buckingham, Oxford University Press.

Apple, M. (1988) 'Work, class and teaching', in J. Ozga (ed.) *Schoolwork*. Milton Keynes, Open University Press.

Apple, M. (2013) *Can Education Change Society?* New York, Routledge.

Arnot, M. and Dillabough, J. (eds) (2000) *Challenging Democracy: International Perspectives on Gender, Education and Citizenship*. London, Routledge Falmer.

Arnot, M., David, M. and Weiner, G. (1999) *Closing the Gender Gap*. London, Blackwell.

Arreman, I. and Weiner, G. (2007). 'Gender, research and change in teacher education: a Swedish dimension.' *Gender and Education*. Vol. 19, No. 3, pp 317–337.

Ashenden, S. (1997) 'Feminism, postmodernism and the sociology of gender', in D. Owen (ed.) *Sociology after Postmodernism*. London, Sage.

Ashley, M. and Lee, J. (2004) *Women Teaching Boys: Caring and Working in the Primary School*. Stoke-on-Trent, Trentham Books.

Aspinall, K. and Drummond, M.J. (1989) 'Socialised into primary teaching', in H. De Lyon and F. Widdowson Migniuolo (eds) *Women Teachers: Issues and Experiences*. Milton Keynes, Open University Press.

Asthana, A. (2009) Schools launch drive to recruit male teachers. *The Observer*, pp 1–2. http://theguardian.com/education/2009/jul/12/primary-schools-male-teachers (06 March 2014).

Australian Bureau of Statistics (2010) *Where Have All the Male Teachers Gone?* www.abs.gov.au (28 September 2010).

Balchin, T. (2002) 'Male teachers in primary education'. *Forum*. Triangle Journals Ltd. Vol. 44, No. 1, pp 28–33.

Ball, S. (2003) *Class Strategies and the Education Market*. London, Routledge Falmer.

Barker, C. (2000) *Cultural Studies*. London, Sage.

Barlin, D. and Hallgarten, J. (2002) 'Supply teachers: symptoms of the problem or part of the solution?', in M. Johnson and J. Hallgarten (eds) *From Victims of Change to Agents of Change*. London, IPPR.

Barton, L. (1999) 'Market ideologies, education and the challenge for inclusion', in H. Daniels and P. Garner (eds) *Inclusive Education*. London, Kogan Page.

Bauman, Z. and May, T. (2001) *Thinking Sociologically* (2nd edition). Oxford, Blackwell.

BBC News UK (2005) *Male Teachers Do Not Help Boys*. news.bbc.co.uk/2/hi/uk_news/education/4230120.stm (9 September 2005).

Beck, U. (1992) *Risk Society: Towards a New Modernity*. London, Sage.

Beckford, M. (2008) The quiet conspiracy: men in primary schools. *The Telegraph*, http://www.telegraph.co.uk/news/uknews/2516986/Quiet-conspiracy-of-society-against-male-teachers-head-of-Government-body-claims.html (20 January 2014).

Beddoe, D. (1983) *Discovering Women's History*. London, Pandora.

Beddoe, D. (1989) *Back to Home and Duty*. London, Pandora.

Beijaard, D., Meijer, P. and Verloop, N. (2004) Reconsidering research on teachers' professional identity. *Teaching and Teacher Education*. Vol. 20, pp 107–128.

Bergen, B. (1988) 'Only a schoolmaster', in J. Ozga (ed.) *Schoolwork*. Milton Keynes, Open University Press.

Bhopal, K. (1994) 'The influence of feminism on black women in the higher educational curriculum', in S. Davis, C. Lubelska and J. Quinn (eds) *Changing the Subject*. London, Taylor & Francis.

Biddulph, S. (1997) *Raising Boys*. London, Thorsons.

Birchenough, C. (1938) *The History of Elementary Education in England and Wales from 1800 to the Present Day* (3rd edition). London, University Tutorial Press.

Blackmore, J. (1999) *Feminism, Leadership and Educational Change*. Buckingham, Open University Press.

Blair, M. (1995) 'Race, class and gender in school research', in J. Holland and M. Blair with S. Sheldon (eds) *Debates and Issues in Feminist Research and Pedagogy*. Avon, Open University Press.

Bloomfield, A. (2000) 'Mrs Roadknight reports... Jane Roadknight's visionary role in transforming elementary education', in M. Hilton and P. Hirsch (eds) *Practical Visionaries: Women, Education and Social Progress 1790–1930*. Harlow, Pearson Education Ltd.

Blumer, H. (1969) *Symbolic Interactionism*. Englewood Cliffs, NJ, Prentice Hall.

Bly, R. (1990) *Iron John: A Book about Men*. New York, Addison-Wesley.

Boffey, D. (2013) Huge rise in numbers of women who are family breadwinners. *The Observer*, Sunday 4th August, http://www.theguardian.com/money/2013/aug/04/mothers-breadwinners-in-family-report-says (07 July 2014)

Bradley, H. (1989) *Men's Work, Women's Work*. Oxford, Blackwell.

Bradley, J. (2000) 'Male elementary teacher candidates: a narrative perspective on their initial career choice'. *McGill Journal of Education*. Vol. 35, No. 2, pp 155–172.

Brah, A. and Phoenix, A. (2004) 'Ain't I a woman? Revising intersectionality. *Journal of International Women's Studies*. Vol. 5, No. 3, May.

Brehony, K. (2000) 'English revisionist froebelians and the schooling of the urban poor', in M. Hilton and P. Hirsch (eds) *Practical Visionaries: Women, Education and Social Progress 1790–1930*. Harlow, Pearson Education Ltd.

Brennan, P. (2007) *The Munitionettes*. Rowlands Gill, Donmouth Publishing.

Bricheno, P. and Thornton, M. (2002) 'Staff gender balance in primary schools'. *Research in Education*. Vol. 68, pp 57–63.

Britton, C. and Baxter, A. (1999) 'Becoming a mature student: gendered narratives of the self'. *Gender and Education*. Vol. 11, No. 2, pp 179–193.

Brookhart, S. and Loadman, W. (1996) 'Characteristics of male elementary teachers in the USA, at teacher education program entry and exit'. *Teacher and Teacher Education*. Vol.12, pp 197–210.

Browne, N. and France, P. (1985) 'Only cissies wear dresses: a look at sexist talk in the nursery', in G. Weiner (ed.) *Just a Bunch of Girls*. Milton Keynes, Open University Press.

Bunting, C. (1999) 'Aussie teachers fly home to party'. *Times Educational Supplement*. p 5, 12 November, London.

Burgess, H. (1989) 'A sort of career: women in primary schools', in C. Skelton (ed.) *Whatever Happens to Little Women?* Milton Keynes, Open University Press.

Burn, E. (1989) 'Inside the lego house', in C. Skelton (ed.) *Whatever Happens to Little Women?* Milton Keynes, Open University Press.

Burn, E. (2000) 'You won't want to get your hands dirty: an early years teacher reflecting on her training experience'. *Education and Social Justice*. Vol. 3, No. 1, Autumn, pp 59–64.

Burn, E. (2001) 'Battling through the system'. *Journal of Inclusive Education*. Vol. 5, No. 1, pp 85–92.

Burn, E. (2002) 'Do boys need male teachers as positive role models?' *Forum*. Triangle Journals Ltd. Vol. 44, No. 1, pp 34–40.

Burn, E. (2005) 'Constructing the male primary school teacher', *Unpublished PhD*, London Metropolitan University.

Burn, E. and Finnigan, T. (2003) 'I made it more academic by adding some snob words from the thesaurus', in J. Satterthwaite, E. Atkinson and K.Gale (eds) *Discourse, Power, Resistance: Challenging the Rhetoric of Contemporary Education*. Stoke-on-Trent, Trentham.

Burr, V. (1995) *An Introduction to Social Constructionism*. London, Routledge.

Butler, J. (1990) *Gender Trouble*. London, Routledge.

Byrne, D. (2006) *Social Exclusion*. Berkshire, Open University Press.

CACE (1967) Central Advisory Council on Education. *Children and Their Primary Schools* (The Plowden Report). London, HMSO.

Cameron, C. (2001) 'A review of the literature on men working in early childhood services'. *Gender, Work and Organization*. Vol. 8, No. 4, pp 430–453.

Cameron, C., Moss, P. and Owen, C. (1999) *Men in the Nursery*. London, Sage.

Canadian Teachers' Federation (2011) *The Voice of Canadian Teachers on Teaching and Learning*. Canada, Canadian Teachers' Federation.

Carrington, B. (2002) 'A quintessentially feminine domain? Student constructions of primary teaching as a career'. *Educational Studies*. Vol. 28, No. 3, pp 287–303.

Carrington, B. and Skelton, C. (2003) 'Re-thinking "role models": equal opportunities in teacher recruitment in England and Wales'. *Journal of Educational Policy*. May–June. Vol. 18, No. 3, pp 253–265.

Carrington, B. Tymms, P. and Merrell, C. (2005) 'Forget gender: whether a teacher is male or female doesn't matter', in *Teacher: Australian Council for Educational Research*, December, pp 32–34.

Carrington, B., Francis, B., Hutchings, M., Reid, S.C. and Hall, B.I. (2007) 'Does the gender of the teacher really matter? Seven-to-eight-year-olds' accounts of their interactions with their teachers'. *Educational Studies*. Vol. 33, No. 4, pp 397–413.

Clarke, K. (1985) 'Public and private children: infant education in the 1820s and 1830s', in C. Steedman, C. Urwin and V. Walkerdine (eds) *Language, Gender and Childhood*. London, Routledge & Kegan Paul.

Clay, J. and George, R. (1993) 'Moving beyond permutation: courses in teacher education', in I. Siraj-Blatchford (ed.) *'Race', 'Gender and the Education of Teachers*. Buckingham, Open University Press.

Clegg, A.B. (ed.) (1972) *The Changing Primary School: Its Problems and Priorities, a Statement by Teachers*. London, Chatto and Windus.

Cockburn, C. (1991) *In the Way of Women*. Basingstoke, Macmillan Education Ltd.

Coffey, A. and Acker, S. (1991) 'Girlies on the Warpath: addressing gender in initial teacher education'. *Gender and Education*. Vol. 3, No. 3, pp 249–261.

Coffey, A. and Delamont, S. (2000) *Feminism and the Classroom Teacher: Research, Praxis and Pedagogy*. London, Routledge Falmer.

Cole, M. (1999) 'Professional issues and initial teacher education'. *Education and Social Justice*. Vol. 2, No. 1, pp 64–65.

Coleman, W. (1990) 'Doing masculinity/doing theory', in J. Hearn and D. Morgan (eds) *Men Masculinities and Social Theory*. London, Unwin Hyman Ltd.

Connell, R.W. (1987) *Gender and Power*. Cambridge, Polity Press.

Connell, R.W. (1995) *Masculinities*. Cambridge, Polity Press.

Connell, R.W. (2000) *The Men and the Boys*. Oxford, Blackwell.

Connell, R.W. (2002) *Gender*. Cambridge, Polity Press.

Connolly, P. (1998) *Racism, Gender Identities and Young Children*. London, Routledge.

Convery, A. (1999) 'Listening to teachers' stories: are we sitting too comfortably?' *Qualitative Studies in Education*. Vol. 12, No. 2, pp 131–146.

Copelman, D. (1996) *London's Women Teachers*. London, Routledge.

Corbetta, P. (2003) (Trans. from Italian) *Social Research*. London, Sage.

Coulter, R. and Greig, C. (2008) 'The man question in teaching: an historical overview'. *The Alberta Journal of Educational Research*. Vol. 54, No. 4, Winter 2008, pp 420–431

Coulter, R. and McNay, M. (1993) 'Exploring men's experiences as elementary school teachers'. *Canadian Journal of Education*. Vol. 18, No. 4, pp 398–413.

Crozier, G. and Menter, I. (1993) 'The heart of the matter? Student teacher experiences in schools', in I. Siraj-Blatchford (ed.) *'Race', 'Gender and the-Education of Teachers*. Buckingham, Open University Press.

Cruickshank, V. (2012) 'Why men choose to become primary teachers'. Proceedings of the 2012 Australian Association for Research in Education Conference, 2–6 December 2012, University of Sydney, Australia, pp 1–10. ISSN 1324–9320.

Cuff, E. C., Sharrock, W.W. and Francis, D.W. (1990) *Perspectives in Sociology* (3rd edition). London, Routledge.

Cunningham, B. and Watson, L. (2002) 'Men in the lives of children: recruiting male teachers'. *Young Children*, November, pp 10–15.

Cunningham, P. (2000) 'The montessori phenomenon: gender and internationalism in early twentieth-century innovation', in M. Hilton and P. Hirsch (eds) *Practical Visionaries: Women, Education and Social Progress 1790–1930*. Harlow, Pearson Education Ltd.

Cunnison, S. (1994) 'Women teachers: career identity and perceptions of family constraints—changes over a recent decade'. *Research Papers in Education*. Vol. 9, pp 81–105.

Curtis, S.J. (1967) *History of Education in Great Britain* (7th edition). London, University Tutorial Press.

Cushman, P. (2005a) 'It's just not a real bloke's job: male teachers in the primary school'. *Asia-Pacific Journal of Teacher Education*. Vol. 33, No. 3, November, pp 321–338.

Cushman, P. (2005b) 'Let's hear it from the males: issues facing male primary school teachers'. *Teaching and Teacher Education*. Vol. 21, pp 227–240.

Cushman, P. (2005c) 'Will a revised code of practice change the practices of male teachers in their interactions with children?'. *New Zealand Journal of Teachers' Work*. Vol. 2, No. 2, pp 83–93.

Cushman, P. (2007) 'The male teacher shortage: a synthesis of research and worldwide strategies for addressing the shortage'. *KEDI Journal of Education Policy*. Vol. 4, No. 1, pp 79–98.

Cushman, P. (2009a) 'Three men teachers, three countries and three responses to the physical contact dilemma'. *International Journal of Education*. Vol. 1, No. 1, E7.

Cushman, P. (2009b) 'Lessons from Sweden: male teachers in the primary school'. *SET – Research Information for Teachers*. Vol. 2.

Cushman, P. (2010) 'Male primary school teachers: helping or hindering a move to gender equity?'. *Teaching and Teacher Education*. Vol. 26, pp 1211–1218.

Davies, B., Dormer, S., Gannon, S., Laws, C., Rocco, S., Taguchi, H.L. and Mccann, H. (2001) 'Becoming schoolgirls: the ambivalent project of subjectification'. *Gender and Education*. Vol. 13, No. 2, pp 167–182.

Davin, A. (1996) *Growing Up Poor*. London, Rivers Oram Press.

Day, C. (2000) 'Stories of change and professional development: the costs of commitment', in C. Day, A. Fernandez, T. Hauge and J. Moller (eds) *The Life and Work of Teachers*. London, Falmer.

De Beauvoir, S. (1988) *The Second Sex*. Harmondsworth, Penguin Books Ltd.

De Corse, C. and Vogtle, S. (1997) 'In a complex voice: the contradictions of male elementary teachers' career choice and professional identity'. *Journal of Teacher Education*. January–February, Vol. 48, No. 1, pp 37–46.

De Lion, H. and Widdowson Migniuolo, F. (eds) (1989) *Women Teachers: Issues and Experiences*. Milton Keynes, Open University Press.

Delamont, S. (1992) *Fieldwork in Educational Settings: Methods, Pitfalls and Perspectives*. London, Sage.

Delamont, S. (1999) 'Gender and the discourse of derision'. *Research Papers in Education*. Vol. 20, pp 99–126.

Delamont, S. (2003) *Feminist Sociology*. London, Sage.

Delamont, S. and Atkinson, P. (1995) *Fighting Familiarity*. New York, Hampton Press.

Denscombe, M. (1998) *The Good Research Guide*. Buckingham, Open University Press.

Department Foe Education and Skills (2000) *Statistics of Education: Teachers England and Wales*. London, The Stationery Office.

Department for Education (DFE) (2014) *School workforce in England: November 2013*. London, Crown

Dillabough, J. (1999) 'Gender politics and conceptions of the modern teacher: women, identity and professionalism'. *British Journal of Sociology of Education*. Vol. 20, No. 3, pp 373–394.

Dillabough, J. (2000) 'Women in teacher education: their struggles for inclusion as 'citizen-workers' in late modernity', in M. Arnot and J. Dillabough (eds) *Challenging Democracy: International Perspectives on Gender, Education and Citizenship*. London, Routledge Falmer.

Dixon, C. (1997) 'Pete's tool: identity and sex-play in the design and technology classroom'. *Gender and Education*. Vol. 9, No. 1, pp 89–104.

Donaldson, M. (1978) *Children's Minds*. Fontana, London.

Drews, D. (2005) Children's mathematical errors and misconceptions: perceptions on-the teacher's role, in A. Hansen et al. (eds) *Children's Errors in Mathematics*. Exeter, Learning Matters Ltd.

Duncan, J. (1996) 'For the sake of the children as the worth of the teacher? The gendered discourses of the New Zealand National Kindergarten Teachers' Employment Negotiations'. *Gender and Education*. Vol. 8, No. 2, pp 159–170.

Eddison, S. (2014) Men, your nurturing skills are sorely needed. *Times Educational Supplement*. Professional, pp 7–8, 7 March.

Edgoose, J. (2009) 'Radical hope and teaching: learning political agency from the politically disenfranchised'. *Educational Theory*. Vol. 59, No. 1, pp 105–121.

Edley, N. and Wetherell, M. (1995) *Men in Perspective*. Hertfordshire, Prentice-Hall/Harvester Wheatsheaf.

Education Canada (2012) 'False accusations: a growing fear in the classroom'. *Education Canada*. Vol. 53, No. 5, 3 July 2012. www.cea-ace.ca. (1 October 2014).

Eng, J. (2004) *Male elementary teachers: Where are they? Educational Insights* 8(3) ccfi.educ.ubc.ca/publication/insights/v08n03/articles/eng.html (1 October 2014).

England, J. (1973). *Forever England*. London, Tom Stacey Ltd.

Epstein, D. (1993) *Changing Classroom Cultures*. Stoke-on-Trent, Trentham Books.

Epstein, D. (1997) 'Boyz' own stories: masculinities and sexualities in schools'. *Gender and Education*. Vol. 9, No. 1, pp 105–115.

Epstein, D. and Johnson, R. (1998). *Schooling Sexualities*. Buckingham, Open University Press.

Epstein, D., Elwood, J., Hey, V. and Mans, J. (1998) *Failing Boys?* Buckingham, Open University Press.

Evetts, J. (1989) 'The internal labour market for primary teachers', in S. Acker (ed.) *Teachers, Gender and Careers*. Lewes, Falmer Press.

Exley, S. (2014) "Teacher supply is failing", warns Institute of Education director'. *Times Educational Supplement*, 02 December 2014. https://news.tes.co.uk/b /news/2014/12/02/school-direct-39-simply-does-not-work-39-academic-claims .aspx (12 December 2014).

Faludi, S. (1992) *The Undeclared War against Women*. London, Chatto and Windus

Farquhar, S. (1997) 'Are male teachers really necessary?' Paper presented at the *NZARE Conference*, Auckland, NZ, December, pp 1–8.

Fielding, N. (1996) 'Qualitative interviewing', in N. Gilbert (ed.) *Researching Social Life*. London, Sage.

Flax, J. (1995) 'Postmodernism and gender relations in feminist theory', in M. Blair and J. Holland with S. Sheldon (eds) *Identity and Diversity: Gender and the Experience of Education*. Avon, Open University Press.

Foucault, M. (1978) *The Will to Knowledge*. London, Penguin.

Fraser, H. and Yeomans, R. (1999) 'Stereotyped minority or endangered species? Male trainee teachers' experiences of working in primary schools'. Paper presented at *BERA*, University of Brighton, 9–11 September.

Freidus, H. (1992) 'Men in a woman's world: a study of male second career teachers in elementary schools'. Paper presented at the annual meeting of the American Educational Research Association, San Francisco.

Freire, P. (1995) *Paulo Freire at the Institute*. Essex, Institute of Education, University of London, Southend on Sea, Formara Ltd.

Freire, P. (1996) *Letters to Cristina*. New York, Routledge.

Freire, P. (2007) *Pedagogy of Hope* (2nd edition). New York, Continuum.

Gaffin, J. and Thoms, D. (1993) *Caring and Sharing. The Centenary History of the Women's Co-operative Guild*. Nottingham, Nottingham Printers Ltd.

Garner, R. (2014) 'Even excellent schools don't help poor catch up with rich'. *The Independent*. p. 22, 23 September, London.

General Teaching Council for Wales (2003) *Action Plan for Teacher Recruitment and Retention in Wales*, September.

Giardiello, P. (2014) *Pioneers in Early Childhood Education*. Routledge, New York.

Gill, J. and Starr, K. (2000) 'Sauce for the goose? Deconstructing the boys-in-education push'. *Discourse: Studies in the Cultural Politics in Education*. Vol. 21, No. 3, pp 323–333.

Giroux, H. (1992) *Border Crossings*. London, Routledge.

Glaser, B. and Strauss, A. (1967) *The Discovery of Grounded Theory: Strategies for Qualitative Research*. New York, Aldine Publishing Co.

Goffman, E. (1959) *The Social Presentation of Self in Everyday Life*. New York, Anchor Books.

Goldstrom, J. M. (1972) *Education-Elementary Education, 1780–1900*. Newton Abbot, David and Charles.

Goodson, I. (2000) 'Professional knowledge and the teacher's life and work', in C. Day, A. Fernandez, T. Hauge and J. Moller (eds) *The Life and Work of Teachers*. London, Falmer.

Goodson, I. and Sikes, P. (2001) *Life History Research in Educational Settings*. Buckingham, Open University Press.

Goseden, P. H. J. H. (1972) *The Evolution of a Profession*. Oxford, Basil Blackwell.

Gosse, D. (2011) 'Race, sexual orientation, culture and male teacher role models: will any teacher do as long as they are good?' *The Journal of Men's Studies*, Vol. 19, No. 2 (Spring), pp 1–17. http://go.galegroup.com/ (29 July 2014).

Grace, G. (1987) 'Teachers and the state in Britain: a changing relation', in M. Lawn and G. Grace (eds) *Teachers: The Culture and Politics of Work*. London, Falmer Press.

Grace, G. (1994) *Education and the City. Theory, History and Contemporary Practice*. London, Routledge and Kegan Paul.

Grant, R. (1989) 'Women teachers' career pathways: towards an alternative model of career', in S. Acker (ed.) *Teachers, Gender and Careers*. Lewes, Falmer Press.

Griffiths, M. (1998) *Educational Research for Social Justice*. Buckingham, Open University Press.

Gubrium, J. and Holstein, J. (1997) *The New Language of Qualitative Method*. New York, Oxford University Press, Inc.

Gutterman, D. (1994) 'Postmodernism and the interrogation of masculinity', in H. Brod and M. Kaufman (eds) *Theorizing Masculinities*. London, Sage.

Hahn, H. J. (1998) *Education and Society in Germany*. Oxford, Berg.

Hall, C. (1995) *White, Male and Middle Class*. Cambridge, Polity Press.

Hall, S. (1997) 'The spectacle of the other', in S. Hall (ed.) *Representation: Cultural Representations and Signifying Practices*. London, Sage/Open University.

Hall, D. and Langton B. (2006) *Perception of the Status of Teachers*. New Zealand, Ministry of Education.

Hamann, G. (2013) *German Government Campaigns for More Male Kindergarten Teachers*. Bonn, Deutsche Welle Akademie.

Hammersley, M. (2002) 'Ethnography and disputes over validity', in G. Walford (ed.) *Debates and Developments in Ethnographic Methodology*. Oxford, Elsevier Science Ltd.

Hammersley, M. (2003) 'Recent radical criticism of interview studies: any implications for the sociology of education?' *British Journal of the Sociology of Education*. Vol. 24, No. 1, pp 119–126.

Hammersley, M. and Atkinson, P. (1990) *Ethnography: Principles in Practice*. London, Routledge.

Hansen, P. and Mulholland, J. (2005) 'Caring and elementary teaching: the concerns of male beginning teachers'. *Journal of Teacher Education*, Vol. 56, No. 2, pp 119–131 (March/April) www.questia.com

Hargreaves, A. (1994) *Changing Teachers, Changing Times: Teachers' Work and Culture in the Postmodern Age*. London, Cassell.

Harris, S. (2010) 'Number of men applying to be primary school teachers soars by more than 50% thanks to recession'. Mail online, pp 1–5.

Harnett, P. and Lee, J. (2001) 'Nurturing the boys: a gendered issue?' Paper presented at *BERA*, University of Leeds, 13–15 September.

Harris, J. (1993) *Private Lives, Public Spirit: Britain 1870–1914*. London, Penguin.

Healy, K. (2000) *Social Work Practices*. London, Sage.

Hearn, J. (2002) 'Men, fatherhood and the state: national and transnational perspectives', in B. Hobson (ed.) *Making Men into Fathers Men, Masculinities, and the Social Politics of Fatherhood*. Cambridge, Cambridge University Press, pp 245–272.

Henry, J. (2000) 'A game for young hearts'. *The Times Educational Supplement*, p 15, 12 May.

Hobson, B. (ed.) (2002) *Making Men into Fathers*. Cambridge, Cambridge University Press.

Helliwell, G. (2013) 'Few men taking up teaching. Tell us what you think'. *Bay of Plenty Times*. New Zealand Herald www.nzherald.co.nz/bay-of-plenty-times/news/article.cfm?c_id... (9 March 2013).

Hepburn, H. (2013) 'Anxious times for male teachers in primary'. *Times Educational Supplement*. Professional, pp 1–6, 16 February.

Hey, V. (1997a) 'Northern accent and southern comfort: subjectivity and social class', in P. Mahony and C. Zmroczek (eds) *Class Matters: Working –Class' Women's Perspectives on Social Class*. London, Taylor & Francis.

Hey, V. (1997b) *The Company She Keeps*. Buckingham, Open University Press.

Hey, V. (2003) 'Joining the club? Academia and working-class femininities'. *Gender and Education*. Vol. 15, No. 3, pp 319–335.

Hilton, M. and Hirsch, P. (2000) 'Introduction', in M. Hilton and P. Hirsch (eds) *Practical Visionaries: Women, Education and Social Progress 1790–1930*. Harlow, Pearson Education Ltd.

Hobson, B. and Morgan, D. (2002) 'Introduction: making men into fathers', in B. Hobson (ed.) *Making Men into Fathers*. Cambridge, Cambridge University Press.

hooks, b. (1984) *Feminist Theory: From Margin to Center*. Boston, South End Press.

hooks, b. (1989) *Talking Back*. Boston, South End Press.

hooks, b. (1994) *Teaching to Transgress*. London, Routledge.

hooks, b. (2000) *Where We Stand: Class Matters*. London, Routledge.

Van-Horn, J., Schaufell, W., Greenglass, E. and Burke, R. (1997) 'A Canadian-Dutch comparison of teachers' burnout'. *Psychological Reports*. Vol. 81, pp 371–382.

Hoyle, E. (1969) *The Role of the Teacher*. London, Routledge and Kegan Paul.

Huggett, F. G. (1986) *Teachers*. London, Weidenfeld & Nicolson.

Hughes, C. (2002) *Women's Contemporary Lives*. London, Routledge.

Hutchings, M., Dalgety, J. and Ross, A. (2002) 'Gender factors in teacher retention'. Paper presented at *BERA*, University of Exeter, 12–14 September.

Hutchings, M., Menter, I., Ross, A., Thompson, D. and Bedford, D. (2000) *Teacher Retention in Six London Boroughs*. London, TTA.

Hutchings. M. (2002) 'A representative profession? Gender issues', in M. Johnson and J. Hallgarten (eds) *From Victims of Change to Agents of Change*. London, IPPR.

Jackson, D. and Marsden, D. (1962) *Education and the Working Class*. London, Routledge, Kegan and Paul.

Jackson, S. (1998) 'Breaking out of the binary trap: boys' underachievement, schooling, and gender relations', in D. Epstein, J. Elwood, V. Hey, and J. Maw (eds) *Failing Boys: Issues in Gender and Achievement*. Buckinghamshire, Open University Press.

Jayaratne, T. E. and Stewart, A. J. (1995) 'Quantitative and qualitative methods in the social sciences: feminist issues and practical strategies', in J. Holland and M. Blair with S. Sheldon (eds) *Debates and Issues in Feminist Research and Pedagogy*. Avon, Open University Press.

Jenson, J. and Brushwood Rose, C. (2003) 'Women@Work: listening to gendered relations of power in teachers' talk about new technologies'. *Gender and Education*. Vol. 15, No. 2, pp 169–181.

Johnson, M. (2002) 'Making teacher supply boom-proof', in M. Johnson and J. Hallgarten (eds) *From Victims of Change to Agents of Change*. London, IPPR.

Johnston, J., Mckeown, E. and Mcewan, A. (1999) 'Choosing primary teaching as a career: the perspectives of males and females in training'. *Journal of Education for Teaching*. Vol. 25, No. 1, pp 55–64.

Jones, D. (1990) 'The genealogy of the urban schoolteacher', in S. Ball (ed.) *Foucault and Education*. London, Routledge.

Jones, D. (2006) 'The "right kind of man": the ambiguities of regendering the key stage one environment'. *Sex Education*. Vol. 6, No. 1, February, pp 61–76.

Jones, K. (1985) 'The national union of teachers (England and Wales)', in M. Lawn (ed.) *The Politics of Teacher Union*. Kent, Croom Helm Ltd.

Jones, O. (2011) *Chavs. The Demonization of the Working Class*. London, Verso.

Jones, R. and Jenkins, A. (2012) *Call Me MISTER: The Re-Emergence of African American Male Teachers in South Carolina*. Charleston, Advantage Media Group.

Kane, R. and Mallon, M. (2006) *Perceptions of Teachers and Teaching*. New Zealand, Ministry of Education.

Kaufman, M. (1994) 'Men, feminism and men's contradictory experiences of power', in H. Brod and M. Kaufman (eds) *Theorizing Masculinities*. London, Sage.

Kean, H. (1990) *Deeds Not Words*. London, Pluto Press.

Kenway, J. (1990) 'Education and the right's discursive politics', in S. Ball (ed.) *Foucault and Education*. London, Routledge.

Kenway, J. (1995) 'Feminist theories of the state: to be or not to be?', in M. Blair and J. Holland with S. Sheldon (eds) *Identity and Diversity: Gender and the Experience of Education*. Avon, Open University Press.

Kenway, J. and Bullen, E. (2001) *Consuming Children*. Buckingham, Open University Press.

Kimmel, M. (1994) 'Masculinity as homophobia', in H. Brod and M. Kaufman (eds) *Theorizing Masculinities*. London, Sage.

King, J. (1998) *Uncommon Caring: Learning from Men Who Teach Young Children*. New York, Teachers College Press.

King, R. (1984) 'The man in the wendy house: researching infants' schools', in R.G. Burgess (ed.) *The Research Process in Educational Settings: Ten Case Studies*. Lewes, Falmer Press.

King, J. (2004) 'The (im)possibility of gay teachers for young children'. *Theory into Practice*, Vol. 43, No. 2, pp 122–127.

Kirsch, G. (1999) *Ethical Dilemmas in Feminist Research*. Albany, NY, SUNY Press.

Labrinth (2014) *My best teacher*. TES, p 29, 22 August.

Lahelma, E. (2000) 'Lack of male teachers: a problem for students or teachers?' *Pedagogy, Culture and Society*. Vol. 8, No. 2, pp 173–186.

Lather, P. (1992) 'Post-critical pedagogies: a feminist reading', in C. Luke and J. Gore (eds) *Feminisms and Critical Pedagogy*. New York, Routledge.

Lather, P. (1995) 'Feminist perspectives on empowering research methodologies', in J. Holland and M. Blair with S. Sheldon (eds) *Debates and Issues in Feminist Research and Pedagogy*. Avon, Open University Press.

Lawn, M. (1987) *Servants of the State: The Contested Control of Teaching, 1900–1930*. London, Falmer Press.

Lawn, M. (1988) 'Skill in schoolwork: work relations in the primary school', in J. Ozga (ed.) *Schoolwork*. Milton Keynes, Open University Press.

Lea, M. and West, L. (1995) 'Motives, mature students, the self and narrative', in J. Swindells (ed.) *The Uses of Autobiography*. London, Taylor & Francis.

Leake, J. (2001) 'Nursery boys "devalued" by female teachers'. *The Sunday Times*, p 9, 9 June London.

Lee, C. (2006) *Language for Learning Mathematics*. Berkshire, Oxford University Press.

Lee, J. (1987) 'Pride and prejudice: teacher, class and an inner-city infants school', in M. Lawn and G. Grace (eds) *Teachers: The Culture and Politics of Work*. Lewes, Falmer Press.

Lees, S. (1993) *Sugar and Spice*. London, Penguin Books Ltd.

Leonard, D. (1989) 'Gender and initial teacher training', in H. De Lion and F. Widdowson Migniuolo (eds) *Women Teachers: Issues and Experiences*. Milton Keynes, Open University Press.

Leonard, D. (1994) 'Transforming the household: mature women students and access to higher education', in S. Davies, C. Lubelska, and J. Quinn (eds) *Changing the Subject*. London, Taylor & Francis.

Lett, D. (2013) *Only Male Teachers Need Apply: New Hiring Policy Based on Speculation, Not Real Data*. Winnipeg Free Press www.winnipegfreepress.com (21 February 2013).

Lewis, P. (2000) 'An enquiry into male wastage from primary ITE courses at a University College and success indictors for retention'. Paper presented at *Regional Issues in Teacher Supply and Retention Conference*. University of North London, 19 January.

Lewis, P. (2001) 'Young, male and absent'. Paper presented at *Teacher Supply and Retention: Emerging Issues Conference*, University of North London, 12 June.

Lewis, P. and Weston, C. (2002) 'Creating boyzones'. Paper presented at *BERA*, University of Exeter, 12–14 September.

Lillis, T. (2001) *Student Writing, Access, Regulation, Desire*. London, Routledge.

Limond, D. (2002) 'Like the spirit of the army: fascistic discourse and the national association of schoolmasters, 1919–1939', in J. Goodman and J. Martin (eds) *Gender, Colonialism and Education*. London, Frank Cass Publications.

Lingard, B. and Douglas, P. (1999) *Men Engaging Feminism*. Buckingham, Open University Press.

Littlewood, M. (1995) 'The makers of men', in L. Dawtrey, J. Holland and M. Hammer with S. Sheldon (eds) *Equality and Inequality in Education Policy*. Avon, Open University Press.

Lofgren, H. (2012) 'Questioning the narrative of more male teachers as the easy solution to problems in Swedish schools', in I. Goodson, A. Loveless and D. Stephens (eds). *Explorations in Narrative Research*. Rotterdam, Sense Publishers, pp 71–82.

Loftland, J. and Loftland, L. (1995) *Analyzing Social Settings, A Guide to Qualitative Observation and Analysis* (3rd edition). Belmont, CA, Wadsworth Publishing Company.

Love, K. (2012) 'Alberta facing shortage of male teachers in rural areas'. *Calgary Herald* (30 August). www.calgaryherald.com/news/Alberta... male+teachers+rural.../story.html (3 August 2014).

Lown, J. (1995) 'Feminist perspectives', in M. Blair and J. Holland with S. Sheldon (eds) *Identity and Diversity: Gender and the Experience of Education*. Avon, Open University Press.

Luke, C. and Gore, J. (eds) (1992) *Feminisms and Critical Pedagogy*. New York, Routledge.

Mac An Ghaill, M.. (1994) *The Making of Men: Masculinities, Sexualities and Schooling*. Buckingham, Open University Press.

Mac An Ghaill, M. (1995) '(In)visibility: 'race', sexuality and masculinity in the school context', in M. Blair and J. Holland with S. Sheldon (eds) *Identity and Diversity: Gender and the Experience of Education*. Avon, Open University Press.

McCann, P. and Young, F. A. (1982) *Samuel Wilderspin and the Infant School Movement*. London, Croom Helm.

McGrath, K. and Sinclair, M. (2013) 'More male primary-school teachers? Social benefits for boys *and* girls'. *Gender and Education*. Vol. 25, No. 5, pp 531–547.

Maclure, J.S. (1965). *Educational Documents: England and Wales 1816–1963*. London, Chapman and Hall.

Maguire, M. (1997) 'Missing links: working-class women of Irish descent', in P. Mahony and C. Zmroczek (eds) *Class Matters: Working-Class' Women's Perspectives on Social Class*. London, Taylor & Francis.

Maguire, M. (1999) 'A touch of class: inclusion and exclusion in initial teacher education'. *Inclusive Education*. Vol. 3, No. 1, pp 13–26.

Maher, F.A. (2001) 'Women's studies in England: mature women students and their educational vision'. *Gender and Education*. Vol. 13, No. 1, pp 7–23.

Mahony, P. (1985) *Schools for the Boys*. London, Hutchinson.

Mahony, P. and Hextall, I. (2000) *Reconstructing Teaching: Standards, Performance and Accountability*. London, Routledge Falmer.

Mallozzi, C. and Campbell Galman, S. (2014) 'Guys and "the rest of us": tales of gendered aptitude and experience in educational carework'. *Gender and Education*. Vol. 26, No. 3, pp 262–279.

Martin, J. (1999) 'Gender and education', in I. Grosvenor and D. Matheson (eds) *An Introduction to the Study of Education*. London, Fulton.

Martin, J. (2000) 'Working for the people? Mrs Bridge Adams and the London School Board, 1897–1904'. *History of Education*. Vol. 29, No. 1, pp 49–62.

Martin J. and Goodman, J. (2004) *Women and Education 1800–1980*. Basingstoke, Palgrave Macmillan.

Martino, W. (2008) Male teachers as role models: addressing issues of masculinity, pedagogy and the re-masculinization of schooling'. *Curriculum Inquiry*, Vol. 38, No. 2, pp 189–223.

Martino, W. (2009). 'The lure of hegemonic masculinity: investigating the dynamics of gender relations in two male elementary school teachers' lives'. *International Journal of Qualitative Studies in Education*. Vol. 21, No. 6, pp 575–603.

Martino, W., Lingard, B. and Mills, M. (2004) 'Issues in boys' education: a question of teachers' threshold knowledges?' *Gender and Education*. Vol. 16, No. 4, pp 235–254.

May, T. (1999) *The Victorian Schoolroom*. Buckinghamshire, Shire Pub. Ltd.

May, T. (2001) *Social Research* (3rd edition). Buckinghamshire, Open University Press.

Mayntz, R., Holm, K. and Hoebner, P. (1976) *Introduction to Empirical Sociology* (Trans. From German). Middlesex, Penguin Books Ltd.

Mcgrath, K. and Sinclair, M. (2013) 'More male primary-school teachers? Social benefits for boys and girls'. *Gender Education*. Vol. 25, No. 5, pp 531–547.

Mead, G.H. (1934) *Mind, Self and Society*. Chicago, Chicago University Press.

Measor, L. and Sikes, P.J. (1992) *Gender and Schools*. London, Cassell.

Medhurst, A. (2000) 'If anywhere: class identifications and cultural studies academics', in S.R. Munt (ed.) *Cultural Studies and the Working Class*. London, Cassell.

Messner, M. (1992) *Power at Play. Sport and the Problem of Masculinity*. Boston, Beacon.

Miller, J. (1996) *School for Women*. London, Virago.

Mills, M. (2001) *Challenging Violence in Schools*. Buckingham, Open University Press.

Mills, M., Martino, W. and Lingard, B. (2004) 'Attracting, recruiting and retaining male teachers: policy issues in the male teacher debate'. *British Journal of Sociology of Education*. Vol. 25, No. 3, pp 355–369.

Mills, S. (2003) *Michel Foucault*. London, Routledge.

Mirza, H. (1995) 'Life in the classroom', in J. Holland and M. Blair, with S. Sheldon (eds) *Debates and Issues in Feminist Research and Pedagogy*. Avon, Open University Press.

Mirza, H. (1998) 'Same voices, same lives?: revisiting black feminist standpoint epistemology', in P. Connolly and B. Troyna (eds) *Researching Racism in Education*. Buckingham, Open University Press.

Mistry, M. and Sood, K. (2013) 'Why are there still so few men within early years in primary schools: views from male trainee teachers and male leaders'. *Education 3-13: International Journal of Primary, Elementary and Early Years Education*. pp 1–13.

Mitchell, C. and Weber, S. (1999) *Reinventing Ourselves as Teachers: Beyond Nostalgia*. London, Falmer Press.

Moi, T. (1999) *What Is a Woman?* Oxford, Oxford University Press.

Montecinos, C. and Nielson, L. (2004) 'Male elementary pre-service teachers' gendering of teaching'. *Multicultural Perspectives*. Vol. 6, No. 2, pp 3–9.

Morgan, D. (2002) 'Epilogue', in Hobson, B. (ed.) *Making Men into Fathers*. Cambridge, Cambridge University Press.

Moriarty, V. (1998) *Margaret McMillan: 'I Learn to Succour the Helpless'*. Nottingham, Educational Heretics Press.

Morley, L. (1997) 'A class of one's own: women, social class and the academy', in P. Mahony and C. Zmroczek (eds) *Class Matters: Working-Class Women's Perspectives on Social Class*. London, Taylor & Francis.

Mulholland, J. and Hansen, P. (2003) 'Men who become primary school teachers: an early portrait'. *Asia-Pacific Journal of Teacher Education*. Vol. 31, No. 3, November, pp 213–224.

Munro, P. (1998) *Subject to Fiction*. Buckingham, Open University Press.

Munt, S.R. (ed.) (2000) *Cultural Studies and the Working Class*. London, Cassell.

National Parents Organisation Canadian Study (2014) *13% of Male Teachers 'Wrongly accused of inappropriate contact with students'*. https:// nationalparentsorganization.org/blog/10449-canadian-study-13 (3 August 2014).

National Post Canada (2013) *Fight the stigma against male teachers*. www.fullcomment.nationalpost.com/.../national-post-editorial-board-fight-the-sti... (19 February 2013).

Neal, S. (1998) 'Struggles with the research self: reconciling feminist approaches to antiracist research', in P. Connolly and B. Troyna (eds) *Researching Racism in Education*. Buckingham, Open University Press.

Nelson, B. (2003) 'Male primary teachers'. *Curriculum and Leadership Journal*. www.earlychildhoodaustralia.org.au/ec0403_male_primary_teachers.pdf (1 January 2003).

Nelson, B. (2008) *Finland: Incentives for Male Teacher Trainees?* (Friday, 4 July 2008) World News.

Nelson, B. (2013) *Schools Attracting More Male Teachers in New Zealand*. www.menteach.org/news/schools_attracting_more_male_teachers Schools attracting more male teachers in New Zealand. (11 April 2013) World News.

Nelson, B. and Shamani-Jeffrey, S. (2010) *Men in Your Teacher Preparation Program: Five Strategies to Recruit and Retain Them*. NAEYC, expanded from Young Children, May, pp 36–41.

Newson Report (1963) *Report of the Central Advisory Committee for Education, (England): Half Our Future*. London, DES.

Nias, J. (1988) 'What it means to feel like a teacher', in J. Ozga (ed.) *Schoolwork*. Milton Keynes, Open University Press.

Nias, J. (1989) *Primary Teachers Talking*. London, Routledge.

NUT (1980) *Promotion and the Woman Teacher*. Manchester, Equal Opportunities Commission, NUT.

Organisation for Economic Cooperation and Development (OECD) (2003) *Attracting, Developing and Retaining Effective Teachers*. Country Background Report for Finland (June) http://www.oecd.org/edu/school/5328720.pdf (28 October 2014).

Organisation for Economic Cooperation and Development (OECD) (2005) *Teachers Matter: Attracting, Developing and Retaining Effective Teachers*. Paris, OECD Publishing. http://www.oecd.org/education/school/34990905.pdf (23 December 2014).

Organisation for Economic Cooperation and Development (OECD) (2012) *What Students Know and Can Do*. http://www.oecd.org/pisa/keyfindings/pisa-2012 -results.htm (28 October 2014).

Ofsted (1996) *Subjects and Standards*. London, HMSO.

Oram, A. (1989) 'A master should not serve under a mistress: women and men teachers 1900–1970', in S. Acker (ed.) *Teachers, Gender and Careers*. Lewes, Falmer Press.

Ord, F. and Quigley, J. (1985) 'Anti-sexism as good educational practice: what can feminists realistically achieve?' in G. Weiner (ed.) *Just a Bunch of Girls*. Milton Keynes, Open University Press.

Orner, M. (1992) 'Interrupting the calls for student voice in "liberatory" education: a feminist poststructuralist perspective', in C. Luke and J. Gore (eds) *Feminisms and Critical Pedagogy*. New York, Routledge.

Osler, A. (1997) *The Education and Careers of Black Teachers*. Buckingham, Open University Press.

Osler, A. and Vincent, K. (2003) *Girls and Exclusion*. London, RoutledgeFalmer.

Ousley, H. (1998) 'Presidential address, north of England education conference'. *Primary Teaching Studies*. Vol. 10, No. 1, p 1. Stoke on Trent, Trentham Books.

Ouston, J. (1999) 'Inner-city life a double burden for the poor'. *Times Educational Supplement*, p 25, 1 October, London.

Oyler, C., Jennings, G. and Lozada, P. (2001) 'Silenced gender': the construction of a male primary educator'. *Teaching and Teacher Education*. Vol. 17, pp 367–379.

Ozga, J. and Lawn, M. (1981) *Teachers, Professionalism and Class: A Study of Organised Teachers*. Lewes, Falmer Press.

Paechter, C. (1998). *Educating the Other*. London, Falmer.

Parker, A. (1996) 'The construction of masculinity within boys' physical education'. *Gender and Education*. Vol. 8, No. 2, pp 141–157.

Parr, J. (1997) 'Women, education and class: the relationship between class background and research', in P. Mahony and C. Zmroczek (eds) *Class Matters: 'Working-Class' Women's Perspectives on Social Class*. London, Taylor & Francis.

Parr, M. and Gosse, D. (2011) 'The perils of being a male primary/junior teacher: vulnerability and accusations of inappropriate contact with students'. *McGill Journal of Education*. Vol. 46, No. 3, Fall, pp 379–393.

Parsons, J. and Larson, N. (2004–5) *Kindness, Warning, Precept and Praise: The Fading Impact of Male Teachers*. Alberta Teachers' Association, Volume 85 2004–05, Number 3.

Partington, G. (1976) *Women Teachers in the Twentieth Century*. Windsor, NFER.

Patin, G. (2010) 'No male teachers in quarter of primary schools'. *The Telegraph*, 3 September http://www.telegraph.co.uk/education/primaryeducation/7978146 /No-male-teachers-in-quarter-of-primary-schools.html (25 October 2014).

Paton, G. (2013) *Just a Fifth of New Primary School Teachers Are Men*. http://www.telegrah.co.uk/education/educationnews/10475749/just-a-fifth (26 November 2013).

Peeters, J. (2007) 'Including men in early childhood education: insights from the European experience'. *New Zealand Research in Early Childhood Education*. Vol. 10, pp 15–24.

Peltzman, B.R. (1998) *Pioneers of Early Childhood Education*. Westport, CT, Greenwood Press.

Pepperell, S. and Smedley, S. (1998) 'Calls for more men in primary teaching: problematizing the issues'. *International Journal of Inclusive Education*. Vol. 2, No. 4, pp 341–357.

Pickering, M. (2001) *Stereotyping: The Politics of Representation*. Basingstoke, Palgrave.

Plummer, G. (2000) *Failing Working-Class Girls*. Stoke-on-Trent, Trentham Books.

Plummer, K. (1983) *Documents of Life: An Introduction to the Problems and Literature of a Humanistic Method*. London, Allen and Unwin.

Pollard, A. (ed.) (2010) *Professionalism and Pedagogy. A Contemporary Opportunity*. London, TLRP.

Powney, J., Wilson, V., Hall, S., Davidson, J., Kirk, S., Edward, S., Mirza, H.S. (2003) *Teachers' Careers: the Impact of Age, Disability, Ethnicity, Gender and Sexual Orientation*. London, DfES. Research Paper 488.

Pratt-Adams, S. and Burn, E. (2004) 'Every good boy deserves football', in W. Mitchell. R. Bunton and E. Green (eds) *Young People, Risk and Leisure*. Basingstoke, Palgrave Macmillan Ltd.

Pratt-Adams, S., Maguire, M. and Burn, E. (2010) *Changing Urban Education*. London, Continuum.

Prevost, K. (2011) 'The shortage of male primary school teachers and the "not-so-hidden" consequences'. *BU Journal of Graduate Studies in Education*. Vol. 3, No. 2, pp 39–43.

Pulsford, M. (2014) 'Constructing men who teach: research into care and gender as productive of the male primary teacher'. *Gender and Education*. Vol. 26, No. 3, pp 215–231.

Purvis, J. (1989) *Hard Lessons: The Lives and Education of Working-Class Women in Nineteenth-Century England*. Cambridge, Polity Press.

Rakhit, A. (1998) 'Silenced voices: life history as an approach to the study of South Asian women teachers', in P. Connolly and B. Troyna (eds) *Researching Racism in Education*. Buckingham, Open University Press.

Ramazanoglu, C. and Holland, J. (2002) *Feminist Methodology*. London, Sage.

Raphael Reed, L. (1995) 'Reconceptualising equal opportunities in the 1990s: a study of radical teacher culture in transition', in M.Griffiths, and B. Troyna (eds) *Antiracism, Culture and Social Justice in Education*. Stoke-on-Trent, Trentham Books.

Raphael Reed, L. (1998) 'Zero tolerance; gender performance and school failure', in D.Epstein, J. Elwood, V. Hey, and J. Mans (eds) *Failing Boys?* Buckingham, Open University Press.

Raphael Reed, L. (1999) 'Troubling boys and disturbing discourses on masculinity and schooling: a feminist exploration of current debates and interventions concerning boys in school'. *Gender and Education*. Vol. 11, No. 1, pp 99–110.

Reay, D. (1990) 'Working with boys'. *Gender and Education*. Vol. 2, No. 3, pp 269–282.

Reay, D. (1998) *Class Work*. London, UCL Press.

Reay, D. (2001) 'The paradox of contemporary femininities in education: combining fluidity with fixity', in B. Francis and C. Skelton (eds) *Investigating Gender*. Buckingham, Open University Press.

Reay, D. (2003) 'A risky business? Mature working-class women students and access to higher education'. *Gender and Education*. Vol. 15, No. 3, pp 301–335.

Ribbins, P. (1990) 'Teachers as professionals: towards a redefinition', in R. Morris (ed.) *Central and Local Control of Education after the Education Reform Act of 1988*. Harlow, Longman Group Ltd.

Riddell, S., Tett, L., Burns, C., Ducklin, A., Ferrie, J., Staffford, A. and Winterton, M. (2005) *Gender Balance of the Teaching Workforce in Publicly Funded Schools*. www.scotedreview.org.uk/pdf/217.pdf (3 August 2014).

Robinson, W. (2000) 'Sarah Jane Bannister and teacher training in transition 1870–1918', in M. Hilton, and P. Hirsch (eds) *Practical Visionaries: Women, Education and Social Progress 1790–1930*. Essex: Pearson Education Limited.

Robinson, M. (2010) *Adam Buckingham, of New Zealand, Receives Grant to Recruit Male Teachers.* www.menteach.org/news/adam_buckingham_of_new_zealand _receives_gr... (29 October 2010).

Russell, K. (2013) 'The gender divide: men in ECE'. *New Zealand Education Review.* www.educationreview.co.nz/nz-teacher/.../the-gender-divide-men-in -ece/ (31 January 2013).

Sagan, A. (2013) 'New Canadian *teachers head abroad amid tight job market*'. *CBS News.* http://www.cbc.ca/news/canada/new-canadian-teachers-head-abroad -amid-tight-job-market (24 February 2014).

Sahlsberg, P. (2010) 'The secret to Finland's success: education teachers'. *Stanford Center for Opportunity Policy in Education – Research brief*, September, pp 1–8.

Salisbury, J. and Jackson, D. (1996) *Challenging Macho Values: Practical Ways of Working with Adolescent Boys.* London, Taylor & Francis.

Sargent, P. (2000) 'Real men or real teachers?' *Men and Masculinities.* Vol. 2, No. 4, April, pp 410–433.

Savage, M. (2000) *Class Analysis and Social Transformation.* Buckingham, Open University Press.

Sewell, T. (1997) *Black Masculinities and Schooling.* Trentham, Stoke on Trent.

Sewell, T. (2000) 'Identifying the pastoral needs of African-Caribbean students: a case of critical antiracism'. *Education and Social Justice.* Vol. 3, No. 1, Autumn, pp 17–26.

Sharp, C., Kendell, L. and Schagen, I. (2003) 'Different for girls? An exploration of the impact of playing for success'. *Educational Research.* Vol. 45, No. 3, pp 309–324.

Showunmi, V. (1995) 'Surely you're imagining things', in V. Showunmi, and D. Constantine-Simms (eds) *Teachers for the Future.* Stoke-on-Trent, Trentham.

Sikes, P. (1991) 'Nature took its course? Student teachers and gender awareness'. *Gender and Education.* Vol. 3, No. 2, pp 145–162.

Sikes, P. (1993) 'Gender and teacher education', in I. Siraj-Blatchford (ed.) *'Race', Gender and the Education of Teachers.* Buckingham, Open University Press.

Silverman, D. (2000) *Doing Qualitative Research.* London, Sage.

Simpson, R. (2009) *Men in Caring Occupations: Doing Gender Differently.* Basingstoke, Palgrave McMillan.

Siraj-Blatchford, I. (ed.) (1993) *'Race', Gender and the Education of Teachers.* Buckingham, Open University Press.

Siraj-Blatchford, I. (1995) 'Racialised and gendered discourses in teacher education', in L. Dawtrey, J. Holland and M. Hammer with S. Sheldon (eds) *Equality and Inequality in Education Policy.* Avon, Open University Press.

Siraj-Blatchford, I., Sylva, K., Muttock, S., Gilden, R. and Bell, D. (2002) *Researching Effective Pedagogy in the Early Years.* London, Department for Education and Skills, Research Report, Brief No:356 (June).

Skeggs, B. (1997) *Formations of Class and Gender.* London, Sage.

Skelton, C. (ed.) (1989) *Whatever Happens to Little Women.* Milton, Keynes Open University Press.

Skelton, C. (1991) 'A study of the career perspectives of male teachers of young children'. *Gender and Education.* Vol. 3, pp 279–289.

Skelton, C. (1994) 'Sex, male teachers and young children'. *Gender and Education.* Vol. 6, No. 1, pp 87–93.

Skelton, C. (1996) 'Learning to be 'Tough': the fostering of maleness in one primary school'. *Gender and Education.* Vol. 8, No. 2, pp 185–197.

Skelton, C. (1998) 'Feminism and research into masculinities and schooling'. *Gender and Education*. Vol. 10, No. 2, pp 217–227.

Skelton, C. (2000) 'A passion for football: dominant masculinities and primary schooling'. *Sport, Education and Society*. Vol. 5, No. 1, pp 5–18.

Skelton, C. (2001) *Schooling the Boys*. Buckingham, Open University Press.

Skelton, C. (2003) 'Male primary teachers and perceptions of masculinity'. *Educational Review*. Vol. 55, No. 2, pp 195–209.

Skelton, C. (2007) 'Gender, policy and initial teacher education'. *Gender and Education*. Vol. 19, No. 6, pp 677–690.

Skelton, C. (2009) 'Failing to get men into primary teaching: a feminist critique'. *Journal of Educational Policy*. Vol. 24 , No.1, pp 39–54.

Skelton, C. (2011) 'Men teachers and the "feminised" primary school: a review of the literature'. *Educational Review*. Vol. 64, No. 1, February, pp 1–19.

Skelton, C. and Hanson, J. (1989) 'Schooling the teachers: gender and initial teacher education', in S. Acker (ed.) *Teachers, Gender and Careers*. Lewes, Falmer Press.

Smedley, S. (1998) 'Perspectives on male student primary teachers'. *Changing English*. Vol. 5, No. 2, pp 147–159.

Smedley, S. (1999) 'Don't rock the boat: men student teachers' understanding of gender and equality'. Paper presented at *BERA*, University of Brighton, 9–11 September.

Smedley, S. (2007) 'Learning to be a primary school teacher: reading one man's story'. *Gender and Education*. Vol. 19 , No.3, pp 369–385.

Smith, L. (2010) 'Where have all the male primary school teachers gone?' *My Daily*, pp 1–3, 9 September.

Spencer, F.D. (1938) *An Inspector's Testament*. London, English Universities Press.

Spender, D. (1982) *Invisible Women*. London, Writers and Readers Pub. Cooperative Society Ltd.

Spender, D. (1990) *Man Made Language* (2nd edition). London, Pandora Press.

Statistics Canada (2013) *Women in teaching-related professions, Canada, 1996 and 2006*. http://www.statcan.gc.ca/pub/89-503-x/2010001/article/11542/tbl/tbl013-eng.htm (28 October 2014).

Stanley, L. (ed.) (1997) *Knowing Feminisms*. London, Sage.

Steedman, C. (1982) *The Tidy House*. London, Virago.

Steedman, C. (1987) 'Prisonhouses', in M. Lawn and G. Grace (eds) *Teachers: The Culture and Politics of Work*. Lewes, Falmer Press.

Steedman, C. (1990) *Childhood, Culture and Class in Britain: Margaret Macmillan, 1860–1931*. London, Virago.

Steedman, C. (1992) *Past Tenses: Essays on Writing, Autobiography and History*. London, Rivers Oram Press.

Strauss, A. and Corbin, J. (1990) *Basics of Qualitative Research*. London, Sage.

Stroud, J., Smith, L., Ealy, L. and Hurst, L. (2000) 'Choosing to teach: perceptions of male pre-service teachers in early childhood and elementary education'. *Early Child Development*. Vol. 163, August, pp 49–60.

Sumsion, J. (2000) 'Negotiating *Otherness*: a male early childhood educator's gender positioning'. *International Journal of Early Years Education*. Vol. 8, No. 2, pp 129–139.

Sutherland, G. (1971) *Elementary Education in the Nineteenth Century*. London, The Historical Association.

Sutherland, R. (2007) *Teaching for Learning Mathematics*. Berkshire, Oxford University Press.

Swindells, J. (ed.) (1995) *The Uses of Autobiography*. London, Taylor & Francis.

Szwed, C. (2010) 'Gender balance in primary initial teacher education: some current perspectives'. *Journal of Education for Teaching: International Research and Pedagogy*. Vol. 36, No. 3, pp 303–317.

The World Bank (2011) *Primary Education, (% Females) Data*. Washington, DC, The World Bank Group. http://data.worldbank.org/indicator/SE.PRM.TCHR .FE.ZS (28 October 2014).

Thomas, D. (ed.) (1995) *Teachers' Stories*. Buckingham, Open University Press.

Thompson, B. (1989). 'Teacher attitudes: complacency and conflict', in C. Skelton (ed.) *Whatever Happens to Little Women?* Milton Keynes, Open University Press.

Thompson, E.P. (1963) *The Making of the English Working Class*. Middlesex, Penguin Bks. Ltd.

Thorne, B. (1993) *Gender Play. Girls and Boys in School*. Brunswick, NJ, Rutgers University Press.

Thornton, A. (1993) 'The accomplishment of masculinities: men and sports', in T. Haddad (ed.) *Men and Masculinities*. Toronto, Canadian Scholars Press Inc.

Thornton, M. (1999) 'Reducing wastage among men student teachers in primary courses: a male club approach'. *Journal of Education for Teaching*. Vol. 25, No. 1, pp 41–53.

Thornton, M. and Bricheno, P. (2000) 'Primary school teachers' careers in England and Wales: the relationship between gender, role, position and promotion aspirations'. *Pedagogy, Culture and Society*. Vol. 8, No. 2, pp 187–206.

Thrupp, M. (2000) 'Compensating for class: are school improvement researchers being realistic?' *Education and Social Justice*. Vol. 2, No. 2, pp 2–9.

Titus, J. (2000). 'Engaging student resistance to feminism: 'how is this stuff going to make us better teachers?' *Gender and Education*. Vol. 12, No. 1, pp 21–37.

Tomlinson, S. (2000). 'Exclusion: the middle classes and the common good', in H. Daniels and P. Garner (eds) *Inclusive Education*. London, Kogan Page.

Topping, A. (8 July 2013). 'Boris Johnson criticised for suggesting women go to university to find husband'. *The Guardian* (London). http://en.wikipedia .org/wiki/Boris_Johnson#Remarks_about_women_in_Malaysian_universities (16 July 2013).

Tropp, A. (1957) *The School Teachers: The Growth of the Teaching Profession in England and Wales from 1800 to the Present Day*. Heinemann, London.

Tremonti, A.M. (2013) *Is the Shortage of Male Teachers a Crisis?* (Canada). The Current www.cbc.ca/thecurrent/episode/.../is-the-shortage-of-male-teachers-a -crisis/ (21 February 2013).

TVNZ (2012) *Male teachers still scarce*. National News tvnz.co.nz/national-news/ male-teachers-still-scarce-4709653 (2 February 2012).

Vancouver Sun (2011) *Number of Male Teachers Continues to Decline*. www.canada.com/vancouversun/news/westcoastnews/story.html?id... (28 March 2011).

Wadsworth, J. (2002) 'The issues facing men working in early childhood education'. *Forum*. Triangle Journals Ltd. Vol. 44, No. 1, pp 41–44.

Walby, S. (1990) *Theorising Patriarchy*. Oxford, Blackwell.

Walford, G. (2001) *Doing Qualitative Educational Research*. London, Continuum.

Walker, A. and Walker, C. (eds) (1997) *Britain Divided*. London, CPAG Ltd.

Walkerdine, V. and Lucey, H. (1989) *Democracy in the Kitchen: Regulating Mothers and Socialising Daughters*. London, Virago Press.

Walkerdine, V. (1989) *Counting Girls Out*. London, Virago.

Walkerdine, V. (1990) *Schoolgirl Fictions*. London, Verso.

Walkerdine, V. (1992) 'Progressive pedagogy and political struggle', in C. Luke and J. Gore (eds) *Feminisms and Critical Pedagogy*. New York, Routledge.

Walkerdine, V. (1997) *Daddy's Girl: Young Girls and Popular Culture*. London, Macmillan Press.

Walkerdine, V., Lucey, H. and Melody, J. (2001) *Growing Up Girl*. Basingstoke, Palgrave.

Walvin, J. (1987) *Victorian Values*. London, Andre Deutsch Ltd.

Walvin, J. (2000) *The People's Game* (2nd edition). Edinburgh, Mainstream Pub. Ltd.

Ward, H. (2001) 'Quality of men entering teaching takes a nose dive'. *Times Educational Supplement*. 19 October. London.

Wardle, D. (1976) *English Popular Education 1780–1975*. Cambridge, Cambridge University Press.

Warrier, S. (1988) 'Marriage, maternity, and female economic activity: Gujarati mothers in Britain', in S. Westwood and P. Bhachu (eds) *Enterprising Women*. London, Routledge.

Weber, S. and Mitchell, C. (1995) *"That's Funny, You Don't Look Like a Teacher": Interrogating Images and Identity in Popular Culture*. London, The Falmer Press.

Weedon, C. (1998) *Feminist Practice and Poststructuralist Theory* (2nd edition). London, Blackwell.

Weiner, G. (1994) *Feminisms in Education: An Introduction*. Buckingham, Open University Press.

Wells, B. and Cunningham, P. (1995) 'I wanted to nurse. Father wanted teachers', in J. Swindells (ed.) *The Uses of Autobiography*. London, Taylor & Francis.

Weaver-Hightower, M. (2011) 'Male preservice teachers and discouragement from teaching'. *The Journal of Men's Studies*. Vol. 19, No. 2 (Spring), pp 97–110.

Widdowson, F. (1980) *Going Up into the Next Class. Women and Elementary Teacher Training 1840–1914*. London, Women's Research and Resources Centre Pub.

Wieler, K. (1999) 'Reflections on writing a history of women teachers', in K. Wieler and S. Middleton (eds) *Telling Women's Lives*. Buckingham, Open University Press.

Wieler, K. and Middleton, S. (eds) (1999) 'Introduction', in K. Wieler and S. Middleton (eds) *Telling Women's Lives*. Buckingham, Open University Press.

Williams, M. and May, T. (1996) *Introduction to the Philosophy of Social Research*. London, Routledge.

Willott, S. (1998) 'An outsider within: a feminist doing research on men', in K. Henwood, C. Griffin and A. Phoenix (eds) *Standpoints and Differences*. London, Sage.

Windass, A. (1989) 'Classroom practice and organisation', in C. Skelton (ed.) *Whatever happens to Little Women?* Milton Keynes, Open University Press.

Wright, C. (1992) *Race Relations in the Primary School*. London, Fulton.

AUTHOR INDEX

SUBJECT INDEX